Global E

N

Although much has been written on the topic of economic globalization, few volumes examine the social foundations of the global economy in a way that puts power and contestation at the forefront of the analysis. This book addresses the gap by emphasizing the contested social processes that underpin global production chains and financial structures. Multidisciplinary in its approach, with perspectives from sociologists, political scientists and political economists, it juxtaposes the examination of global trends with the diverse contexts of specific regions and countries. It features a range of case-studies from North and Latin America, Europe, Africa, East and South-East Asia and Post-Communist Russia to explore the issues surrounding:

- global production chains and the international division of labour
- corporate social responsibility and socially responsible investing
- new forms of labour organising and internationalism.

The book will be of interest to students and researchers in international political economy, the sociology of globalization, development studies, economic geography and labour studies.

Marcus Taylor is an Assistant Professor in the Department of Global Development Studies at Queen's University, Canada.

Rethinking Globalizations

Edited by Barry K. Gills
Newcastle University, UK

This series is designed to break new ground in the literature on globalization and its academic and popular understanding. Rather than perpetuating or simply reacting to the economic understanding of globalization, this series seeks to capture the term and broaden its meaning to encompass a wide range of issues and disciplines and convey a sense of alternative possibilities for the future.

1 **Whither Globalization?**
The vortex of knowledge and globalization
James H. Mittelman

2 **Globalization and Global History**
Edited by Barry K. Gills and William R. Thompson

3 **Rethinking Civilization**
Communication and terror in the Global Village
Majid Tehranian

4 **Globalisation and Contestation**
The new great counter-movement
Ronaldo Munck

5 **Global Activism**
Ruth Reitan

6 **Globalization, the City and Civil Society in Pacific Asia**
Edited by Mike Douglass, K.C. Ho and Giok Ling Ooi

7 **Challenging Euro-America's Politics of Identity**
The return of the native
Jorge Luis Andrade Fernandes

8 **The Global Politics of Globalization**
'Empire' vs 'Cosmolis'
Barry K. Gills

9 **The Globalization as Evolutionary Crisis**
Edited by Jan Oosthoek and Barry K. Gills

10 **Globalization as Evolutionary Process**
Modeling global change
Edited by George Modelski, Tessaleno Devezas and William R. Thompson

11 **The Political Economy of Global Security**
War, future crises and changes in global governance
Heikki Patomäki

12 **Cultures of Globalization**
Coherence, hybridity, contestation
Edited by Kevin Archer, M. Martin Bosman, M. Mark Amen and Ella Schmidt

13 **Globalization and the Global Politics of Justice**
Edited by Barry K. Gills

14 **Global Economy Contested**
Power and conflict across the international division of labour
Edited by Marcus Taylor

15 **Rethinking Insecurity, War and Violence**
Beyond savage globalization?
Edited by Damian Grenfell and Paul James

Global Economy Contested

Power and conflict across the international division of labour

Edited by
Marcus Taylor

LONDON AND NEW YORK

First published 2008
by Routledge
2 Park Square, Milton Park, Abingdon, Oxon OX14 4RN

Simultaneously published in the USA and Canada
by Routledge
270 Madison Avenue, New York, NY 10016

Routledge is an imprint of the Taylor & Francis Group, an informa business.

Typeset in Times by
Taylor & Francis Books
Printed and bound in Great Britain by
TJ International Ltd, Padstow, Cornwall

British Library Cataloguing in Publication Data
A catalogue record for this book is available from the British Library

Library of Congress Cataloging in Publication Data
Global economy contested : power and conflict across the international division of labor / edited by Marcus Taylor.
p. cm. – (Rethinking globalizations)
Includes bibliographical references and index.
1. Labor market. 2. Globalization–Economic aspects. 3. Capitalism–Social aspects–Case studies. I. Taylor, Marcus (Marcus Edward).
HD5702.G56 2008
331.1–dc22 2007046489

ISBN 978-0-415-77548-9 (hbk)
ISBN 978-0-415-77549-6 (pbk)
ISBN 978-0-203-92724-3 (ebk)

Contents

Illustrations

Figures

Tables

Contributors

Étienne Cantin is a researcher at the Inter-University Research Centre on Globalization and Work and Assistant Professor of Labour and Industrial Relations at Laval University, Québec, Canada. For his PhD, he studied comparative and international political economy at York University, Toronto, Canada. His current work deals with the history of industrial capitalism and trade unionism in the United States, as well as the impact of global dynamics of uneven capitalist development on the restructuring of industrial and labour relations in North America's low-wage manufacturing sector.

Marlea Clarke is a postdoctoral fellow in the Labour Studies Programme at McMaster University, Hamilton, Canada. She is currently working on project funded by the Workers' Safety and Insurance Board (WSIB) entitled 'Employment Strain: The Hidden Costs of Precarious Employment'. She is also a research associate of the Labour and Enterprise Project, Institute of Development and Labour Law at the University of Cape Town. Her articles on labour markets and worker struggles in South Africa have appeared in various journals including *Canadian Journal of African Studies* and *Law, Democracy & Development*. She has also published numerous policy documents on labour in South Africa for international organisations including the ILO and Oxfam.

Simon Clarke is Professor of Sociology at the University of Warwick and Scientific Director of the Institute for Comparative Labour Relations Research, Moscow. His recent research has focused on aspects of labour and employment in post-socialist countries, with particular reference to worker organisation and the development of trade unionism, in collaboration with national and international trade union and labour organisations. His main publications include *Marx, Marginalism and Modern Sociology* (Macmillan, 1982); *Keynesianism, Monetarism and the Crisis of the State* (Edward Elgar, 1990); *Marx's Theory of Crisis* (Macmillan, 1994); (with Vadim Borisov and Peter Fairbrother) *The Workers' Movement in Russia* (Edward Elgar, 1995); *The Formation of a Labour Market in Russia* (Edward Elgar, 1999); and *The Development of Capitalism in Russia* (Routledge, 2006).

Ryan Foster is a PhD student in the Department of Political Science at York University, Toronto. His current research focuses on the relationship between US-based corporate philanthropy directed at recent post-disaster reconstruction in New Orleans and Banda Aceh, and the privileged position of market-based solutions in rebuilding the delivery of basic social services to low-income communities in these cities.

Paul Langley is Senior Lecturer in International Politics at the School of Arts and Social Sciences, Northumbria University, UK. Paul's research interests are in finance, political economy and social theory. He is the author of *World Financial Orders: An Historical International Political Economy* (Routledge, 2002), and *The Everyday Life of Global Finance: Saving and Borrowing in Anglo-America* (forthcoming, Oxford University Press). He is also currently serving as Convenor of the International Political Economy Group (IPEG) of the British International Studies Association (BISA).

Jeroen Merk works for the Clean Clothes Campaign, is a lecturer at the University of Amsterdam and completed his PhD in International Relations at the University of Sussex, Brighton. His publications include 'Regulating the Global Athletic Footwear Industry: The Collective Worker in the Product Chain', in Libby Assassi, Duncan Wigan, and Kees van der Pijl (eds), *Global Regulation: Managing Crises After the Imperial Turn* (Palgrave, 2004).

Ronaldo Munck is Theme Leader for internationalisation, interculturalism and social development in the President's Office of Dublin City University, and visiting Professor of Sociology at Liverpool University. He is the author of a trilogy on the globalisation problematic: *Globalisation and Labour: The New 'Great Transformation'* (Zed Books, 2002), *Globalisation and Social Exclusion: A Transformationalist Perspective* (Kumarian Press, 2005), and *Globalisation and Contestation: The New Great Counter-Movement* (Routledge, 2007). He is currently researching labour migration in Ireland and has launched a new journal *Translocations: The Irish Migration, Race and Social Transformation Review* (www.translocations.ie).

Viviana Patroni is Associate Professor in the Division of Social Science at York University and the former Director of the Centre for Research on Latin America and the Caribbean, also at York. Her work has focused on the experience of development in Latin American, the changing nature of state–labour relations under neoliberalism and the emergence of new forms of unionism in Argentina. Her articles have appeared in journals including *Capital and Class* and *Research in Political Economy.* She is currently also the co-director of a Canadian-funded project of activities aimed at supporting the development of a Latin American network for human rights education and research.

Susanne Soederberg is a Canada Research Chair in Global Political Economy and Associate Professor in the Department of Global Development Studies at Queen's University, Canada. She is the author of *The Politics of the New International Financial Architecture: Reimposing Neoliberal Domination in the Global South* (Zed Books, 2004), and *Global Governance in Question: Empire, Class, and the New Common Sense in Managing North–South Relations* (Pluto, 2006). She is currently completing a book manuscript entitled *Corporations, Power and Ownership in Contemporary Capitalism: The Politics of Governance, Activism and Social Responsibility* (Routledge, forthcoming).

Marcus Taylor is an Assistant Professor in the Department of Global Development Studies at Queen's University, Kingston, Ontario, Canada. He has written on a wide range of issues related to the political economy of development, including neoliberalism in Latin America and the changing theory and practice of the World Bank. He is the author of *From Pinochet to the Third Way: Neoliberalism and Social Transformation in Chile* (Pluto, 2006) and is currently undertaking a comparative study of labour market transformation in Mexico and China.

Acknowledgements

The impetus for this volume derived from an annual series of panels on global labour issues held at the International Studies Association annual conventions from 2005 to 2007. From our discussions at these meetings it became clear that there was a need for a volume that could address both theoretical and empirical issues relating to the challenges facing workers and communities in an era of notable change within global capitalism. I would like to thank all participants in those sessions and look forward to continuing our debates in future years. During the production of the volume, Étienne Cantin and Jeroen Merk offered encouragement and very useful ideas (often without their knowing) and Paul Langley most helpfully provided the 'Global Economy Contested' title. My sincerest thanks go to Victoria Henderson, who provided excellent editorial services on numerous chapters. Finally, Susanne and Sydney Soederberg offered continual support, worthy distraction, and great humour throughout the project!

All author proceeds from this book are donated to the Clean Clothes Campaign – an international campaign focused on improving working conditions in the global garment and sportswear industries, and empowering the workers in it: www.cleanclothes.org/

Abbreviations

ACFTU	All China Federation of Trade Unions
ACWU	Amalgamated Clothing Workers' Union
AEC	Anti-Eviction Campaign
AFDC	Aid to Families with Dependent Children
AFL-CIO	American Federation of Labor-Congress of Industrial Organizations
AMRC	Asia Monitor Resource Centre
ANC	African National Congress
APEC	Asia-Pacific Economic Cooperation
APF	Anti-Privatisation Forum
ATR	Association of Public Employees
BCEA	Basic Conditions of Employment Act 75
BIT	Building Investment Trust
CalPERS	California Public Employees Retirement System
CCC	Clean Clothes Campaign
CCC	*Corriente Clasista Combativa*
CDS	Coastal Development Strategy
CGT	*Confederación General del Trabajo*/General Confederation of Labour
CIS	Commonwealth of Independent States
CODESA	Convention for a Democratic South Africa
COSATU	Congress of South African Trade Unions
CPC	Communist Party of China
CROC	Confederación Revolucionario de Obreros y Campesinos
CSR	corporate social responsibility
CTA	*Central de Trabajadores Argentinos*/Central of Argentinian Workers
CTERA	Central of Education Workers
DB	defined benefit
DC	defined contribution
DoL	Department of Labor
EAP	Economically Active Population
EEA	Employment Equity Act 55

ECC	Employment Conditions Commission
ETIs	economically-targeted investments
FDI	foreign direct investment
FRENAPO	National Front Against Poverty
FTV	Federation of Land, Housing and Habitat (*Federación de Tierra/ Vivienda y Habitat)*
GATT	General Agreement on Tariffs and Trade
GCC	global commodity chains
GEAR	Growth, Employment and Redistribution
GUF	Global Unions Federations
GWC	Garment Workers Center
HIT	Housing Investment Trust
HSE	health, safety and environment
ICEM	International Federation of Chemical, Energy, Mine and General Workers Union
ICFTU	International Confederation of Free Trade Unions
IFC	International Finance Corporation
ILGWU	International Ladies' Garment Workers' Union
ILO	International Labour Organisation
IMF	International Monetary Fund
ITUC	International Trade Union Confederation
LRA	Labour Relations Act 66
NAFTA	North American Free Trade Agreement
NCL	National Consumers' League
Nedlac	National Economic Development and Labour Council
NEF	National Economic Forum
NGOs	non-governmental organisations
NIC	Newly Industrialising Countries
NLC	National Labour Committee
NMC	National Manpower Commission
NP	National Party
PCI	Permissible Country Index
PRI	Partido Revolucionario Institucional
PRWORA	Personal Responsibility and Work Reconciliation Act
ROCE	Return on capital employed
SACTU	South African Congress of Trade Unions
SDA	Skills Development Act 97
SEC	Securities and Exchange Commission
SECC	Soweto Electricity Crisis Committee
SEZs	Special Economic Zones
SITEKIM	Sindicato de los Trabajadores de la Empresa Kukdong International de Mexico
SOEs	state-owned enterprises
SRI	socially responsible investing
TANF	Temporary Aid to Needy Families

TNCs	transnational corporations
TUC	Trade Union Congress
TVEs	town and village enterprises
UNITE!	Union of Needletrades, Industrial, and Textile Employees
USAS	United Students Against Sweatshops
WCL	World Confederation of Labour
WOTC	Work Opportunity Tax Credit
WRC	Workers' Rights Consortium
WTO	World Trade Organisation
WtWTC	Welfare to Work Tax Credit

Introduction

Global economy contested

Marcus Taylor

When visiting Coventry in the UK a few years back, a prominent advertising campaign run by a major international bank across the city's billboards captured my attention. On top of a striking red background was the slogan 'Making your money work harder for you'. This message was accompanied by an image of an elderly man dressed in nineteenth-century garb (apparently the personification of 'money') performing mundane household tasks that changed from one billboard to the next. Although unintentional, this advertisement drew attention to several important facets of the contemporary global economy that commonly remain obscured in such venues. Despite personifying money as a droll old man, it nonetheless signalled that money is power; or, more specifically, that money can be profitably turned into command over other people's labour. While there remains a remote possibility that the international bank who commissioned the adverts was indeed investing in friendly old men to undertake gentle domestic labour, it is eminently more plausible that a deposit at this institution would circulate through international financial markets to facilitate high-return activities in boom areas of the global economy, such as labour-intensive export sectors in contemporary China or India. Of course, in this context, the notion of 'making your money work harder for you' assumes a far more direct and disconcerting embodiment in the various disciplinary mechanisms that induce workers to labour long and intensive hours for low wages in the production of goods for distant Western consumers. Contrary to its intentions, the advert was indicative of a chain of power relations that interlace the realms of global finance, production and consumption and therefore run through the global economy at large.

While it might be expected that the advertising campaigns of international banks would not normally emphasise that the global economy is founded upon and functions through a complex succession of power relationships, this myopia towards relationships of power and domination is also notably present in much mainstream academic writing. In particular, large quantities of recent output on the topics of 'globalisation' and the 'global economy' within the broad field of political economy present the issue in terms of finding a suitable balance between the relative influence of states and markets that can facilitate a more efficient global economy. In such presentations, the central notion of 'the global economy' is left as an abstract and obscure entity whose social foundations are not questioned and whose constitutive forms of power are left concealed. Such analytical blind spots emerge in part because these writings take for granted the somewhat fanciful vision of the economy perpetuated in mainstream economics. Within the principal strands of neoclassical economics, 'the global economy' is used interchangeably with 'the global marketplace', and the latter is viewed through a series of convenient assumptions used to construct models of rational, utility-maximising individuals and firms who engage in mutually beneficial exchanges in markets characterised by liberty, stable preferences and perfect foresight. From this perspective, a global market society represents the perfection of 'economic freedom' and globalisation is viewed as the unfolding of progressive market forces on a global scale that simply provides opportunities for all individuals, firms and countries willing to embrace it. As a consequence, issues of power and contestation are reduced to the status of social anomalies or special interest politics. While the latter may retard the natural and harmonising economic forces of supply and demand, they are not seen as intrinsic to the dynamics of the market itself.

Even a casual glance at the social relationships on which the global economy is founded, however, finds overwhelming evidence to reject this view. Not only are the dynamics of power and contestation inseparable from everyday material life, they are also driving forces that shape the processes of production, exchange and consumption on a global level. As the following chapters indicate, key sectors of the global economy are characterised by heavy concentrations of ownership and market power – a situation in which oligopolistic corporations, born of centralised financial control, deploy a range of strategies to restrict competition and structure their supply lines to further their accumulation of capital. Moreover, the operations of firms are in turn predicated on conflictual social relations. In the realm of production, conflicts between capital and labour are endemic over issues such as the length and intensity of the working day, the deployment of technology and the organisation of the labour process. In the labour market, the relative bargaining power of employers and employees intersect with state institutions and forms of discrimination along the basis of gender, race and class. In the sphere of consumption, corporations spend vast sums of money in an attempt to manipulate the symbolic capital attached to their brand and to construct new consumer needs. These everyday power relationships exist as the social foundations of the global economy, and the dynamics of power and contestation they invoke shape the global economic edifice that is constructed upon them.

The starting point of this volume, therefore, is that the very notion of 'the global economy' as employed in much mainstream literature is an analytical abstraction that clouds our comprehension of the social relations, institutions and processes through which commodities are produced, distributed and consumed. This volume consequently seeks to contest mainstream understandings of the global economy and to highlight the complex relationships of power and contestation on which it is founded. In particular, we focus on how different social actors struggle to redefine the institutional structures and relationships through which they are integrated into and reproduced within the global economy. On the one hand, we examine how multinational corporations, financial institutions and state organisations have sought to reshape the contemporary international division of labour by restructuring labour markets, expanding the power of capital and altering the conditions of work on a global level in order to allay competitive pressures and preserve profit rates. On the other, we also look at the ways in which workers and communities have responded, including an emphasis on new forms of local and international labour unionism and the contested terrains of corporate social responsibility and socially responsible investing. In so doing, the volume demonstrates not only how the uneven effects of global economic integration impact upon workers and communities across the globe, but simultaneously how the agency of these individual and collective actors have reciprocal effects that reconfigure the terrain of global capitalism.

To accomplish this task, the chapters draw upon a wide range of case studies divided into four related parts that examine, respectively: (1) the remaking of the international division of labour; (2) global commodity chains and corporate social responsibility; (3) global finance and socially responsible investing; and (4) new directions in labour organising.

Part I – Reworking the international division of labour

Part I examines the restructuring of the social foundations of the global economy over the past three decades, with a focus on how different branches of production have been reorganised across a new international division of labour. Mainstream accounts view the structure of global production arising simply from the complementarities of comparative advantages between countries engaged in trade, and tend to emphasise trade and financial liberalisation as the keys to this process. In contrast, we place production within a much wider spectrum of social relations and institutions. Specifically, the chapters that follow examine how global productive structures rest upon the creation and reproduction of labour forces that are socially embedded in local power relations and institutional contexts. Refashioning the international division of labour has therefore involved transforming a wide range of social institutions ranging from the level of the household, factory, through to labour market institutions and state social policies. Using case studies of the high-profile cases of China and Russia, Part I illustrates how integration into global capitalism has occurred through profound social transformations including the rapid construction of labour markets, the restructuring of established labour forces, new state policies for

regulating social reproduction, dramatic changes within household relations, and the creation of new cultural values. Moreover, such processes have been widely contested and have had dramatically uneven results both within and outside of these countries, empowering and enriching some social groups while marginalising and impoverishing others.

Marcus Taylor begins this discussion in Chapter 1 by asking which conceptual tools are useful to help us make sense of these processes. By surveying the contributions of various schools of thought – including economic sociology and institutional economics – Taylor suggests that an analysis of the changing structures of global production needs to focus on both the social embedding of economic activities within local power relations and institutional contexts; and the concurrent abstraction of these relationships in the form of market prices and the dynamics of inter-firm competition. By examining the tensions between these simultaneous and ongoing social processes, we can better grasp both the social foundations of capitalist production and the way in which the resulting social struggles shape the contours of the broader global economy.

Simon Clarke deepens this discussion in Chapter 2 by examining the troubled nature of Russia's integration into global capitalism in the post-Soviet era. Clarke takes issue with mainstream accounts of this transformation, which argue that market-driven systems of production and exchange emerge spontaneously once previous institutional contexts are removed. In contrast, Clarke highlights how the transformation of post-Soviet Russia has occurred largely on the basis of integrating existing institutions and productive relations into global capitalism. This has led to profoundly uneven development, repeated crises and the further restructuring of productive structures, social institutions and of the country's labouring population.

In contrast to the crisis-stricken trajectory of post-Soviet Russia, China's embrace of global capitalism has been widely championed as stimulating an 'economic miracle' represented in over two decades of strong and sustained economic growth. While the mainstream literature attributes this growth primarily to the liberalisation of trade and investment, Cantin and Taylor indicate in Chapter 3 that many of the most fundamental transformations underscoring China's integration into global capitalism have been in the world of work. The chapter examines the contested creation of new institutions that regulate the production, distribution, deployment and remuneration of workers. Such profound institutional change is neither simply a cause nor consequence of industrial transformation. Rather, it is an ongoing process inextricably bound up with the transformation of productive structures, the effects of which are experienced far beyond China as the creation of specific Chinese work forces reverberates across the international division of labour in the form of new competitive pressures for various sectors of industrial manufacturing. While the Chinese case is often labelled an unqualified success, Cantin and Taylor emphasise the frequently severe disciplinary labour systems in force in China and the uneven effects of productive restructuring on various parts of the country's workforce. Simultaneously, they focus on the ways in which Chinese workers have sought to actively challenge the intensification of their labour within the global economy.

Part II – Commodity chains, labour standards and corporate social responsibility

Whereas the previous part focused on country-level case studies, Part II deepens the analysis of change in the global economy by examining the evolution of several sectors that are transnational in scope, namely, the global footwear, garment and consumer good retail industries. All three sectors have undergone dramatic restructuring over the past three decades and have been reorganised spatially – by relocating supply lines into the developing world – and organisationally – by implementing new forms of subcontracting within global inter-firm networks. One of the motivations of this restructuring has been to dramatically reduce labour costs through relocating production to cheap labour zones and by increasing the intensity of labour throughout the commodity chain. Alongside detailing these transformations, the chapters each examine the reactions of workers and communities to these processes, focusing on both the actions of local worker organisations alongside the broader movement that has emerged as an attempt to enforce corporations to act in social responsible manners. In particular, the phenomenon of 'corporate social responsibility' (CSR) is seen as a field of power in which various social groups – from consumers, to workers, to the corporations themselves – struggle to shape its meanings and impact.

First, Jeroen Merk commences with a sectoral examination of the global athletic footwear industry in Chapter 4. The latter has undergone a growing functional split through which the activities of design and marketing, on the one hand, and production, on the other, have been separated and distributed between networked firms across a commodity chain. To emphasise this division of labour, the chapter focuses on the relationships between Nike and their major subcontractor, Yue Yuen. The latter is a giant yet largely unrecognised Taiwanese company that undertakes the labour-intensive production for close to 20 per cent of global athletic shoes. Merk illustrates the specific spatial fragmentation of labour processes within the production of global footwear and the varied socio-political conditions in which these activities are embedded in countries such as China and Indonesia. Turning to a discussion of the effectiveness of corporate codes of conduct for protecting workers, Merk demonstrates the weaknesses of the latter in promoting the freedom of association of local labour organisation in explicitly authoritarian and anti-labour political environments. This, he concludes, greatly problematises the ability of workers to struggle for basic labour rights and therein weakens the notion that corporate social responsibility is a suitable tool in and of itself for raising global labour standards.

Étienne Cantin pursues similar themes in the context of the transnationalisation of the apparel industry. In so doing, Chapter 5 provides a specific case of how changes across the international division of labour have impacted upon – and been contested by – the workers involved in commodity production. Cantin employs a long-term perspective, detailing the establishment of garment production in the US as a sweated industry in the early 1900s and the movements that were frequently successful at raising conditions across the industry in the subsequent decades. He then focuses on the ways in which various worker movements have challenged the effects of the deepening transnationalisation of garment production since the 1960s on their employment and working conditions. While the US garment industry has undergone a significant dissolution of jobs and a lowering of pay and conditions, Cantin examines how the experience of previous defeats inflicted on worker movements has led to a greater acknowledgement of workers of the necessity to mobilise on an international basis to complement and strengthen local forms of organisation. He suggests that these lessons are starting to lead to cautious yet important attempts to change the strategies pursued by organised labour in the North American garment industry.

In Chapter 6, Ryan Foster sheds light on workers at the other end of the commodity chain – namely, the low-wage retail and service sector employees in the United States whose function in the international division of labour is to facilitate the circulation of goods in the West. Foster highlights the increasingly precarious position of low-wage workers in the USA and their growing dependence on charity to secure their social existence. Ironically, to an increasing extent charity is now provided under the guise of 'corporate philanthropy' by giant retail conglomerates despite their status as low-wage employers. By introducing the notion of 'divide and sponsor', Foster indicates how this seeming contradiction is part of a sophisticated strategy of legitimisation by corporations stung with growing criticism of their impacts on workers and communities both at home and abroad. In this manner, the chapter charts the contradictions at play between the operation of disciplinary labour markets, low-paying employers and struggles over the meaning and practices of corporate social responsibility on the circulation end of global commodity chains.

Part III – Global finance and socially responsible investing

The subsequent two chapters by Paul Langley and Susanne Soederberg shift focus to questions of power and social conflict in the realm of global finance and investment. The relationship between global financial markets and the international division of labour is of paramount importance. In order to expand operations and upgrade technologically, enterprises need repeated access to financing either through recycling profits, borrowing from banks, or raising revenue through equity on financial markets. Over the last three decades, the latter solution has become increasingly important. As a result, the channels and conditions through which companies attain credit have changed greatly, as has the range of actors who can influence these processes. Significantly, the accumulated pensions savings of Western workers now provides an important and growing proportion of the capital within the global financial system. This is a contradictory process as workers become dependent on the profitability of corporations active both at home and abroad for the accumulation of their retirement savings. The pivotal question that both Langley and Soederberg engage, therefore, is whether workers and unions can use the potential power embodied in their accumulated pension funds to achieve progressive social change by influencing the conduct of corporations and governments.

In Chapter 7, Langley focuses on the role of pension-fund capital in the USA and Britain, arguing that various forms of dissent have arisen to contest the short-term mentality of investment practices. The drive to ensure high-returns on financial investment often comes at the expense of the security and conditions of worker employment. This leads to a paradox in which workers' savings become the driving force for corporate restructuring that is often prejudicial to worker interests. Langley outlines these contradictions and assesses the two proposed solutions. In critiquing the notions and practices of 'pension fund capitalism' and 'pension fund socialism', Langley points to the diffusion and diversity of forms of contestation that elude definition in simple class terms. Expanding this discussion, Soederberg tackles similar questions yet on a global scale in Chapter 8. Specifically, she asks whether the socially responsible investing (SRI) practices of Western public pension funds can promote social justice in the global South, or whether they reinforce long-standing relations of domination between the West and the rest. Using the case study of CalPERS, the California Public Employees Retirement System that controls an investment portfolio of over US$240 billion, Soederberg emphasises the contradictions inherent to the practice of socially responsible investing. Despite its oft-proclaimed activist orientation, CalPERS' variant of SRI builds on and reinforces existing forms of power inherent in the attempt of Western investors to ensure profitable rates of return on investment in the global South. This analysis leads to Soederberg's call for a radicalisation of SRI practices and their linkage with other social justice movements in order to help overcome their present limitations.

Part IV – New directions in labour organising

The final three chapters of this volume return to politics of labour and focus directly on the ways in which workers have reacted to the challenges that integration into the global economy brings. Specifically, they examine the possibilities of and challenges to the collective organisation of workers on local, national and potentially international levels. Chapters 9 and 10, written by Marlea Clarke and Viviana Patroni, use case studies to highlight new forms of labour unionism that emerged in South Africa and Argentina over the 1990s and beyond. In both cases, the challenges of precarious labour conditions led to the formation of new collective organisations that attempted to link both formal and informal sector workers with other social movements that had common goals. As such, these new movements circumvented the older 'managerial' style of union organisation that appeared to be floundering in the face of the changed power structures of globalised capitalism. While recognising the potentialities latent within these new social movements and the ways in which they addressed the failures of older unions, both authors nonetheless underline the serious barriers that remain to be overcome before such movements can expand their political influence in the search for new and more humane ways of making ends meet for the working poor.

In this respect, one of the key challenges facing new union movements is how to build international solidarity. Ronaldo Munck concludes the volume in Chapter 11 by analysing the seeds of new labour internationalisms that can be discerned in the contemporary era. Through a discussion of older forms of labour internationalism and the current dynamics of global capitalism, Munck examines how globalisation has created conditions favourable to global solidarity by linking workers across the international division of labour. At the same time, however, the unevenness of global economic integration serves to divide working classes, both internally and across borders, because the restructuring of capital repeatedly pressures specific groups of workers to protect their status at the expense of others. This leaves us asking how to fashion unifying internationalist responses to global capitalism that operate on both local and global scales, thereby reacting to both the embedded and abstracted nature of capitalism. There are no easy answers to these questions – if there were, we would live in a drastically different world. However, as Munck indicates, it is important to start posing the right questions. It is hoped that this volume will provide steps in that direction.

Part I

Reworking the international division of labour

1 Power, conflict and the production of the global economy

Marcus Taylor

One of the most remarkable aspects of the global capitalist economy is that it rests on a continuously evolving and ever-more complex international division of labour. While the consumption of finished products remains concentrated in the West, the production of this increasing range of commodities is increasingly conducted by workers located across the far reaches of global capitalism. For example, while Apple design and market the iPod, they outsource the entire manufacturing process for each of the 451 components across a wide network of companies spanning North America and Asia. These companies range from multinationals such as Toshiba, who produce the hard drive, through to small producers based in countries such as China and the Philippines whose workforces either make or assemble small, yet essential, components of the final product (Linden *et al.* 2007). What we are faced with in the case of the iPod is an enormously complex division of labour across social space that collectively orchestrates the production of one of the prominent consumption icons of the current decade. This division of labour incorporates a great number of diverse and spatially separated workforces who undertake specific compartmentalised tasks and who are connected to the larger process through various forms of social organisation – ranging from the bureaucratic control of multinational firms, to market exchanges, social networks of subcontracting firms, and intricate webs of financing – that facilitate complex flows of goods, money and information.

Faced with the complexity of this contemporary international division of labour, the chapter introduces a series of analytical perspectives that help to shed light on the social foundations that underpin this global economic edifice. Following a brief critique of how mainstream economics conceptualises the global economy, I examine two contemporary approaches that attempt to transcend the limitations of the former. First, the chapter surveys the global commodity chains approach, which has sought to blend political-economy perspectives with insights drawn from economic sociology to explain how the international division of labour functions. Second, it examines the canon of critical institutional economics, which has stressed the importance of social institutions in determining the processes and outcomes of a range of economic activities within the global economy. These two perspectives have gained considerable influence over contemporary debates outside of the mainstream and their importance can be discerned in the chapters that follow. Used together, I argue, the global commodity chains and institutional economics literature provide useful analytical tools for understanding how economic activities such as production are socially embedded in specific institutional contexts that rest on distinct relations of power and contestation. In so doing, these approaches are valuable for opening empirical research agendas that can draw out the dynamics of power and conflict that shape the global economy and account for its profoundly uneven nature. I elaborate this point through an examination of the institutions and social processes through which labour forces are produced, reproduced and utilised.

In spite of the insights that these perspectives provide, however, the chapter identifies some important limitations in their analytical frameworks. To fully appreciate how the global economy is produced and reproduced, including the relationship between power and contestation that runs through the international division of labour, it is necessary to integrate the former approaches with the theory of 'social abstraction' developed by Karl Marx. I argue that Marx's notion of social abstraction helps puts the concept of social embedding in motion by forcing us to consider how the embedded activities of production and social reproduction are simultaneously subsumed under the abstract dynamics of global capitalism. Fluctuations in the price system, which acts as the nerve centre of the global economy, force producers across the international division of labour to continually disembed, restructure and re-embed their productive activities in an ongoing process that repeatedly generates social struggles. Focusing on the dynamic interplay between social embedding and social abstraction, moreover, allows us not only to understand how social conflict is endemic to the capitalist global economy, but also how the outcomes of such struggles serve to reshape the social foundations of productive activities across the international division of labour.

The global economy in mainstream economics

The terms in which the global economy is discussed in mainstream economics tend to follow the agenda set by the classical political economists who correlated the onset of capitalist modernity with dramatic increases in the productivity of human labour (cf. Cowen and Shenton 1996). Adam Smith's foundational exposition, for example, tied the essence of modernity to an extended and ever-more specialised division of labour that was driven by the growth of the market. This process was seen as a virtuous circle wherein specialisation induces greater productivity, higher national income and, therein, the further enlargement of the market: a formulation that parallels the current neoclassical orthodoxy. For Smith, the increasing productivity of labour constituted the material basis of what is now termed 'development'. Becoming part of an expanded division of labour, according to Smith, allowed an 'industrious and frugal peasant' to accommodate his needs in a manner that exceeded 'many an African king, the absolute master of the lives and liberties of ten thousand naked savages' (Smith 1990).

Smith's focus on market expansion and an expanding division of labour remains central to contemporary mainstream discourses on economic development. The World Bank, for example, celebrated the expansion of the international division of labour that would draw some 90 per cent of global workers into the 'economic mainstream' of global market relations, a process which they see as raising incomes and contributing to global prosperity (World Bank 1995: 50). As in Smith's time, the expanding productivity of labour is matched by the expanding production of labourers as proletarianisation accelerates apace through rural to urban migration, aided by the aggressive commodification and private ownership of land and other resources in rural areas (cf. Harvey 2004, and Chapter 3 in this volume). It is also matched with expanding inequality on a global level and the reproduction of vast levels of absolute and relative poverty (cf. Wade 2004). Such workers – and by extension the familial and community support systems that help to socially reproduce them – have indeed become cogs in a system of global production that is able to churn out ever greater numbers of commodities. However, the productive potentiality that appears innate to capitalism remains closely tied to uneven development, vast inequalities, and the poverty of an expanding global working class.

Although the substantive irrationalities of capitalist development were discussed by the classical political economists, they tended to be seen as a tangential and temporary evil that would be overcome by the productive revolution through which growing numbers of socially useful items (use-values) could be produced and hence expand the limits of social wealth. In so doing, capitalist development offered a potential solution to scarcity and therefore paved the way for social, cultural and political progress, a formulation that remains the implicit basis for liberal theories of development (Weisband 1989). In the contemporary era, institutions such as the IMF and the World Bank have deployed mainstream neoclassical economics to present development as the result of a transhistorical spread and growing efficiency of markets innate to humankind's assumed need to 'truck, barter and trade'.[1] For contemporary neoliberals, ensuring liberalised markets for all goods – including labour itself – and supplemented by a streamlined yet efficient state apparatus to uphold property rights, remains the only manner of providing for the material needs of humanity and ending global poverty. By integrating productive activities into a global division of labour, the expansion of a global market society is seen as a purely beneficial force that allows market forces to distribute resources into the areas of highest productivity and returns. Using simplifying microfoundations, the approach proclaims that, under proper macroeconomic management including trade liberalisation and fiscal responsibility, global productive structures naturally take shape through rational and mutually beneficial market exchanges in a manner that reflects national comparative advantages, leading to long run complementarities, income convergence and global equilibrium (Weeks 2001; Chang and Grabel 2004; Dunkley 2004). This conclusion, moreover, has been forcibly deployed to legitimate the rapid liberalisation of trade and capital markets on a global level since the 1980s.

Not only do these models fly against the history of profoundly uneven development across the capitalist world economy, they offer a pointedly incomplete understanding of the social dynamics that underpin the organisation of material life within global capitalism. On an analytical level, the focus on idealised models of exchange and market expansion wilfully erases any appreciation of the important qualitative differences between the social relationships though which production, distribution and the consumption of material items occurs (cf. Clarke 1991; Sayer 1995; Hodgson 2002; Reinert 2004). In particular, the abstract model of individuals and firms voluntarily exchanging goods in idealised market settings gives little room for understanding how power and conflict are integral to the functioning of economic activities; vary greatly between different social contexts; and are driving forces within global capitalism. As two critics put it in a blistering critique of the neoclassical mainstream:

> It leaves out almost everything social about the division of labour and modern production: the great varieties of people at work, the social integument that binds together their activities, and the social context in which production and circulation proceed. In effect, this shorthand denies the exigencies of power and domination, coordination and conflict, economic development and social change.
>
> (Sayer and Walker 1992: 3)

Without doubt, the methodological assumptions of neoclassical economics have been sharply critiqued from across the social sciences. The following sections focus on two specific contributions: (1) the 'global commodity chains approach'; and (2) critical institutional economics. These two approaches are particularly important due to the influence they have in setting the terms of contemporary debates on the global political economy.

Global commodity chains and the organisation of production

In recent years, the 'global commodity chains' (GCC) approach has become an increasingly fashionable method of analysing the organisation of production in contemporary capitalism (cf. Bernstein and Campling 2006b). In distinction to the abstractions of neoclassical economics, GCC analysis aims to take seriously the social dimensions of global production in a way that combines theoretical rigour with detailed case studies. Although it is possible to distinguish different trends within GCC analysis – including a variant that draws more strongly upon the business literature concerning transaction costs – they nonetheless share several central features including: (1) a sensitivity to the multiple ways of organising the production and distribution of commodities in a globalised economy; (2) the forms of power that permeate these different types of economic organisation, and (3) the implications for socio-economic development entailed in different types of commodity chains (cf. Bair 2008, for a concise history of the GCC approach).

Whereas the original theorists of the division of labour – from Weber to Durkheim and Marx – tended to focus on the increasing specialisation of labour tasks within the firm and between firms across society, the global commodity chains approach argues that the most important contemporary trend is the way that the assorted processes for producing a single commodity are divided up (modularised) and distributed across a network of firms. While the iPod example used in the introduction to this chapter is an excellent example of this process, such processes have been undertaken for the manufacture of an encompassing range of commodities – from bicycles and refrigerators through to blue jeans and tennis shoes. GCC analysis therefore focuses upon, first, the modularisation of the varied labour processes necessary for the creation of such commodities and, second, the subsequent distribution of these tasks between a network of firms. The metaphor of the 'commodity chain' is used to capture the technical and administrative methods by which firms are able to coordinate the various interlinked labour processes across the network. Central to GCC studies, therefore, is the question of how these distinct production processes performed by diverse companies in numerous locations can be effectively integrated and coordinated across a network of formally independent firms despite important logistical and organisational challenges, not to mention questions of power regarding the relative valuation of different modules of the production and distribution process.

This leads us to the second key aspect of GCC approaches, which is a focus on the economic, political and social ties that permit networks to function despite these constraints. GCC analysts are particularly interested in the governance structures that allow control to be exercised and efficiency maintained across the network without lead firms requiring direct ownership of the chain. To do so, they draw upon the notion of 'social embedding' as developed in economic sociology. For the GCC approach, the concept of social embedding is used to examine how a broad range of social relations affects economic behaviour. While mainstream economics assumes that market actors operate in a universally rational manner in terms of pursuing self-maximising exchanges, economic sociology rejects this assumption by asking how the social context and the social values held by economic agents affect various types of economic activities. For GCC analysis, this is reflected in the emphasis on how production networks rely on the 'embedded' nature of their relationships in order to achieve control, stability, and efficiency. In a manner that escapes mainstream economic theory, GCC emphasises how the pursuit of efficiency relies not simply on economic rationality but on a wide range of social relationships through which business is done:

> Network actors in many instances control opportunism through the effects of repeat transactions, reputation, and social norms that are embedded in particular geographic locations or social groups . . . trust, reputation, and mutual dependence dampen opportunistic behavior, and in so doing they make possible more complex inter-firm divisions of labor and interdependence than would be predicted by transaction costs theory.
>
> (Gereffi *et al.* 2005: 81)

Owing to their embedded nature, network relationships can lead to the formation of trust between firms and therefore facilitate mutual coordination for joint problem-solving activities. However, while embedded relationships may be ones of relative equality, longevity, mutual dependence and trust, they can also reinforce hierarchy, power asymmetries, and the uneven appropriation of rents and, ultimately, profit.

As part of its analysis of social embedding, GCC analysis interrogates the power relations that pervade such networks and mediate the vertical and, to a lesser degree, horizontal linkages that compose commodity chains. Commodity chains are consequently identified according to the governance structure and power relationships that bind the network together. The particular depth of social embedding and types of power relations differentiate network types. They range from un-embedded 'arm's-length' market relations that function through formal market exchanges, to modular, relational and captive value chains that operate through gradations of social embedding and levels of power between networked firms (Gereffi *et al.* 2005).[2] For example, the governance structures of 'captive value chains' are characterised by lead firms that use their financial and technological advantages to institutionalise dominant relationships with suppliers. The latter are left dependent in terms of technology, information and market access and are rendered more vulnerable to market shifts.

Commodity chains are therefore structured around significant power imbalances through which lead firms seek to control market access, shape the technical organisation of production and influence the distribution of costs associated with relative production stages so as to maximise their control over the appropriation of value across the chain as a whole. Within these relationships, the exercise of power is shaped by the way in which information about market opportunities, quality standards and production technologies is centralised, codified and controlled (Ponte and Gibbon 2005;

Heintz 2006). Access to and control of such knowledge help define the relative capacity of firms across the commodity chain to upgrade their technological capabilities and produce directly for markets (Gereffi *et al.* 2005). Moreover, the exercise of power affects the geographical distribution of productive activities – with the technology and branding functions held by companies in the advanced industrial countries and low-cost, labour-intensive processing peripheralised to the developing world – thereby feeding into the uneven development of global capitalism.

This leads to the third concern of GCC analysis, which is to analyse the consequences of commodity chains on the socio-economic development of regions or nations. In particular, GCC authors are interested in the possibilities for firms in lesser-developed countries to upgrade their role in the production process by assuming more technologically advanced functions that allow for a greater value appropriation and further horizontal and vertical linkages with local firms (Gibbon 2001; Bair and Gereffi 2003). Technological upgrading is recognised to play a central – although not straightforward – role in socio-economic development in an era of globalisation. Whereas early contributions tended to focus upon the possibilities and limits to industrial upgrading, recent studies have begun to question the presumed benefits of this form of 'catch-up' by considering wider questions about the concentration of wealth within 'total package' sectors in the developing world (Bair and Dussel Peters 2006; cf. Bernstein and Campling 2006a).

The insights of the GCC exploration of network dynamics and the power relations that traverse transnational supply chains are instructive and its influence can be found in many of the following chapters. Despite these attributes, however, GCC approaches provide only a partial view of the social relations and institutional contexts that shape global production and mediate its developmental impacts. This derives largely from the methodology of the GCC approach which prioritises the governance structures of commodity chains (cf. Gereffi *et al.* 2005). At a conceptual level, the complexity of the social relations through which commodities are produced tend to be reduced to ideal-type categories of network governance that vary according to the degree of embedding between firms. The latter are seen to spring from a combination of technological imperatives – i.e. methods of modularisation, information coordination, relative technological capacity, and the character of market access and demand for a given commodity – that define the parameters in which networked firms attempt to shape the distribution of knowledge, resources and profits. On this basis there is a tendency to view the dynamics of global commodity chains as being determined by the functional characteristics of governance networks.

Although governance mechanisms are important, this analytical focus is problematic because it provides little theoretical purchase on the wider social and institutional contexts that shape the production and distribution of commodities beyond the level of inter-firm relationships. Specifically, by focusing on inter-firm governance, the process of production itself tends to be reduced to a technical task of modularising and distributing labour tasks across a network of firms and production sites. In so doing, analysis is focused on the power relations and distribution of surplus between networked firms. What this misses is the prior issue of the character of production relations within firms, including the question of how value is produced before its subsequent distribution among networked firms. Production is an infinitely more complex social process than a focus on inter-firm networks would indicate. It involves not just the production of material goods but also the simultaneous reproduction of workforces constructed and utilised within particular social institutions and power relations – a process that occurs at multiple social levels including within firms, within the larger society, and within the context of the reproduction of profitability on a global level (Clarke 1980; Burawoy 1985; Lee 1998).

As such, the approach gives little quarter to the relationships through which specific labour forces are reproduced with attributes and characteristics that make them suitably disposed for incorporation into global commodity chains. GCC analysis is, of course, not entirely muted on labour issues and GCC analysts often consider, albeit briefly, the impact of changes in global commodity chains upon workforces in terms of their effects on wages and technological upgrading within the workplace (e.g. Bair and Gereffi 2001; Czaban and Henderson 2003; Palpacuer and Parisotto 2003; Bair and Dussel Peters 2006). The latter are undoubtedly pertinent issues in need of elaboration and discussion. Nonetheless, studies within the genre tend to consider labour forces as an *a priori* factor in the spatial disbursement of productive processes within chains. This is often undertaken with the implicit assumption of the availability of cheap and/or disciplined labour-power without consideration of the processes that socially construct and reproduce labour in the form of a commodity with particular qualities in specific locations.

By handling labour as a static input into production, the approach sidelines important questions about power and subjectivity both in the labour process and within the wider context of the creation and reproduction of labour forces. In the GCC approach, labour is constructed as a passive object that is moulded through shifts within the overarching categories of networks and technological change central to GCC analysis. Often such studies are addressed within the paradigm of the 'effects of the global economy' upon labour markets and workforces (Jenkins 2004; Manda and Sen 2004) whereas insufficient attention is paid to the inversion of this question: what are the constitutive effects of constructed and contested workforces, labour markets and production processes upon the global economy? In short, rather than see the global economy as an autonomous entity that shapes the social world around itself, it is important to ask what the social foundations on which the global economy is constructed and which shape its dynamics.

Institutions, capitalism and social power

Sympathetic critiques of the GCC approach suggest that, in order to overcome its limitations, it is necessary to consider a much fuller spectrum of institutions in which productive activities are embedded (Henderson *et al.* 2002; Bair 2005). The literature stemming from critical institutional economics is useful in this respect.[3] Within this body of work, institutions are understood as 'durable systems of established, embedded and potentially codifiable social rules and conventions that structure social interactions' (Hodgson 2002: 297). This formulation casts a wide net that transcends the restricted notion of social embedding found in the GCC approach. It draws our attention to how economic activities are both embedded within and facilitated by a range of social institutions that are formed historically, evolve in path-dependent manners, and that are shaped by the power relations within societies while simultaneously institutionalising those same relationships.

Institutionalists tend to demarcate firms, markets, the family and the state as the most important institutions that determine the dynamics of capitalist society owing to their primacy in shaping production and distribution. Nonetheless, a range of underlying social institutions and cultural practices mould the particular character of these primary institutions. As Henry Yeung has argued, while the central institutions of capitalist society exist in contemporary China – including private enterprises and labour markets – they operate in a qualitatively distinct manner owing to their embedding in distinct social institutions and cultural practices that are unique to the Chinese context (Yeung 2004). Institutions therefore tend to manifest sharp qualitative differences across social space, leading to divergence in both process and outcome of the economic activities that they structure.

On this basis, for institutionalists, it is not possible to accept the proposition of mainstream economics that capitalist economies have a universal set of dynamics and outcomes but rather analysis must focus on particular character of the historically and socially specific institutions that exist in different locations. In this sense, the neoclassical vision of 'the market' – a universal institution that operates through the interaction of rational individuals engaged in the activity of exchanging goods, and which tends toward a single efficient form through the harmonisation of supply and demand – is rendered problematic. Markets are not natural and spontaneous institutions that operate according to a universal logic, but are social constructs that depend on a range of other social institutions – including money, property rights, collective behavioural norms, relationships of trust and numerous forms of institutional regulation and information provision. All of the latter vary greatly across social contexts and, as a consequence, the process and outcomes of markets change depending upon the character of these supporting institutions (cf. Sayer 1995). Global capitalism may well subordinate economic activities to a similar logic of the accumulation of capital through the appropriation of profit, but it does so in-and-through divergent institutional contexts that perpetuate the diversity of capitalist social relations within, between and across nation states (cf. Hall and Soskice 2001).

The institutionalist canon helps not only in broadening our understanding of social embedding but also influences our perception of the exercise of power in the global economy. By structuring social interactions, institutions not only serve to facilitate certain activities but simultaneously to restrict others. In shaping the bounds of what is normal and legitimate in a given social context, institutions are integrally related to the way in which power is exercised within and across societies. For example, while many of the following chapters question the ability of corporate codes of conduct to make sustained improvements to the rights of workers on a global level, they nonetheless recognise how codes of conduct have changed the institutional structure in which the contemporary dynamics of conflict and accommodation between workers and factory managers occurs (cf. Sum and Ngai 2005). Like other institutional forms, codes of conduct serve to normalise and legitimise certain forms of behaviour while delegitimising others. It is therefore notable that transnational corporations have concertedly attempted to institutionalise criticism of their activities into these structures of 'corporate social responsibility' that facilitate self-regulation and weak forms of monitoring and enforcement (Wells 2007). As this indicates, relationships of power not only shape the creation of social institutions, they are simultaneously reproduced by the very functioning of those institutions.

One area in which an institutionalist perspective is essential is in the analysis of the social institutions and processes through which labour forces in different regional and national settings are produced, reproduced and utilised. Mainstream economics tends to see labour as a ready-made commodity, which simply exists and can be added to the other ingredients of production as if baking a cake. GCC analysis also gives little quarter to labour, tending to take its existence across the commodity chain for granted. As both Karl Marx and Karl Polanyi emphasised, however, labour in commodity form (labour-power) is a fictitious commodity that is produced and reproduced through a wide range of historically-specific social institutions. Its existence not only has to be constituted through the separation of workers from alternative means of subsistence, but also labour forces with specific attributes and characteristics must be socially constructed as resources that can be profitably employed within the international division of labour. In this way, the analysis of the production of commodities is inseparable from an analysis of the production of labouring bodies and this forces us to examine the regionally-specific social institutions that are pivotal to this process.

To do so, it is useful to draw upon what Fred Deyo has termed 'labour systems'. In this usage, labour systems comprise the mechanisms through which labour is 'socially reproduced, mobilised for economic ends, utilised in production and controlled and motivated in support of economic goals' (Deyo 2001: 259). This involves the interaction of contested material, social and cultural processes that are filtered through the specific institutional contexts of different locales. By bringing labour systems into the analysis of social embedding and institutional contexts, we can begin to understand how productive activities are not reducible to simply adding capital and pre-existing labour as in mainstream economics; nor are they merely embedded in the networked relationships between interrelated firms that compose a commodity chain. Rather, they are embedded in both the social fabric of the relationships between capital and labour within the process of production, and in the social reproduction of waged labour in its commodity form, mediated by historically-specific institutions such as the household, labour markets and the state.

The role of the state in fashioning the social context within which labour forces are created and deployed is pivotal. While some authors have suggested that a new era of global capitalism has rendered it necessary to dispense with the centrality of the nation state and think in terms of transnational classes and transnational states (Robinson 2002), this perspective tends to downplay the magnitude of the national state's role in creating the conditions within which economic activities are embedded. It therefore underestimates the continued prevalence of the national state in socially differentiating productive activities across space. In particular, retaining a focus on the *international* (rather than global) division of labour helps to emphasise the foundational element of state influence over the production, reproduction and utilisation of labour. At a very minimum, this includes fashioning the institutional basis for the contracting of labour, the legal basis on which industrial relations occur, and its function in the reproduction of differentiated labouring bodies through various interventions in social reproduction, including social security, education and 'anti-poverty' policies (cf. Edwards and Elger 1999).

Notwithstanding its centrality, the state is one of a number of institutions that configure the social context in which labour forces are constructed, reproduced and put to work. The complex interplay between the social embedding of production and the social reproduction of labour forces is shaped by struggles across a range of social institutions including: (1) the institutional environment established by national and regional state bodies through social, labour and industrial policies; (2) the hiring and labour control strategies of employers in their attempt to forge a cohesive, efficient and disciplined workforce; (3) practices of exclusion or inclusion that structure workforces based on social origin, age, gender or ethnicity; and (4) social relationships within the family unit that shape which family members will enter paid labour and under what conditions. Intrinsic to these relationships are important issues of power and conflict associated with class and patriarchy that shape both the dynamics and spatial division of economic activity. They permeate the very forms assumed by production relations, such as the development of modes of labour control within the factory and their integration with the technologies of production.

While the following chapters illustrate case studies of such conflicts in considerable detail, it is useful to highlight two aspects here. First, class conflicts over the nature and functioning of institutions that regulate labour markets and mediate the exercise of power within firms are endemic across both the advanced industrial countries and the global South. In many countries conflicts have revolved around attempts by the state and capital to introduce 'labour flexibilisation' which is predicated on the notion that a free market economy can only function successfully if barriers to the treatment of labour as a commodity are removed. Institutions that are seen to restrict market-determination of the price and subsequent utilisation of labour-power are remodelled, therein allowing capital greater flexibility to hire, fire and utilise workers within the firm (see Taylor 2006, and Chapter 9 in this volume). Second, in other branches of the international division of labour – particularly in the context of migrant and predominantly female labourers drawn into export production zones such as coastal China – workers have been less concerned with safeguarding institutionalised rights as with trying to establish their implementation in the first place (see Chapters 3, 4 and 5).

The outcomes of struggles over flexibilisation and worker rights tend to be both path-dependent and profoundly uneven, forging major qualitative and quantitative differences between workforces across social space. Anita Chan and Hong-zen Wang, for example, have illustrated the starkly different forms of labour control employed by Taiwanese firms producing the same labour-intensive goods in China and Vietnam respectively (Chan and Wang 2004). Whereas a brutally militaristic form of worker discipline was employed in the Chinese factories under study – including extensive working hours, widespread rights abuses and habitually unpaid wages – the factories studied around Hanoi and Ho Chi Minh City in Vietnam were characterised by a somewhat 'softer' form of labour management where the above abuses were notably less present. The authors relate such differences – which belie the notion of a homogenous global 'cheap labour army' – to the distinct institutional contexts for production established by the interaction between firms, state and workers and as reflected in vastly different levels of worker right awareness and divergent strategies of contestation pursued by workers at the level of the factory, through unions in the national ambit, and through global consumer campaigns that attempt to enforce corporate social responsibility in terms of labour rights. By influencing the conditions under which labour-power is put to work and remunerated, such struggles have determinate effects upon the constitution of global commodity chains.

Concurrently, as highlighted by feminist studies of work and labour markets, the distinct ways in which gender is socially constructed is pivotal to this creation of socially specific labour forces. For example, Leslie Salzinger has closely elaborated how the ongoing creation and contestation of gender identities within Mexico's *maquiladora* zones have been crucial processes in the attempt of capital and the state to reproduce a profitable assembly sector. Reproducing the trope of a female *maquila* worker in Ciudad Juárez – cheap, docile and productive owing to her femininity – created a battlefield over the construction of gender that stretched from the household to the factory, labour market and into the mechanisms of cultural production including the local and international media:

> In this context, gender certainly shapes the export-processing labor market, but not through transnationals' capacity to leverage the ineluctable productivity of young, third-world women. Rather, gender intervenes because it is the terrain upon which the question of who looks like a maquila worker, and who doesn't, is decided, thus establishing the context within which hiring takes place and production is initiated.
>
> (Salzinger 2003: 35–36)

Salzinger therein builds on an impressive body of feminist scholarship that highlights how the gendered nature of social institutions – ranging from the household to the state – has an unequivocal impact upon the process and outcomes of the production, distribution and consumption of commodities (e.g. Mies 1986; Elson 1995).

Social embedding meets social abstraction

The above section has indicated some of the constructive ways in which critical institutionalist analysis expands the notion of social embedding found in the global commodity chains literature. The production and distribution of commodities are not simply embedded within the governance structures of inter-firm networks. Rather, they are embedded in a much wider spectrum of social institutions and relationships, including those through which specific labour forces are created, reproduced and utilised. Widening the scope of analysis therein provides important tools for critically examining the global economy. Nonetheless, this final section of the chapter argues that it is also necessary to proceed beyond a conceptualisation of economic relationships that focuses solely on social embedding. I argue that if we wish to take the concept of social embedding seriously, we must not only engage a much fuller and richer spectrum of institutions and relationships in which economic activities are embedded, but also consider how these activities undergo a repeated process of *abstraction* and *re-embedding* within the framework of global capitalism. By extension, this approach permits us to analyse not only how the uneven effects of global economic integration impact upon workers and communities across the globe, but also how the struggles that surround embedded economic activities have reciprocal effects upon the wider terrain of global accumulation.

To elaborate this relationship between embedding and abstraction, it is useful to draw upon Marx's critique of political economy and his notion of the dual form of commodity-producing labour within capitalism. For Marx, labour within capitalist production has both concrete and abstract qualities. On the one hand, labour is concrete and private because production involves a specific type of labour (e.g. stitching together jeans or assembling electronic parts) that is undertaken by waged labourers within the context of a capitalist enterprise operating with distinct conditions of production in a specific social setting. The concept of concrete labour thereby reflects the embedded quality of production, whereby productive activities are embedded in specific social, cultural and institutional contexts that include the relationships and institutions through which labour forces are reproduced and put to use. The unique social context in which every act of production takes place provides the basis for the qualitatively and quantitatively distinct economic activities and outcomes upon which the uneven productive structures of global capitalism are mapped out. They shape the contracting process by which capital purchases labour-power, the production process through which labour-power is put to work in qualitatively and quantitatively distinct manners, and the forms and strategies through which this power is contested by workers, either individually or collectively.

Alongside being embedded as concrete and private, however, labour within capitalism is simultaneously abstract and social because every private and concrete process of production forms one moment of the social division of labour that is mediated through the exchange of commodities. As such, production must be understood not solely as a conjuncture of concrete, embedded relationships but also – simultaneously – as one moment in a circuit of capital that spans production and circulation. Within the circuit of capital, moreover, the concrete products of embedded production enter the realm of abstract social relationships in which their value is ascribed through market forces that appear as a dominating social power without concrete subject. The distinct qualitative and embedded relationships of production are reduced to the homogenous and abstract form of market prices whose fluctuations exercise power over the concrete relationships of production (Clarke 1991: 136). The embedding-abstraction relationship illuminates that capitalist production is indivisibly material and social (Clarke 1980: 6). Every act of production not only produces a material item but also produces abstract social relations – the formation of a new social average for production – that conditions the production of future commodities of that type.

This abstract social power is manifested through the price system that is the regulatory nexus of global capitalism. Through the circulation of commodities on the market, the concrete social relations and labouring practices through which an individual act of production occurs are abstracted into the form of value, represented through the interplay of market prices. The concrete and abstract moments of global capitalism are therefore locked into a relationship of mutual constitution. Through the circuit of capital each concrete act of production enters into a disciplinary feedback loop with the social whole through which it must be socially validated by way of the sale of commodities. As Massimo de Angelis (2005) puts it:

> It is by pursuing value within the confinement of market relations that individual 'actors' compare values of different products or compare among values of the same products produced with different methods and conditions of production and act upon this comparison. The effect of this acting enters into feedback relations with millions of others, it contributes to produce new average prices and profit and produces effects that act as material forces for other actors making similar comparisons and acting upon them. The ongoing process of this act of measurement of value and action upon it, is what gives rise to what we value socially regardless of our individual or collective aggregate ethical standpoint.

The market operates as an abstract disciplinary mechanism through which concrete productive activities are compared and value is socially ascribed, a process in which individual producers are either rewarded or punished in accordance with their ability to meet the quantitative and qualitative requirements of social reproduction.

The qualitative requirements of social production signify the need for producers to match the social validation of what constitutes a socially useful item, or 'use value' in Marx's terminology. As Marx (1976: 48) stated: 'If the thing is useless, so is the labour contained within it; the labour does not count as labour, and therefore creates no value.' As Marx did not put it, however, the ascription of social utility to a commodity involves complex struggles over the social construction of consumption needs through such techniques as product differentiation and branding through sophisticated advertising techniques (Lefebvre 1971; Bourdieu 1984; Fine 2002). This is extremely important because companies selling such products frequently attempt to mediate the social discipline imposed by the market by either creating new social needs – and thereby expanding the market – or by attempting to manipulate the symbolic capital associated with their particular product in an attempt to capture market share and displace competition, a technique known as 'branding'. Although companies seek to institutionalise the branded quality of their product, the ability to do so is often provisional. Consumers become savvy to marketing ploys while other producers mimic the same branding techniques, a process which tends to reconstitute the social average around a new definition of social utility and thereby re-launch the process of differentiation anew.

Simultaneously, the quantitative dimension of value is imposed through the constant struggle of capitals to cut costs and to increase the productivity of labour in the production of a given commodity. This is reflected in the notion of 'socially necessary labour time', which was used by Marx to indicate how the value of any generic commodity is established by the labour-time socially necessary to produce that item under the normal conditions of production with the average degree of skill and intensity prevalent at the time (Marx 1976: 47). For Marx, therefore, value was not embodied in each individual commodity but rather described a social average for a particular class of commodity. The imposition of value upon commodities, as determined by socially necessary labour-time, forces firms to make their embedded conditions of production conform to this social norm of productivity on pain of extinction. Firms whose concrete production relations allow them to produce quicker the socially necessary labour-time will be able to offer lower prices, capture a greater market share and force competitors to attempt to catch up in a continuous competitive struggle to maintain profitability. To do so, they will have to attempt to reorganise the locally embedded social relations through which their production is realised. In so doing, however, a new social average for production will be established and this will reinitiate the competitive pressures and drive the process of value formation onwards.

What we find, therefore, is a continual process of mutual constitution between the embedded and abstracted elements of production. This is inevitably a conflict-ridden process that applies not merely to the production of material goods, but also to the production of 'immaterial products' as predominates in the so-called service economy (Sayer and Walker 1992). When the socially embedded relations of production for a specific firm no longer meet the social ascription of value, production must be disembedded from its existing social context, and those social relations must be restructured and re-institutionalised if production is to be profitably re-embedded. Recognising the dynamics of social abstraction, therefore, helps us put social embedding in motion. The result is an uneven and conflict-driven process in which various social actors attempt to respond to the abstract demands of the market by restructuring the concrete relationships in which they are embedded. While, capitals respond to the pressures of competition by internally restructuring their labour processes and organisational structures, state bodies respond to a potential drop in regional or national competitiveness by attempting to restructure a wide range of social relations and institutions that lay the social foundations for economic activities.

Global economy in motion: restructuring and social conflict

The abstract world of capital – objectified in the form of global economic forces such as shifting market prices for commodities and fickle investment flows – is locked into a dialectical relationship with the embedded world of concrete institutions and labour processes: it is impossible to understand one without the other. The pressures of social abstraction compel periods of social restructuring which necessitate repeated revolutions in the social, technical and frequently spatial organisation of production in an ongoing process. As Marx emphatically argued, capitalism contains within it an 'endless and limitless drive to go beyond its limiting barrier. Every limit appears as a barrier to be overcome' (Marx 1973: 408).

As the above sections have emphasised, however, these limiting barriers are not simply a question of technical innovations nor are they simply overcome through the automatic response of rational actors to economic signals, therein leading naturally to a new equilibrium state as assumed by mainstream economics. Rather, overcoming the barriers to the accumulation of capital requires the restructuring of the social relationships and institutional forms through which the production, distribution and consumption of commodities are embedded. The success or failure of these restructuring strategies is not simply a function of the economic system; but rests on the outcome of social conflicts in which varied social actors attempt to reshape the institutionalised and embedded relationships through which capitalism operates (Taylor 2006). The tension between embedding and abstraction across the global economy therefore generates constant social conflicts and is driven by their outcomes.

Within the realm of production, the restructuring of the social foundations on which commodities and services are produced necessitates an analytical focus on class relationships. In particular, generations of Marxist authors have highlighted how capital is repeatedly forced to restructure its foundational class relationships in attempt to impose extensive (longer, harder work) and/or intensive (productivity increase through mechanisation) methods of increasing the surplus extracted from labour (cf. Fine 2004). These pressures operate on a quotidian level and force firms to constantly seek to anticipate and mitigate the effects of competition through organisational restructuring. Indeed, the very creation of global commodity chains are a response to precisely these kind of pressures which became particularly pronounced within the context of the pronounced social and economic crisis in the 1970s.

For example, companies such as Nike have outsourced the entire production process for their shoes in an attempt to shed the pressures of productive reorganisation onto its suppliers and use its market position to displace any incurred costs onto the latter, as typically described in the GCC literature (cf. Merk, Chapter 4 in this volume). In short, large firms attempt to shelter from the pressures of social abstraction by institutionalising themselves as the lead player in a network. However, the dynamics of spatial reorganisation cannot be adequately comprehended outside of the context of the ongoing wide-scale restructuring of labour forces in the global South (specifically China, in this case) within which such production processes are embedded (cf. Cantin and Taylor, in this volume). The outcomes of restructuring – and therefore the very dynamics of the global economy – are predicated on the complex social struggles that interlock production and social reproduction through which actors – ranging from firms and state organisations (national and international) through to individual and collective bodies of workers, families and communities – attempt to redefine the institutional structures and processes through which they are integrated into the international division of labour.

Of particular concern in the chapters that follow, therefore, are how workers in various branches of the international division of labour have been the target of restructuring yet have also contested and sought to shape the nature and effects of this process. The outcome of struggles in one site are refracted across the international division of labour through the abstraction process and this raises notable challenges for workers seeking to either safeguard or improve their working lives. For example, the absorption of the vast and strongly disciplined Chinese labour force into global capitalism has unleashed deflationary pressures on prices of many manufactured commodities, leading to intense competition and restructuring across the international division of labour. The success of capital in lowering costs and heightening the intensity of work in one location only increases competitive pressures in others and workers in industries from textiles to automobiles have found it difficult to withstand the demands of globally mobile capital to find ways to cut costs or intensify labour processes.

It is precisely this division of labour – in which workers find themselves in a relationship of competition with other workers – that creates great obstacles for building solidarity and coherent political positions between groups of workers. The uneven development of capital on a global level therefore raises a greater need for international labour solidarity at the same time as it constructs significant barriers to it (cf. Arrighi and Silver 2000). However, as the following chapters elaborate, various labour and social movements have taken up these challenges through forms of contestation that extend from new forms of collective organisation at the level of production; building international solidarity across union movements separated by national boundaries; to movements that aim to impose various forms of corporate social responsibility on a global level through the imposition of labour codes of conduct and socially responsible investment criteria. The important facet of these struggles is that, while they emphasise the importance of localised organisation to counter the exercise of locally-embedded power relations; they equally recognise the need to build linkages upwards and outwards in an attempt to better meet the global and more abstract forms of power within capitalism. To be sure, many of these initiatives are tentative at best and are limited by prevailing forms of power and internal divisions; yet at the same time they suggest that new and promising avenues to overcome such problems are being explored.

Notes

1 It is useful to follow Arnsperger and Varoufakis (2006), who define neoclassical economics as a body of thought predicated on the axioms of: (1) methodological individualism; (2) methodological instrumentalism; and (3) methodological equilibration.

2 The fifth and final ideal type production network is 'hierarchy', which relates to the complete vertical integration of production within a unitary transnational enterprise. Given that this form of economic organisation does not involve a network, it has received less attention within the approach. See Jenkins (1987).

3 By 'critical institutional economics', I exclude the 'New Institutional Economics', as popularised by Douglas North and heralded by international institutions such as the World Bank. See Fine (2001).

References

Arnsperger, C. and Varoufakis, Y. (2006) 'What Is Neoclassical Economics?', *Post-Autistic Economics Review* 38: 2–12.

Arrighi, G. and Silver, B. (2000) 'Workers North and South', in L. Panitch and C. Leys, *Socialist Register 2001: Working Classes, Global Realities*, London: Merlin Press, pp. 51–74.

Bair, J. (2005) 'Global Capitalism and Commodity Chains: Looking Back, Going Forward', *Competition & Change* 9(2): 153–180.

—— (2008) 'Global Commodity Chains: Genealogy and Review', in J. Bair, *Frontiers of Commodity Chains Research*, Ithaca, NY: Cornell University Press.

Bair, J. and Dussel Peters, E. (2006) 'Global Commodity Chains and Endogenous Growth: Export Dynamism and Development in Mexico and Honduras', *World Development* 34(2): 203–221.

Bair, J. and Gereffi, G. (2001) 'Local Clusters in Global Chains: The Causes and Consequences of Export Dynamism in Torreon's Blue Jeans Industry', *World Development* 29(11): 1885–1903.

—— (2003) 'Upgrading, Uneven Development, and Jobs in the North American Apparel Industry', *Global Networks* 3(2): 143–169.

Bernstein, H. and Campling, L. (2006a) 'Commodity Studies and Commodity Fetishism I: Trading Down', *Journal of Agrarian Change* 6(2): 239–264.

—— (2006b) 'Commodity Studies and Commodity Fetishism II: "Profits with Principles"?' *Journal of Agrarian Change* 6(3): 414–447.

Bourdieu, P. (1984) *Distinction: A Social Critique of the Judgement of Taste*, London: Routledge & Kegan Paul.

Burawoy, M. (1985) *The Politics of Production: Factory Regimes under Capitalism and Socialism*, London: Verso.

Chan, A. and Wang, H.-Z. (2004) 'The Impact of the State on Worker's Conditions: Comparing Taiwanese Factories in China and Vietnam', *Pacific Affairs* 77(4): 629–646.

Chang, H.-J. and Grabel, I. (2004) *Reclaiming Development: An Alternative Economic Policy Manual*, London: Zed Books.

Clarke, S. (1980) 'Althusserian Marxism', in S. Clarke, *One Dimensional Marxism*, London: Allison and Busby, pp. 5–102.

—— (1991) *Marx, Marginalism and Modern Sociology*, London: Macmillan.

Cowen, M. and Shenton, R.W. (1996) *Doctrines of Development*, London: Routledge.

Czaban, L. and Henderson, J. (2003) 'Commodity Chains, Foreign Investment and Labour Issues in Eastern Europe', *Global Networks* 3(1): 171–196.

De Angelis, M. (2005) 'Values, Measures and Disciplinary Markets', *The Commoner* 10: 66–86.

Deyo, F. (2001) 'The Social Construction of Developmental Labour Systems: South-East Asian Industrial Restructuring', in G. Rodan, K. Hewison and R. Robinson, *The Political Economy of South-East Asia: Conflicts, Crises and Change*, Oxford: Oxford University Press, pp. 235–249.

Dunkley, G. (2004) *Free Trade: Myth, Reality and Alternatives*, London: Zed Books.

Edwards, P. and Elger, T. (eds) (1999) *The Global Economy, National States and the Regulation of Labour*, London: Mansell.

Elson, D. (1995) *Male Bias in the Development Process*, Manchester: Manchester University Press.

Fine, B. (2001) 'Neither the Washington Nor the Post-Washington Consensus', in B. Fine, C. Lapavitsas and J. Pincus, *Development Policy in the Twenty-First Century: Beyond the Post-Washington Consensus*, London: Routledge, pp. 3–37.

—— (2002) *The World of Consumption: The Material and Cultural Revisited*, London, Routledge, pp. 3–22.

—— (2004) 'Value Theory and the Study of Contemporary Capitalism', in R. Westra and A. Zuege, *Value and the World Economy Today: Production, Finance and Globalization*, London: Palgrave.

Gereffi, G., *et al.* (2005) 'The Governance of Global Value Chains', *Review of International Political Economy* 12(1): 78–104.

Gibbon, P. (2001) 'Upgrading Primary Production: A Global Commodity Chain Approach', *World Development* 29(2): 345–363.

Hall, P.A. and Soskice, D.W. (2001) *Varieties of Capitalism: The Institutional Foundations of Comparative Advantage*, Oxford: Oxford University Press.

Harvey, D. (2004) 'The "New" Imperialism: Accumulation by Dispossession', in L. Panitch and C. Leys, *Socialist Register 2004*, London: Merlin Press, pp. 46–62.

Heintz, J. (2006) 'Low-wage Manufacturing and Global Commodity Chains: A Model in the Unequal Exchange Tradition', *Cambridge Journal of Economics* (30): 507–520.

Henderson, J. *et al.* (2002) 'Global Production Networks and the Analysis of Economic Development', *Review of International Political Economy* 9(3): 436–464.

Hodgson, G. (2002) *How Economics Forgot History: The Problem of Historical Specificity in Social Science*, London: Routledge.

Jenkins, R. (2004) 'Vietnam in the Global Economy: Trade, Employment and Poverty', *Journal of International Development* 16: 13–28.

Jenkins, R.O. (1987) *Transnational Corporations and Uneven Development: The Internationalization of Capital and the Third World*, London: Methuen.

Lee, C.K. (1998) *Gender and the South China Miracle: Two Worlds of Factory Women*, Berkeley, CA: University of California Press.

Lefebvre, H. (1971) *Everyday Life in the Modern World*, New York: Harper & Row.

Linden, G. *et al.* (2007) *Who Captures Value in a Global Innovation System? The Case of Apple's iPod*, Irvine, CA: Personal Computing Industry Center, University of California, Irvine..

Manda, D. and Sen, K. (2004) 'The Labour Market Effects of Globalization in Kenya', *Journal of International Development* 16: 29–43.

Marx, K. (1973) *Grundrisse*, London: Penguin Books.

—— (1976) *Capital*, vol. 1, London: Penguin Books.

Mies, M. (1986) *Patriarchy and Accumulation on a World Scale: Women in the International Division of Labour*, London: Zed Books.

Palpacuer, F. and Parisotto, A. (2003) 'Global Production and Local Jobs: Can Global Enterprise Networks Be Used as Levers for Local Development?' *Global Networks* 3(2): 97–120.

Ponte, S. and Gibbon, P. (2005) 'Quality Standards, Conventions and the Governance of Global Value Chains', *Economy and Society* 34(1): 1–31.

Reinert, E.S. (2004) *Globalization, Economic Development and Inequality: An Alternative Perspective*, Cheltenham: Edward Elgar.

Robinson, W.I. (2002) 'Remapping Development in Light of Globalization: From a Territorial to a Social Cartography', *Third World Quarterly* 23(6): 1047–1071.

Salzinger, L. (2003) *Genders in Production: Marking Workers in Mexico's Global Factories*, Berkeley, CA: University of California Press.

Sayer, A. (1995) *Radical Political Economy: A Critique*, Oxford: Blackwell.

Sayer, A. and Walker, R. (1992) *The New Social Economy: Reworking the Division of Labor*, Oxford: Blackwell.

Smith, A. (1990) *An Inquiry into the Nature and Causes of the Wealth of Nations*, Chicago: Encyclopedia Britannica, Inc.

Sum, N.-L. and Ngai, P. (2005) 'Globalization and Paradoxes of Ethical Transnational Production: Code of Conduct in a Chinese Workplace', *Competition and Change* 9(2): 181–200.

Taylor, M. (2006) *From Pinochet to the Third Way: Neoliberalism and Social Transformation in Chile, 1973–2003*, London: Pluto Press.

Wade, R. (2004) 'Is Globalization Reducing Poverty and Inequality?' *World Development* 32(4): 567–589.

Weeks, J. (2001) 'The Expansion of Capital and Uneven Development on a World Scale', *Capital & Class* 74: 9–31.

Weisband, E. (1989) *Poverty Amidst Plenty: World Political Economy and Distributive Justice*, Boulder, CO: Westview Press.

Wells, D. (2007) 'Corporate Codes of Conduct, Non-Governmental Organizations and the Regulation of International Labour Standards', *Global Social Policy* 7(1): 51–74.

World Bank (1995) *World Development Report 1995: Workers in an Integrating World*, Oxford: Oxford University Press.

Yeung, H. W.-C. (2004) *Chinese Capitalism in a Global Era: Towards Hybrid Capitalism*, London: Routledge.

2 Globalisation and the uneven subsumption of labour under capital in Russia

Simon Clarke

There has been a great deal of largely inconclusive discussion over the past twenty years around the appropriate theoretical framework within which to conceptualise the transformation of the former state socialist economies.[1] The commonly used notion of 'transition' has often been questioned as doubly problematic. On the one hand, it is a teleological notion in implying that the process is determined by its end point, whereas critics have emphasised the dependence of the process on the initial conditions, summed up in the notion of 'path dependence' (Stark 1992). For this reason some commentators prefer to use the term 'transformation' rather than 'transition' (Buroway 1999). On the other hand, it begs the question of the characterisation of the end point of transition. The transition is most commonly characterised as the 'transition to a market economy', which is usually a euphemism for the transition to capitalism, but this leaves open the question of what kind of capitalism is developing in Russia. Is the capitalism that is emerging in Russia modelled on one of the existing 'varieties of capitalism' (Hall and Soskice 2001)? Or does Russian capitalism have its own original character, based on the incorporation of capitalist practices into soviet/Russian traditions, values and institutions? If this is the case, how does Russian capitalism measure up to its competitor varieties of capitalism when it confronts them on the world market?

Most commentary on the transition in Russia has been based on a dualistic interpretation of the transition in terms of the interaction of liberalising reforms and state socialist legacies, the latter being seen as barriers to and distortions of the former. Recognition that the path of liberal reform is not necessarily strewn with roses has been accommodated within a vulgarised notion of 'path dependence', according to which the path is littered with obstacles inherited from the past which have to be assimilated or removed, but the past plays a purely negative role in such an analysis. This analysis underpins a voluntaristic interpretation of transition as the outcome of political conflicts between reformers and conservatives. In the first half of the 1990s discussion focused on the role of the 'young reformers', who assumed a pivotal position in successive Moscow governments under Yeltsin, and their western allies, who set the agenda for the involvement of the international financial institutions that provided and financed the blueprint for reform. Assessments of the Putin regime have been much more ambivalent, ranging from those who give Putin credit for institutionalising the achievements of liberal reform in a law-governed state, to those who see him as embedding the corruption of the Yeltsin years in the authoritarian apparatuses of a kleptocratic state. However, a voluntaristic and dualistic approach, which analyses the emerging forms of capitalism as a synthesis of an ideal model and an alien legacy, fails to identify the indigenous roots and real foundation of the dynamic of the transition from a state socialist to a capitalist economy and so fails to grasp the process of transformation as a historically developing social reality.

The theoretical basis of this kind of dualistic analysis has been provided by the classical liberal analysis of the development of capitalism out of feudalism provided by Adam Smith. Many commentators have compared the soviet system to that of feudalism in being based on the appropriation of a surplus by the exercise of political power. For Adam Smith and Friedrich Hayek, the central feature of feudalism was the distortion of the natural order of the market economy by the superimposition of political rule, and the transition from feudalism to capitalism depended on sweeping away the political institutions of the old regime in order to establish the freedom and security of property – what Smith referred to as 'order and good government' – which would allow the market economy to flourish as the expression of unfettered individual reason. This was the ideology that informed the neoliberal project of the transition to a capitalist market economy in the former state socialist economies.

Smith, in *The Wealth of Nations*, had provided a blueprint for a liberal reform programme, but had been very pessimistic about the possibility of such a programme ever being adopted against the resistance of popular prejudice and vested interest:

> To expect, indeed, that the freedom of trade should ever be entirely restored in Great Britain is as absurd as to expect that an Oceania or Utopia should ever be established in it. Not only the prejudices of the public, but what is much more unconquerable, the private interests of many individuals, irresistibly oppose it ... master manufacturers set themselves against any law that is likely to increase the number of their rivals in the home market ... [and] enflame their workmen to attack with violence and outrage the proposers of any such regulation ... they have become formidable to the government, and upon many occasions intimidate the legislature.
>
> (Smith 1910: 414–415)

Despite Smith's pessimism, within a generation of the publication of *The Wealth of Nations*, the mercantile system had collapsed and the system of regulation had been dismantled by the state itself, not on the basis of the triumph of an enlightened individualism but on the basis of a social transformation which had radically altered the balance of class forces and undermined the old regime (Clarke 1988). In the same way, the liberal theorists of totalitarianism were taken completely by surprise when the apparently all-powerful soviet state disintegrated, not as a result of any liberal critique but under the weight of its own contradictions (Clarke 1990).

The promotion of 'shock therapy' by the young reformers was motivated by a similar fear to that of Adam Smith of the power of the old regime to block reform, the idea being that a radical programme of liberalisation and privatisation would completely destroy the old system and all possibilities of resistance, and that a new system would arise, phoenix-like, from its ashes. In reality, the battle promoted by the young reformers between the 'new Russians' and the 'red directors' turned out not to be a battle between the new and the old orders, but a struggle over the appropriation of public assets in the disorder of transition. The old system was certainly destroyed; however, it was replaced not by 'freedom of trade' and 'order and good government', but rather by a corrupt kleptocracy in which great fortunes were made by the theft of public property and the diversion of public revenues.

In retrospect, even the most ardent liberal reformers in the former Soviet Union came to recognise that they had put too much emphasis on destroying the old regime and too little on establishing 'order and good government'. However, the failure of the liberal reformers does not lie merely in their political misjudgement; it is rooted in the dualistic model of the transition derived from Adam Smith's ideal liberal model of a capitalist economy. According to this model, the freedom of the market and the security of private property and the person are sufficient conditions for a dynamic capitalism to develop on the basis of the universal pursuit of individual self-interest. This model does not recognise that the individuals who are creating the new system are characterised by values, motivations, and perceptions that are marked by their own past and that they act within the framework of institutions and on the basis of a disposition of resources inherited from the past. The past is not merely a barrier to the achievement of the glorious future – a depiction shared by the Communist Party of the Soviet Union and the 'market bolshevik' (Reddaway and Glinsky 2001) neoliberal reformers – the future is simply another stage in the development of the past. The driving force of this development is not the spontaneous expression of individual self-interest, but the incorporation of the former Soviet Union into the global capitalist system through the progressive integration of the soviet system into the structures of the world market. It is not to Adam Smith or Friedrich Hayek that we should look to understand the development of capitalism, but to Smith's most cogent critic, Karl Marx.

Contrary to the expectations of the neoliberal theorists of 'shock therapy', the collapse of the soviet system did not lead to the rapid and spontaneous development of the institutions and practices typical of a capitalist market economy. This has led some critics to doubt whether Russia was in transition to industrial capitalism at all. Michael Burawoy, for example, has argued that the collapse of the soviet system led to the transformation of the 'relations of production through which goods and services are appropriated and distributed', but had reinforced the traditional soviet 'relations in production that describe the production of those goods and services' (Burawoy and Krotov 1992: 18). What was emerging was 'merchant capitalism', which, far from being a stage in the development of bourgeois industrial capitalism, tends, quoting Marx, 'to preserve and retain [the old mode of production] as its precondition' (ibid.: 35). This led Burawoy to characterise the developmental trajectory of the Russian economy as one of 'involution', akin to Weber's 'booty capitalism', in which profits are extracted by banks and trading monopolies while nothing is reinvested in production, which continues to be conducted in traditional soviet ways (Burawoy 1996). Richard Ericson (2000) has similarly characterised the emerging system as an 'industrial feudalism'. Clifford Gaddy and Barry Ickes (1998) argued in an influential, if overblown, article that 'Most of the Russian economy has not been making progress toward the market ... It is actively moving in the other direction.' Industrial enterprises have adapted 'to protect themselves against the market rather than join it', characterising demonetisation as a way of sustaining the derelict soviet economy; although, as David Woodruff (1999) has argued, this was a perfectly rational response to neoliberal policies.

These arguments are reminiscent of those invoked in the debate among Marxist historians around 'the transition from feudalism to capitalism', where the point at issue was whether or not the development of a market economy necessarily precipitated the collapse of feudalism and the transition to capitalism in early modern Europe. The debate was first engaged between Maurice Dobb and Paul Sweezy (Dobb 1946; see also Hilton 1976), and was then resumed by Bob Brenner, with Dobb and Brenner arguing, against Sweezy's 'neo-Smithian' approach, that merchant capital made its profits by buying cheap and selling dear, and was not interested in how its commodities were produced (Aston and Philpin 1985). While merchant capital eventually penetrated into production in Western Europe, increasing world trade led to the reinforcement of pre-capitalist modes of production in the rest of the world: slavery in the Americas; feudalism, with the 'second serfdom' in Eastern Europe and debt peonage in Latin America; and household peasant agriculture and landlordism in the 'underdeveloped' world. According to Burawoy, in a repetition of the 'second serfdom', the incorporation of the soviet system of production into the world capitalist market led not to the dissolution but to the reinforcement of soviet relations in production.

While Burawoy's analysis is certainly supported by the experience of the 1990s, it is doubtful whether the analysis can be applied to the former state socialist industrial countries over an extended period of time. The fundamental difference is that the slave plantation, feudal estate, and peasant household were largely self-sufficient and so were able, within limits, to secure their continued reproduction and to continue to produce a surplus, to be appropriated in the form of commodities for sale by merchant capitalists. State socialist industrial enterprises, on the other hand, depended on the state socialist system of distribution for their inputs of parts and raw materials, for the payment of wages and provision of means of subsistence for their workers and, most importantly in the longer term, for investment to sustain or expand their productive capacity. The collapse of the state socialist system, therefore, implied the collapse of the conditions for the reproduction of the industrial enterprise and so for the reproduction of Burawoy's system of merchant capitalism or Ericson's industrial feudalism.

Burawoy is quite right to insist that the collapse of the soviet system led to a transformation of what he calls the 'relations *of* production', without leading to any fundamental change of the 'relations *in* production'. He is quite right to argue that the rise of capitalist intermediaries initially reproduced and even reinforced the 'soviet' character of the 'relations in production', and he is largely right that institutions and households resorted to 'involution' and increasing self-sufficiency in their struggles to survive (Burawoy *et al.* 2000), although they survived primarily by cutting consumption and expenditure, rather than by finding new productive resources (Clarke 2002). However, the system of merchant capitalism that he describes is not sustainable. If profits are extracted by banks and trading monopolies and are not reinvested in production, the production process will gradually grind to a halt as plant and equipment wear out and are not replaced.

The appropriate model for the theorisation of the transformation of state socialism is not merchant capitalism or industrial feudalism, but Marx's account of the development of capitalism in Western Europe. The development of capitalism, for Marx, was not Smith's realisation of individual reason but an expression of the development of commodity production within the feudal order, which was hugely accelerated by the dispossession of the mass of the rural population, who became the wage labourers for capital and the consumers of the products of capitalist industry and agriculture. The dispossession of the rural population by force and by the commercialisation of agriculture provided an ample reserve of cheap wage labour which could be profitably employed by the capitals accumulated at the expense of the landed class through trade and plunder. At this first stage of capitalist development, however, capitalists did not change the handicraft methods of production which they had inherited, so the subsumption of labour under capital was purely formal. Competition between capitalist producers forced them to cut their costs, but they did so not by transforming methods of production but by forcing down wages and extending the working day. Capital penetrated the sphere of production only when competition between producers induced and compelled them to revolutionise the methods of production in order to earn an additional profit, or resist the competition of those who had already done so. It was only with this 'real subsumption' of labour under capital that the characteristic dynamic of the capitalist mode of production got under way.

The process described by Marx as that of 'primitive accumulation' was interrupted in Russia by the October Revolution, but it was completed in the soviet period when the peasants were dispossessed and transformed into wage labourers, not for capital but for the state, which launched a programme of industrialisation based on the introduction of the most advanced capitalist technology. This has led some to characterise the soviet system as 'state capitalist' (Cliff 1970), which leads to a view of the transition as involving merely a transition from state to private monopoly capitalism through the transfer of juridical ownership of property in the privatisation programme. However, the social form of the production and appropriation of a surplus in the soviet system was quite different from that characteristic of the capitalist mode of production, and the dynamics of the system were correspondingly different.

The contradictions of the soviet system

The soviet system had many features in common with the capitalist system of production. It was based on advanced technology and a high degree of socialisation of production, which was the social and material basis of the separation of the direct producers from the ownership and control of the means of production. As in the capitalist system, labour was employed by enterprises and organisations in the form of wage labour and the production of goods and services for individual and social need was subordinated to the production and appropriation of a surplus. However, the two systems differed fundamentally in the form of the surplus and correspondingly in the social organisation of the production and appropriation of that surplus.[2]

The soviet system was not based on the maximisation of profit, nor was it based on planned provision for social need. It was a system of surplus appropriation and redistribution subordinated to the material needs of the state and, above all in its years of maturity, of its military apparatus. This subordination of the entire socio-economic system to the demands of the military for men, materials, and machines dictated that it was essentially a non-monetary system. The strategic isolation of the Soviet Union meant that no amount of money could buy these military commodities, so the soviet state had to ensure that they were produced in appropriate numbers and appropriate proportions, and correspondingly that all the means of production required to produce them were available at the right time and in the right place.

Soviet social relations of production were supposed to overcome the contradictions inherent in the capitalist mode of production in being based on the centralised control of the planned distribution and redistribution of productive resources. However, the soviet system was marked by its own system of surplus appropriation and associated contradictions. The fundamental contradiction of the soviet system lay in the separation of production and distribution, which led to a contradiction between the production and appropriation of the surplus. The development of the forces of production was constrained by the exploitative social relations of production, and it was this specific contradiction that underpinned the collapse of the 'administrative-command' system.

The central planning agencies sought to maximise the surplus in their negotiations with ministries and departments, enterprises, and organisations over the allocation of resources and determination of production plans. However, the enterprises and organisations that were the units of production had an interest in minimising the surplus by inflating the resources allocated to them and reducing their planned output targets. The softer the plan that they could negotiate, the easier it was for the enterprise directors and their line managers to induce or compel the labour force to meet the plan targets. Since neither the worker, nor the enterprise, nor even the ministry, had any rights to the surplus produced, they could only reliably expand the resources at their disposal by inflating their demand for productive resources, and could only protect themselves from the exactions of the ruling stratum by concealing their productive potential. Resistance to the demands of the military–Party–state apparatus for an expanding surplus product rested ultimately on the active and passive resistance of workers to their intensified exploitation, but it ran through the system from bottom to top and was impervious to all attempts at bureaucratic reform. The resulting rigidities of the system determined its extensive form of development, the expansion of the surplus depending on the mobilisation of additional resources. When the reserves, particularly of labour, had been exhausted, the rate of growth of production and of surplus appropriation slowed down.

The fundamental contradiction of the soviet system was between the system of production and the system of surplus appropriation. The centralised control and allocation of the surplus product in the hands of an unproductive ruling stratum meant that the producers had an interest not in maximising but in minimising the surplus that they produced. The contradiction between the forces and relations of production was also expressed in chronic shortages. Enterprises were oriented purely to meeting their formal plan targets, not to meeting the needs of their customers. Thus, while the centre could allocate rights to supplies, it could not ensure that those supplies were delivered to the place, at the time, in the quantity and of the quality desired. The endemic problems of shortages and of poor quality of supplies were an inherent feature not of a system of economic planning, but of a system based on the centralised allocation of supplies as the means of securing the centralised appropriation of a surplus. Like capitalism, but in a quite different way, state socialism was a system within which the practice of individual rationality led to socially irrational outcomes. These irrational outcomes were not defects that could be remedied by introducing reforms into the system, for they were inherent in the system itself.

The transition to a market economy

As in the case of feudalism, the contradictions inherent in the soviet system meant that money, the market, and quasi-market relations developed spontaneously out of attempts to overcome the contradictions of the system and were tolerated, however reluctantly, by the authorities.

First, even if the supplies allocated to an enterprise by the plan were adequate, securing these supplies was a major problem, for the resolution of which enterprises used informal personal connections with their suppliers, often backed up by local Party *apparatchiki*, and came increasingly to draw on the services of unofficial intermediaries, the so-called *tolkachi* (pushers), who were the pioneers of market relations within the soviet economy. The central directives which nominally regulated inter-enterprise transactions within the soviet system were, therefore, only realised in practice through exchanges within networks of personal, political, and commercial connections.

Second, Trotsky's early attempts at the 'militarisation of labour' were unsuccessful and, although wages were regulated centrally, workers were always in practice free to change jobs in search of higher wages. Labour shortages put increasing pressure on the centralised regulation of wages as employers sought to attract the scarcest categories of labour, so that wage-setting had to take account of labour market conditions, with 'coefficients' providing higher wages in priority branches of production and in the more remote regions (Clarke 1999).

Third, although social reproduction was as far as possible subordinated to the imperatives of production, with housing, items of collective consumption, a wide range of social and welfare benefits, and the right to buy goods and services which were not on free sale being provided through the workplace, labour power was partially commodified and workers were paid a money wage with which they bought their heavily subsidised means of subsistence and which they saved in the hope of acquiring the right to buy consumer durables, to take a holiday, or to provide for retirement. Money in the hands of workers lubricated the black market for consumer goods and for the private production of agricultural produce for the market, which was tolerated and even encouraged.

Fourth, the need to acquire advanced means of production from the west meant that the Soviet Union had to export its natural resources in order to finance its essential imports of machinery. Although the state retained a monopoly of foreign trade, this made the soviet system very vulnerable to fluctuations in world market prices and so to the instability of global capitalism. The 1930s industrialisation drive was made possible by the massive export of grain forcibly expropriated from the peasantry, which led to the devastating famines of the 1930s. By the Brezhnev period, the Soviet Union had become dependent on its exports of oil and gas to finance its imports of machinery and even of food.[3] The share of world trade in the net material product of the Soviet Union increased from 3.7 per cent in 1970 to almost 10 per cent in 1980 and a high of 11 per cent in 1985, while oil and gas production doubled between 1970 and 1980. At the same time, the Soviet Union saw a sharp improvement in its terms of trade, the net barter terms of trade improving by an average of 5 per cent per annum over the period 1976–80 and 3 per cent per annum between 1980 and 1985, helping to offset the decline in productivity growth and allowing the Soviet Union to increase its import volume by one-third, while export volume increased by only 10 per cent (IMF, World Bank, and OECD 1991, vol. I, pp. 86, 105). The improved terms of trade also made a substantial contribution to the buoyancy of government revenues through the price equalisation system. This opening of the soviet economy to the world market, and the corresponding political processes of détente, were by no means a sign of fundamental change in the soviet system, but were rather the means by which change was constantly postponed as the soviet system was sustained by the vagaries of world capitalism (Lavigne 1999: 55). However, such favourable circumstances could not last: production of gas and oil peaked in 1980, so that the Soviet Union was increasingly dependent on improvement in the terms of trade to sustain its economy. When the terms of trade turned sharply against the Soviet Union from 1985, the system moved into a deepening crisis.

Proposals for reform of the soviet system were always based on providing direct producers with material incentives to increase production and to make suppliers more responsive to the needs of consumers. Such reforms necessarily implied giving more independence to enterprises and allowing them to retain a portion of the revenue received from the sale of their output, which necessarily implied in turn an increasing role for money and market relations, since producers had to have the freedom to dispose of the incentive funds put at their disposal.

The dilemma that all such reforms soon presented to the centre was that they necessarily eroded centralised control, so even if they were successful at encouraging the development of the forces of production, this was at the expense of the erosion of the system of surplus appropriation. Moreover, once reform was under way it tended to acquire a dynamic of its own, as enterprises that had received a taste of independence demanded more. For these reasons, every reform initiative prior to Gorbachev had been reversed in order to preserve the system. In the same way, Gorbachev also came under pressure to reverse his reforms, but Gorbachev's reforms soon acquired an unstoppable momentum, particularly as the erosion of the administrative-command system of economic management undermined the authoritarian political system with which it was enmeshed.

The 'transition to a market economy' was not an alien project imposed on the soviet system by liberal economists, but was an expression of the fundamental contradiction of the soviet system. Gorbachev never had a coherent reform programme. *Perestroika* was reactive, pragmatic, and fragmented, each reform responding to pressures created by the previous stage of reform. The first stage of market reforms sought to improve the balance of external trade by ending the state monopoly of foreign trade, licensing enterprises and organisations to engage in export operations and to retain a portion of the hard currency earned. The idea was that this would give industrial enterprises an incentive to compete in world markets and to use the foreign exchange earned to acquire modern equipment. In practice, it provided a windfall for exporting enterprises, at the expense of the state, and opportunities for those with the right connections to make huge profits by acting as intermediaries.

Once the precedent had been set, other enterprises sought the right to sell above-plan output on export or domestic markets, and to retain a growing proportion of the proceeds. This aspiration was met with the proposed replacement of plan deliveries by state orders at fixed state prices, with the control of prices replacing the control of quantities. But the emergence of new structures of distribution further undermined the centralised control of the system. Allowing enterprises to sell on the market provided an alternative source of supply to the centralised allocations which the state could not guarantee, and if the state could not guarantee supplies, why should enterprises continue to deliver their state orders when they could sell more profitably at market prices? Thus the development of market relations undermined the control of the centre, created a space for the development of capitalist commercial and financial enterprise, and precipitated the collapse of the administrative-command system. Rather than resolving the contradictions inherent in the soviet system, the 'transition to a market economy' brought those contradictions to a head. While market reforms might provide an incentive for enterprises to develop the forces of production, the loss of centralised control undermined the system of surplus appropriation. The surplus which had previously been appropriated by the state was now retained by enterprises and/or appropriated by the new financial and commercial intermediaries that arose to handle the emerging market relations.

The collapse of the administrative-command system of economic management under the pressure of growing demands for economic independence also undermined the centralised political system of which it was an integral part, as national and regional authorities asserted their independence of the centre. Yeltsin ruthlessly exploited these tendencies in his struggle with Gorbachev, but once he had seized power in Russia his priority was to strengthen rather than to undermine a centralised Russian state. If the Russian Federation was to survive, it was essential to detach the state from its responsibility for the economy, which meant that it had to give free rein to the market relations and market actors which had emerged. Yeltsin's decision to free wages and most prices from state control at the end of 1991 was no more than a recognition that the state had already lost control of wages and prices.

Corporatisation and privatisation of state enterprises were equally inevitable consequences of the disintegration of the administrative-command system. Privatisation did not give enterprises any more rights than they had already appropriated for themselves, while it allowed the state to abdicate those responsibilities which it no longer had the means to fulfil. Thus, the ideology of neoliberalism and radical reform was little more than a rhetoric to cover what was essentially a bowing to the inevitable.

Integration into global capitalism

It is tempting to see the rapid collapse of the soviet system and the equally rapid emergence of market relations as a cataclysmic event marking a radical break between the past and the future. However, in retrospect we can see that the pattern of collapse and emergence was prefigured in the developmental tendencies of the soviet system which expressed its fundamental contradictions. The Stalinist system had been created on the basis of exhortation and repression, backed up by dramatic political penalties and rewards, but even under Stalin it had proved necessary to allow a role for material incentives and horizontal quasi-market relations in an attempt to compensate for the deficiencies of a repressive authoritarian system. With the bureaucratisation of the system from the 1950s, repression was increasingly tempered by negotiation, and attempts to overcome the deficiencies of the system by providing material incentives to workers and managers necessarily implied the expansion of market relations and the further weakening of centralised control. This was the stumbling block of reform throughout the Brezhnev period. As export growth slowed and the terms of trade turned against the Soviet Union in the 1980s, the new wave of reform was unleashed, the dynamic of which rapidly eroded the entire economic and political system. The course of reform, from ending the state monopoly of foreign trade to abandoning state control of prices and wages, was not simply the transition from an administrative-command system to a market economy in Russia, but was more specifically a process of integration of the soviet economy into the global capitalist economy through its subordination to the world market.

The collapse of the soviet system transformed the environment within which enterprises and organisations had to operate. Enterprises and organisations were now subject to the constraints of the market: in order to reproduce themselves they had to secure sufficient revenues to cover the costs of wages and the purchase of means of production and raw materials and, to the extent that they did not receive subsidies and subventions from government, this could only be achieved by selling their products as commodities on the market at a price sufficient to cover their costs. To this extent, enterprises and organisations were subordinated to capital through their subordination to the rule of money, but this did not have any immediate impact on their internal practices and procedures, which did not immediately adjust to the capitalist demands of profit maximisation. In the first instance, the immediate priority of the workers and managers of enterprises and organisations, who in the majority of cases were soon to be recognised as their owners, was to secure their own reproduction. The watchword of the 1990s was 'survival'.

The integration of the soviet economy into the global capitalist economy provided opportunities for some, and presented barriers to others. The opportunities were primarily seized by commercial intermediaries, who were able to make enormous profits through arbitrage as a result of the disparity between domestic and world market prices, reflecting differences between domestic and global production conditions. This was the basis of the 'primitive accumulation of capital' during the late 1980s and early 1990s, which led to the rapid growth of new capitalist companies in trade and finance. The emergence of private commercial and financial capitalist enterprises represented a change in the form of surplus appropriation, or at least a change in the identity of those appropriating the surplus, since the appropriation of the surplus was still based on the exercise of monopoly power and divorced from the production of the surplus. The new capitals were formed by the commercial and financial intermediaries which had their roots in the soviet system and had been given free rein by *perestroika*. They appropriated their profits by establishing the monopoly control of supplies which had formerly been the prerogative of the state. They acquired this control on the basis of rights assigned to them by state bodies, and they maintained their control by the corruption of state officials and enterprise directors, backed up by the threat and use of force. This was not a matter of the corruption of an ideal capitalist system; it was a normal adaptation of capitalism to the conditions it confronted. However, the change in the form of surplus appropriation was not matched by any change in the social relations of production.

The surplus was not appropriated on the basis of the transformation of the social organisation of production or the investment of capital in production. It was appropriated on the basis of trading monopolies, above all in the export of fuels and raw and processed raw materials (which, by 1998, made up 80 per cent of Russian exports) though also in domestic trade. It was appropriated through the banking system, which made huge profits through commercial intermediation and speculation in currency and government debt. Meanwhile, the bulk of enterprise profits were annihilated by taxation, leaving little or nothing to pay out as dividends to shareholders. The windfall profits which enterprises could make in the late 1980s, when they could buy at state prices and sell at market prices, were annihilated by the liberalisation of prices at the end of 1991. With the collapse of the soviet system, enterprises inherited the land and premises, their capital stock and their stocks of parts and raw materials, which substantially reduced their costs and enabled many to remain in profit by trading on their inherited assets. But even so, by 1996, the majority of enterprises were loss-making.

This is the phenomenon that Burawoy characterises as 'merchant capitalism', in which capitalists make their profits through intermediation, exploiting the divergence between Russian and world market prices, without making any investment in production. But the merchant capitalists were not the driving force of the development of the Russian economy and society through the 1990s, they were merely the intermediaries with global capital. The experience of the 1990s was the experience of integration into the capitalist world market, into a system dominated by the dynamics of capital accumulation on a world scale. The first stage of Russia's incorporation into global capitalism from the late 1980s was as a source of fuel and raw materials, extracted and processed by traditional soviet enterprises on the basis of existing production facilities, with virtually no productive investment in the expansion or even the renewal of production capacity; however, the dynamics of the Russian economy through the 1990s showed that this phase of pure exploitation could not be sustained. Continuing economic and social collapse was quite possible: Russia would not be the first country to suffer from 'the development of underdevelopment' (Frank 1966). But the default and devaluation of the 1998 crisis transformed the terms of Russia's integration into the global economy, reduced the opportunities for rentier capitalism, and provided more favourable conditions for economic growth and social stabilisation based on the penetration of capital into production. While the first stage of the incorporation of Russia into global capitalism was associated with the purely formal subsumption of production units under capital, the penetration of capital into production opens up the possibilities of their real subsumption and the systematic subordination of the production process to the logic of capital.

Following the Smithian logic, the neoliberal literature places most emphasis on 'order and good government', in the form of corporate governance structures, transparency, and the rule of law, as the conditions for the renewal of economic growth in Russia, but it is notable that the recovery since 1998 has not been based on or associated with marked improvements in corporate governance, accountancy, and legal practices. These institutional arrangements are undoubtedly important for outside investors, who need to be able to evaluate investment opportunities and have some guarantees of being able to exercise ownership rights, and so the large Russian companies which want to gain access to international capital markets have, at least formally, adopted international practices. But just as important for the direct investors who play the predominant role in productive investment in Russia is the development of appropriate management structures and practices which permit the subordination of the production of use values to the production and appropriation of surplus value.

What management structures and practices are appropriate for Russia? Recent discussion of the 'varieties of capitalism' has shown that capitalism can adapt to a wide range of institutional and cultural contexts. In different countries and at different times, and even within the same country at the same time, capitalism has shown itself to be compatible with different systems of financing (stock markets, retained profits, or bank-lending), different forms of regulation of labour relations (individualistic, collectivist), different payment systems (money, in-kind; individual, collective; piece-rate, time-based), different forms of social and welfare provision (employer-based, state-based, insurance-based). But to compete, capital has to subordinate the production of use values to the production of surplus value. This means that it has to install systematic management structures and practices through which it can obtain relevant information and take and implement appropriate decisions. These are not purely formal bureaucratic structures; they are social structures through which the divergent interests of different managers and workers have to be subordinated to the accumulation of capital. To what extent has capital penetrated production in Russia, and what are the barriers to this penetration?

The ultimate barrier to the production and appropriation of a surplus is the resistance of the direct producers to their exploitation, but this resistance does not necessarily appear immediately as such, and class antagonism certainly does not necessarily result in class polarisation and class confrontation. We have seen that the soviet system of production was oriented primarily to the fulfilment of the production plan, with little regard for cost or quality. To achieve the plan, formal management structures were systematically subverted by informal negotiations and the formal centralisation of power was undermined by the practical devolution of responsibility. Shop-floor workers were responsible for overcoming all the obstacles to making the production plan, in exchange for which management guaranteed to pay wages and provide social benefits and was tolerant of disciplinary infractions. The resistance of the direct producers to their exploitation was expressed primarily in recalcitrance rather than overt resistance, in absenteeism, quitting, and disciplinary violations rather than in collective mobilisation, although workers could show their strength by tacitly colluding in order to fail to make the plan (Kiblitskaya 1995). In this framework, managers faced the resistance of workers as an objective constraint on their ability to realise their primary task of delivering the plan, which they represented as such in their negotiations with higher levels of management. Capitalist production, on the other hand, has quite different priorities, it has to meet targets for cost and quality, not just for gross output, and competition means that capitalist producers cannot treat the resistance of workers to the intensification of their exploitation as an objective constraint, but have to find the means of overcoming that resistance through appropriate systems of personnel and production management. This requires a fundamental change in the balance of power on the shop-floor, but this in turn requires a fundamental change in management structures and practices at all levels.

Recent research, based on case-studies of more than fifty advanced enterprises of all forms of ownership in seven regions across Russia, has shown that the development of capitalist management structures and practices has rarely penetrated beyond the level of senior management, even in foreign-owned companies.[4] Production and personnel management continues to assume traditional soviet forms, based on informal relationships and informal negotiation between workers and line managers, reinforced by the persistence of the problems of unreliable equipment and uneven supplies that plagued the soviet system. The collapse of wages and employment through the 1990s has substantially changed the balance of power on the shop-floor, so that where soviet managers had to make concessions to hold on to scarce workers, the watchword of today's managers is 'if you don't like it, you can go'. But at the same time, the collapse of industrial training has meant that employers still face shortages of the skilled and experienced workers who are the key to the production process, though today they seek to retain such workers by paying them higher wages rather than by showering them with honours.

The increasing insecurity of employment and differentiation of wages facilitate the exercise of managerial authority on the shop-floor in the more successful enterprises, enabling them to meet tightened quality standards and diffuse worker resistance on the basis of soviet management methods, but at the same time the failure to transform the structure and practices of management is a barrier to the introduction of new production systems. This sets up a vicious circle as new owners are reluctant to make the substantial investments that are required to achieve world standards of productivity while they have not achieved full control of the labour process, but in the absence of such comprehensive re-equipment workers and line-managers have to be allowed the discretion that alone makes it possible to work in soviet conditions of production. Investment in the vast majority of Russian enterprises, therefore, continues to be piecemeal, make-do and mend, investment in the replacement of worn-out equipment and the mechanisation or automation of individual production processes.

Continuously rising energy and metal prices, driven by the growth of the Chinese economy, have created favourable conditions for the continuing profitability of the extractive sector, even if productivity in that sector does not match world standards. But the failure to secure the real subsumption of labour under capital has meant that profitability and investment prospects in the rest of the economy have remained unfavourable, sustained only by the protection of the domestic market by tariff and transport barriers. This protection is the condition not only for the sustainability of domestic production, but also for the continued reproduction of soviet social relations in the sphere of immediate production and hence for the appearance of social stability that is based on those social relations. Solidarity of workers in the workplace is undermined by high levels of wage differentiation and by the complex status hierarchies based on skill, occupation, position, age, tenure, and gender, which are the basis of the relationships through which the production process is managed, while direct expressions of worker resistance are constrained by the fear of losing a job. Thus, there is as yet little tendency to the transformation of class relations or the emergence of new forms of class struggle more typical of a developed capitalist economy.

The relative absence of overt class conflict, despite the catastrophic decline in living and working conditions and deterioration of public services, has been one of the most striking features of Russian capitalism since the collapse of the soviet system. The traditional trade unions have lost half their members, and the new (and more militant) alternative trade unions have made very little headway. After the wave of strikes and protests of public sector workers over the non-payment of wages in the middle of the 1990s, the reported level of strikes has declined year by year. Some put the relative quiescence of Russian workers down to a fatalism that supposedly lies at the heart of Russian culture, but the analysis presented above suggests that this apparent quiescence is a reflection of the limited extent of the subsumption of labour under capital in Russia.

The incomplete subsumption of labour under capital means that class conflicts are still diffused through the structure of management, appearing primarily in divisions within the management apparatus rather than in a direct confrontation between capital and labour. The completion of the subsumption of labour under capital is only really possible where there is substantial new investment, which makes it possible on the one hand to reduce reliance on the commitment of skilled and experienced workers by introducing more reliable modern production technologies and, on the other hand, to pay relatively good wages to provide workers with positive work incentives and line managers with effective levers of management. Although foreign direct investment in the productive sphere of the Russian economy, outside the extractive sectors, has been directed almost entirely at supplying the domestic market and the 'near abroad' of the Commonwealth of Independent States (CIS) countries, the sustained growth of the domestic market since the 1998 crash has created the basis for new import-substituting investment by western multinational companies, building new modern plants on greenfield sites or adjacent to the plants of Russian partners. These new plants are radically different from the earlier brownfield investments based on foreign acquisition of Russian companies in that they are based from the start on imported production technologies and imported management practices, including in the spheres of production and personnel management.

The modernisation of production facilities and management methods does not result in the elimination of class conflict, but facilitates the assimilation of line managers to the hierarchical management structure so that patterns of class conflict take on a more familiar form, as conflicts between labour and management rooted in the conflict over the terms and conditions of employment. We can see an example of such a development at the new Ford assembly plant at Vsevolozhsk, near St Petersburg. Soon after the Ford plant went into production, the leader of the traditional trade union was replaced by a young worker, Alexei Etmanov, who had been sponsored by Transnational Information Exchange (TIE) to participate in a meeting in

Brazil of trade union activists from Ford plants in North and South America. Etmanov was astonished to find in Brazil something very different from the Marxism of the Soviet Union and the trade union practices of post-Soviet Russia. As he explained on his return:

> They speak about Marxism, about the struggle of the working class against capital. But, well, that is how it really is. They drag as much out of us as they can. Their aim is to pay us as little as possible, and ours is the opposite, to get as much as possible. It really is a struggle ... I listened and gradually I began to understand that there really is strength in unity, that people achieve things themselves ... It has become Russia's shame. We are people, not some kind of monkeys! Brazilians are the same as Russians. They like a drink just the same. Absolutely similar people, although more impulsive. I saw. I was ashamed. I was inspired.
> (cited in Ilyin 2006)

Etmanov and his young colleagues were elected to the trade union committee and immediately launched a recruiting campaign to secure the membership of half the labour force (required to guarantee negotiating rights), which they achieved within a month, increasing membership from 112 to 800. They then began aggressively pursuing demands for higher wages and improved conditions, with a series of extremely well-organised strikes and work-to-rules, in which they appealed successfully for international solidarity when the management threatened to break the most recent strike by importing cars from Germany. The struggle of the Ford workers soon attracted the attention of workers in neighbouring foreign-owned greenfield plants, leading to the establishment of a local 'association of trade unions in multinational companies', and in other Russian plants set up by foreign auto manufacturers, with the formation of new trade union organisations at GM Avtovaz in Togliatti and Avtoframos (Renault-owned) in Moscow, and an interregional autoworkers' union within the All-Russian Confederation of Labour (VKT), an ITUC-affiliated alternative trade union federation, with the expectation that new unions would be established at the new Toyota and Nissan plants outside St Petersburg and at VW in Kaluga as soon as they go into production. It would be foolish to exaggerate the significance of these developments, let alone to imagine that history is repeating itself, but it is indicative of the fact that capitalism in Russia is not in the end so different from capitalism everywhere else and that Russian workers are ready to take their place in the global struggle of workers to resist the tyranny of capital.

Notes

1 This chapter draws heavily on the introductory chapter of my book *The Development of Capitalism in Russia* (2006).

2 This section draws on the analysis I developed in Clarke *et al.* (1993) and Clarke (1996).
3 In 1985, fuel accounted for more than half the Soviet Union's exports, with another quarter being accounted for by raw and semi-processed raw materials, while machinery accounted for a third of imports and food for one-fifth (IMF *et al.* 1991, vol I, p. 86).
4 The principal findings of the research are reported in Clarke (2006).

References

Aston, T.H. and Philpin, C. (eds) (1985) *The Brenner Debate: Agrarian Class Structure and Economic Development in Pre-Industrial Europe*, Cambridge: Cambridge University Press.

Burawoy, M. (1996) 'The State and Economic Involution: Russia Through a Chinese Lens', *World Development* 24: 1105–1117.

—— (1999) 'Transition Without Transformation: Russia's Involutionary Road to Capitalism', *East European Politics and Societies* 15(2): 269–290.

Burawoy, M. and Krotov, P. (1992) 'The Soviet Transition from Socialism to Capitalism: Worker Control and Economic Bargaining in the Wood Industry', *American Sociological Review* 57, February: 16–38.

Burawoy, M., Krotov, P. and Lytkina, T. (2000) 'Involution and Destitution in Capitalist Russia', *Ethnography* 1(1): 43–65.

Clarke, S. (1988) *Keynesianism, Monetarism and the Crisis of the State*, London and Brookfield: Edward Elgar.

—— (1990) 'Crisis of Socialism or Crisis of the State', *Capital and Class* 42, Winter: 19–29.

—— (1996) *The Russian Enterprise in Transition: Case Studies*, Cheltenham: Edward Elgar.

—— (1999) *The Formation of a Labour Market in Russia*, Cheltenham: Edward Elgar.

—— (2002) *Making Ends Meet in Contemporary Russia: Secondary Employment, Subsidiary Agriculture and Social Networks*, Cheltenham: Edward Elgar.

—— (2006) *The Development of Capitalism in Russia*, London: Routledge.

Clarke, S., Fairbrother, P., Burawoy, M. and Krotov, P. (1993) *What About the Workers? Workers and the Transition to Capitalism in Russia*, London: Verso.

Cliff, T. (1970) *Russia: A Marxist Analysis*, London: Pluto Press.

Dobb, M. (1946) *Studies in the Development of Capitalism*, London: Routledge & Kegan Paul.

Ericson, R. (2000) *The Post-Soviet Russian Economic System: An Industrial Feudalism*, Helsinki: Bank of Finland, BOFIT Online, 8.

Frank, A.G. (1966) *The Development of Underdevelopment*, New York: Monthly Review Press.

Gaddy, C.C. and Ickes, B.W. (1998) 'Russia's Virtual Economy', *Foreign Affairs* 77 (5): 53–67.

Hall, P.A. and Soskice, D. (eds) (2001) *Varieties of Capitalism: The Institutional Foundations of Comparative Advantage*, Oxford: Oxford University Press.

Hilton, R. (ed.) (1976) *The Transition from Feudalism to Capitalism*, London: NLB.

Ilyin, V. (2006) 'Interview with Alexei Etmanov' (February). Available at: www.warwick.ac.uk/russia/Intas/FORD.doc (accessed 8 June 2007).

IMF, World Bank, and OECD (1991) *A Study of the Soviet Economy*, 3 vols, Washington, DC: World Bank, Washington, DC: IMF, Paris: OECD.

Kiblitskaya, M. (1995) 'We Didn't Make the Plan', in S. Clarke (ed.) *Management and Industry in Russia: Formal and Informal Relations in the Period of Transition*, London and Brookfield: Edward Elgar, pp. 198–223.

Lavigne, M. (1999) *The Economics of Transition*, 2nd edn, Houndmills: Macmillan.

Reddaway, P. and Glinsky, D. (2001) *Tragedy of Russia's Reforms: Market Bolshevism Against Democracy*, Washington, DC: U.S. Institute of Peace Press.

Smith, A. (1910) *The Wealth of Nations*, vol. I, London: Dent.

Stark, D. (1992) 'Path Dependence and Privatization Strategies in East Central Europe', *East European Politics and Societies* 6(1): 17–54.

Woodruff, D.M. (1999) 'It's Value That's Virtual: Bartles, Rubles, and the Place of Gazprom in the Russian Economy', *Post-Soviet Affairs* 15(2): 130–148.

3 Making the 'workshop of the world'

China and the transformation of the international division of labour

Étienne Cantin and Marcus Taylor

> [A]ccording to estimates by the World Bank, China's share of world garment exports will increase from about 20% today to 50% by the end of the decade. Shoes, semiconductors and televisions are expected to follow. China already makes over half of the world's shoes, and Malaysia frets over the exodus of electronics factories ... Comparisons are made with Manchester during the Industrial Revolution. China, it is said, is becoming the 'workshop of the world'.
>
> (*The Economist*, 13 February 2003)

Prompted by internal reforms to China's state-socialist system and propelled by ongoing changes in the functioning of global capitalism, China's socio-economic structures have undergone a profound transformation over the past three decades. The results have been nothing short of dramatic: a largely autarkic and centrally planned economy has been transformed into a major labour-intensive export economy centred on the production of manufactured goods. Since the beginning of the 1990s, China's share of global manufactured exports has grown from 1.7 per cent to almost 7 per cent in 2003. As a consequence, it has become East Asia's largest exporter and by 2008 China is predicted to be the world's foremost goods exporter, surpassing both the United States and Germany (cf. Lall and Albaladejo 2004; Adams *et al.* 2006). These transformations have made China a central cog in the 'global factory' of contemporary capitalism, with uneven effects in China and across the international division of labour. Should we expect, as predicted by orthodox economic theory, the expansion of Chinese exports to lead to a new global equilibrium that is mutually beneficial for all (e.g. Blázquez-Lidoy *et al.* 2006)? Or, are we witnessing a 'race to the bottom' in which the rise of China as an export powerhouse will 'intensify economic tensions and contradictions throughout the region to the detriment of workers everywhere' (Hart-Landsberg and Burkett 2005: 94)? Moreover, what are the social processes that lie behind the rapid transformation of China's productive structures and the concurrent shift in the international division of labour?

To begin to frame answers to these questions, the chapter analyses the construction of China as a 'workshop of the world'. We focus on the interaction between two processes: first, changes in the international division of labour that catalysed China's integration into global capitalism; and, second, the construction of new labour forces within China. As Michael L. Blim (1992: 1) notes, the development of the 'global factory' is marked not only the spread of industrialisation but also 'the incorporation of vast new populations of workers in novel production and labour processes manufacturing goods for the world capitalist market'. In short, producing suitable workers that can be profitably deployed within production is a prerequisite to integration into global capitalism. China's transition and its integration into the circuits of global capitalism, we argue, have therefore been predicated not simply upon liberalising reforms but upon a transformation of the context in which Chinese workers find, experience, and are remunerated for their labour. The implications of this transformation reach globally because the specific conditions under which Chinese workers have been embedded within global productive structures drive competitive pressures across the division of labour, promoting global restructuring, uneven development, and conflict.

The following sections examine these changes in more detail. The first two sections unpack the dominant narratives on China's economic transformation and growth and discuss the nature of China's integration within global capitalism, detailing the local and global conditions leading to its emergence as 'the workshop of the world'. The third section complements this analysis by considering the social construction of workforces suitable for incorporation within the Chinese 'global factory'. The fourth and final section looks at how workers have reacted to and contested new forms of institutionalised discipline in both the labour market and the workplace. Specifically – with an emphasis on understanding the social processes that may transform the desperately poor labour standards that characterise much of industrial China –we examine the interplay between protest movements, corporate social responsibility practices, and local labour organising, including the changing role of the All China Federation of Trade Unions (ACFTU).

Beyond the 'miracle' of China's 'socialist market economy'

To begin to understand the causes and effects of China's integration with global capitalism it is necessary to go beyond the two dominant narratives of this transition. The latter respectively emphasise the role of markets and the state in catalysing structural change. According to the first account, embraced by neoliberals, China has undergone an 'economic miracle' through market-orientated reforms since 1978. The 'miracle' has been conjured through the removal of restrictions on private economic activity, permitting prices to be set by markets, the expansion of the private sector, and the liberalisation of foreign trade and investment. When added to a comparative advantage in cheap labour and the latent capital and technological know-how found within the global Chinese diaspora, these reforms are understood to have liberated market forces to marshal resources in an efficient and rational manner, leading to dramatic and sustained economic growth (e.g. Lardy 2007).

Institutionalists take issue with a perceived over-emphasis on market forces in the former account. They credit the Chinese state with maintaining a pervasive presence across the economy, fostering economic transformation by deliberately distorting market forces in order to build up infant industries, forcing technological transfer, and directing a gradual opening of the economy though significant controls on the movement of goods, investment, and finance. Some authors (e.g. Yeung 2004) have gone so far as to suggest that the resulting synergy between state and private enterprise, linked by social networks and institutionalised bureaucratic power relations, represents a distinct 'hybrid capitalism' that is unique to China. Similarly, as Martin Hart-Landsberg and Paul Burkett (2005a, 2005b) point out, many left-leaning academics and commentators have argued that China's reform programme offers a 'third way' model of development in the guise of a 'socialist market economy' that maintains a core role for state enterprises, reduces central planning of the economy, creates new forms of enterprise organisation, and promotes profit- and productivity-based worker-compensation incentives and market relations.

Despite their differences in emphasis, both the neoliberal and institutionalist explanations tend to view transformation within China as a largely indigenous process, driven by a convergence of state authority and private enterprise. Without doubt, the role of the Chinese state and the issues of liberalisation, privatisation, and technological transfer are indeed important factors that have shaped China's post-1978 socio-economic landscape. However, explanations that emphasise one or the other factor are too narrow to explain fully the social processes that underscore China's transformation. First, they do not adequately place Chinese transformation within the context of global capitalism. China's industrial transformation has not been simply a case of liberated Chinese entrepreneurs making the most of the 'opportunities of globalization' (to use the International Monetary Fund's term). Rather, the character and timing of transformation within China and the attendant restructuring of production in other countries are linked and collectively shaped by broader processes within global capitalism. China's transformation is not an exclusively indigenous process that subsequently interacts with international factors, but the result of an articulation between locally embedded conditions and their integration into capitalist circuits of production, commerce, and finance on a global scale. This integration has led to a specific pattern of industrial development within China, including a marked duality between a small sector of capital-intensive production with high technology levels – often characterised by state-ownership in partnership with foreign investors – and the majority of industrial expansion that is concentrated in labour-intensive firms producing basic manufactured exports and which compete largely on the basis of cost cutting and exploitative and oppressive conditions of work and employment.

This leads to a second aspect that is often neglected within mainstream accounts of China's transformation: the particular social and political context in which production is embedded. Specifically, it is necessary to understand China's integration within global capitalism in terms of the ongoing creation and reproduction of new Chinese workforces that can be profitably incorporated within the changing international division of labour. Whereas economists tend to see production simply as the innate offshoot of adding capital to a universal, pre-existing labour force (see Chapter 1 in this volume), this ignores the way in which labour forces with particular attributes are socially constructed and reproduced. In the Maoist era, China's working classes in both rural and urban spheres were formed within a series of institutional arrangements that made incorporation within capitalist production relations problematic. As a consequence, (re)making workforces suited to integration within the circuits of global capitalism has proved an essential yet tension-laden undertaking for the Chinese state and capital in the reform period. Existing urban labour forces, previously protected by state or collective enterprises, have been profoundly restructured and subjected to new forms of institutionalised discipline and work relations. Concurrently, new labour forces pivotal to the expansion of Chinese manufacturing have been constructed and managed through rural-to-urban migration, effectively being 'captured' within new labour processes that are themselves shaped by the restructuring of global capital.

Such transformations are not merely 'economic' in nature, nor can they be simplified to administrative issues of 'human resource management'. They are predicated upon a range of complex social, political, and cultural processes that have proved central to the formation and mobilisation of a new workforce of rural migrant workers who poured into the newly industrialised zones that serve as hubs for China's integration with global capital. This commodification of labour within 'socialism with Chinese characteristics' is laden with contradictions and has generated notable political repercussions. There is a profound political reluctance to pronounce that labour-power can be bought and sold on the market like any other commodity – not merely because of the manifold differences between labour markets and others, but also because of the ideological confusion which such a pronouncement might generate. As a result, the future of China's so-called socialist market economy will be deeply influenced by the government's ability to manage the contested political consequences of its labour and industrial relations reforms.

Positioning China in the changing international division of labour

Since the late 1970s, the ruling Communist Party of China (CPC) has pursued a series of reforms designed to integrate Chinese productive structures into global capital in an attempt to boost productivity levels and stimulate national economic development. Known as the 'Open Door' policy, the initial reforms constituted an attempt to follow the trajectory charted by the 'Newly Industrialising Countries' (NICs) in East Asia. The NICs had experienced profound structural transformations over the previous two decades through the development of export-orientated industrial sectors (Burkett and Hart-Landsberg 2000). Extremely cautious in scope, China's 'Open Door' policy established a small number of Special Economic Zones (SEZs) that could operate under distinct institutional rules designed to promote export-orientated industrialisation. Shenzhen was selected by the Chinese government as the first SEZ in 1979 owing to its remoteness from the capital and its proximity to Hong Kong and Macao and, the following year, the province of Guangdong was permitted to create two further SEZs. By decentralising regulatory functions to local officials, the central government aimed to create incentives conducive to the development of export-orientated industry, including low corporate taxes, minimal environmental or urban planning regulations, and relatively unrestricted movement of goods, capital, and profits. The SEZs were intended to attract FDI from transnational corporations (TNCs) in the form of joint ventures with Chinese companies as a means to induce technology transfer that would aid the construction of a more modern industrial sector throughout the province. Concurrently, industrial development in the SEZs was seen as a vehicle to expand the market for inland industries that produced raw material inputs and consumption goods.

Despite these intentions, US and Japanese TNCs proved reluctant to invest heavily in what they saw as an uncertain environment (So 2001). The immediate result of the 'Open Door' was to establish the region as a labour-intensive manufacturing centre through its subsumption under the existing productive structures, trading linkages, and financial networks of Hong Kong capital (Sung 1991; Smart and Smart 1992). Since the late 1950s, Hong Kong had experienced rapid industrialisation as part of a shift in global productive structures that authors termed the 'New International Division of Labour' (e.g. Fröbel *et al.* 1980). This shift was attributed to a confluence of factors, including: the crisis of many manufacturing sectors in the advanced industrialised countries; the development of technology that fragmented production and facilitated the worldwide sourcing of manufacturing; the development of a 'world market for labour' and industrial sites; and production shifts to areas of the developing world where labour is relatively 'cheap' and subordinated to cut unit costs, resulting in a corresponding deindustrialisation of the advanced capitalist economies. Hong Kong, like other NICs in East Asia, benefited from precipitous geopolitical conditions to attract foreign investment and rapidly became a centre for the production of labour-intensive manufactures for Western markets. Based primarily on small and medium enterprises operating with conditions of low labour standards and subsidised labour costs, Hong Kong companies began to export a diverse range of parts and goods, from textiles and toys to electronics and eventually computer parts (Henderson 1989).

By the late-1970s and early-1980s, however, the expansion of production in these sectors led to mounting competitive pressures and protectionism in key markets. At the same time, labour shortages began to drive up costs and increased pressure on Hong Kong's manufacturing sector. Unable to compete through technological upgrading owing to a lack of government subsidies, this sector began to restructure through spatial relocation into China's coastal province of Guangdong. Here it found a potentially expansive cheap labour force that could be subjected to despotic regimes of labour control – conditions that facilitated an intensity of labour and wage rates impossible to achieve in most other production sites. As a result, the bulk of Hong Kong's established manufacturing base moved into Guangdong, either into the SEZs or, more commonly, through joint ventures with town and village enterprises (TVEs) that are owned by rural collectives and managed by local officials. This movement propelled the rapid rise of the non-state-owned industrial sector in China. By 1987, 6,600 of 7,800 foreign-funded enterprises in China were from Hong Kong, accounting for 65 per cent of foreign investment and incorporating as many as 2 million workers in China (Heartfield 2005). Hong Kong quickly began to serve as a managerial, financial, and trading hub for investments into the Pearl River Delta, particularly as foreign companies preferred to find partners in Hong Kong in order to avoid the cultural politics surrounding investments on the mainland (Tsui-Auch 1999). In addition, Hong Kong served as a convenient export label for goods made in China as it circumvented tariffs imposed by the USA prior to China joining the WTO. By 1995, over two-thirds of Hong Kong's exports were re-exports of Chinese goods that had undergone packaging or minor processing within Hong Kong (Sung 1997).

In spite of the integration of the Pearl River Delta within Hong Kong capital as a centre for export-orientated manufacturing, China's 'Open Door' policies did not match the expectations of Chinese leadership. The failure of the policies to stimulate high-tech investment led to tensions within the Communist Party over the direction of reforms (Naughton 1997). After a period of uncertainty within the political leadership, the second phase of China's incorporation into global capitalism came in the mid-1980s and accelerated throughout the 1990s. Internal reforms were expanded through the Coastal Development Strategy (CDS), which aimed to amplify the industrial sector for labour-intensive light-manufactures for export. The CDS extended the liberalised trade system operating in the Pearl River Delta across all coastal regions, thereby allowing the unrestricted import of inputs destined for the export industry and the export of finished and semi-finished goods. Additionally, it gave local governments decentralised authority to take further measures – including tax breaks, provisions for the sale of land use rights and the establishment of foreign trading firms – to promote foreign investment and trade. Limitations on the type of Chinese enterprises that could form joint ventures with foreign firms were lifted, as were the *de facto* restrictions placed on foreign companies setting up subsidiaries. Indeed, foreign companies were granted preferential rights for investment. Mandates concerning both the transfer of technology and embargos on selling to Chinese consumers, for example, were relaxed in a bid to buttress investor confidence.

These reforms coincided with a substantial reworking of global capitalism that triggered massive investment flows into China in the late 1980s and, particularly, throughout the 1990s. Many industrial sectors predicated on the manufacturing of consumer goods were undergoing extensive restructuring through a large-scale and extended shake-out of high cost, low profit means of production in manufacturing, technological reorganisation, and spatial relocation. This was a consequence of worsening overcapacity and overproduction in global manufacturing due to the over-accumulation of capital in sectors that offered few entry barriers and initially provided good returns. Jeroen Merk and Etienne Cantin highlight in Chapters 4 and 5 of this volume, respectively, how competitive pressures that heightened in the 1970s and 1980s drove a functional split in many consumer goods industries, whereby Western retailers attempted to shore up profit rates by severing what were once integrated production and retail processes. Concentrating on design and brand building, Western retailers have attempted to restructure the organisation of production in order to achieve maximum flexibility and extract surplus profit by squeezing the supply chain. As Wong and Chang detail in terms of 'lean production' within the garment industry:

> Computerized sales and logistics control enabled retailers to minimize cost in between production and sales. Higher production and labour flexibility was in demand as off-shore production was now directly linked to stores in the US through just in time delivery, zero inventory, vertical integration and quick response system for a faster turnaround time . . . This strategy goes together with cutting the procurement price through high volume ordering and a more sophisticated global sourcing network.
>
> (2005: 133)

The restructuring of power and production within retail chains occurred alongside a more general transformation of productive structures in the East Asian region. In 1985, the Plaza Accord between Japan and the US served to raise the value of the Yen, precipitating an outflow of Japanese investment into low-wage zones of Southeast Asia. Japanese industries felt the pinch of higher costs and a reduced American market, and turned to Southeast Asia as an escape valve, investing huge amounts of capital in factories throughout the region. By the mid-1990s, Japanese companies began to focus on outsourcing to China, where, drawn by low labour and land costs for electronics production in locations such as the Pearl River Delta, they became the third largest investor (Taylor 1999). Soon after,

Taiwan also experienced a strong appreciation of its currency alongside the ongoing growth of its nominal wage rate. The latter grew 13.7 per cent annually between 1975 and 1985, whereas labour productivity grew only half as fast (Naughton 1997: 92). As a consequence – and in spite of turbulent political relations with the mainland – the relocation of labour-intensive aspects of Taiwanese productive capital to the coastal provinces of China appeared a necessary solution to rising competitive pressures. Guangdong and Fujian proved to be the key destinations for Taiwanese investment, with Hong Kong often serving as a routing hub.

The sharp recession in the advanced industrial countries during the early-1990s prompted further restructuring of capital on a global level and exponentially increased the flow of investment into key regions of the developing world (see Chapter 8 in this volume). FDI into China increased dramatically, from $12 billion in 1991 to $58.7 billion and $111.4 billion in 1992 and 1993 respectively (Yam 1997: 123). The majority of foreign investment in China was – and remains – by ethnic Chinese (58 per cent in 1999), composed mostly of Hong Kong Chinese followed by Taiwanese Chinese. The factories that they own and manage are the principal suppliers of the 'Made in China' goods sold to Western brand-name multinational corporations and retailers of the developed world. In other words, much of the FDI in China is invested in these Asian-owned factories that constitute a link in transnational production chains. Following the patterns set by the early SEZs, most foreign-funded enterprises – either through joint ventures or fully owned subsidiaries – have located in China's south-eastern coastal provinces, with the heaviest concentration throughout the 1990s remaining in Guangdong province, followed by Fujian. More recently Shanghai and the Yangtze River Delta have attracted new investment flows, becoming the greatest regional recipient of FDI in China in the mid-2000s.

The effects of this substantial inflow of investment in coastal China were dramatic and exemplified by the further development of the Pearl River Delta. A primarily agricultural region in the 1970s, the Delta currently boasts China's highest concentrations of manufacturing, the largest factories, the greatest influx of labour from rural areas, the world's third and fourth busiest ports (Hong Kong and Shenzhen), and the world's largest freight facility (Enright *et al.* 2005). With more than 40 million migrant workers, 130,000 apparel factories, and new cities like Shenzhen, which has mushroomed to more than seven million people in just a quarter century, Guangdong lays an arguable claim to being the contemporary 'workshop of the world', following in the footsteps of nineteenth-century Manchester and early twentieth-century Detroit. Gross domestic product in the Pearl River region leaped from $US8 billion in 1980 to $US113 billion in 2002 as the region was transformed into a raw entrepreneurial engine that linked a vast new industrial working class to American retailers who put billions of Chinese-made products on North American and European discount store shelves every day (Ross 2006). Guangdong produces a third of China's total exports and 10 per cent of that finds its way to Wal-Mart's US shelves (Appelbaum and Lichtenstein 2006; Lichtenstein 2006).

Although the industrial expansion of coastal China appears breathtaking in its rapidity and scope, it has largely followed the pattern of integration into global capital circuits established with the initial influx of Hong Kong's manufacturing sector. Edward Steinfeld refers to this process as China's 'shallow integration':

> Only 15% of the manufacturing firms surveyed by the World Bank in 2001 reported engaging in any design efforts for foreign customers, a sign that the respondents are essentially 'rule takers' in open, modularized production processes. Only 7% reported providing customers R&D or other specialized services. The figures are noteworthy given that the sample specifically targeted higher-tech sectors, the very ones in which we should expect high degrees of innovation, networking, and development of firm-specific proprietary knowledge. Overall, the figures are consistent with Rosen's observations at the macro-level regarding China's continued dependence on high-tech imports to fuel its low value-added manufacturing activities.
>
> (2004: 1975)

The claim that China has moved up the 'value chain' by expanding its export of hi-tech manufactures must be taken with caution as the country's exports are characterised by a disproportionate share of assembly processes and of relatively simple products, rather than highly sophisticated complex capital goods and chips (Adams *et al.* 2006). Moreover, the most dynamic export sectors of the economy are increasingly controlled and driven by foreign ownership. Direct foreign affiliates account for one-third of manufacturing output and over half of China's exports. In some sectors, such as IT, foreign-produced goods account for almost 80 per cent of exports. On this basis, Hart-Landsberg and Burkett (2005a, 2005b, 2006) have argued that Chinese productive structures remain subordinated within transnational production chains that accentuate their dependence on foreign ownership and consumption – including the unsustainable expansion of consumption through debt in US households and the expanding US trade deficit.

Certainly there exist a number of Chinese firms that are state-owned and supported by a range of industrial policies aimed at building global leaders. This follows the Chinese state's policy of reforming its state-owned industrial sector by a process of '*zhua da fang xiao*' ('grasping the large, and releasing the small') through which it has attempted – with mixed success – to build globally competitive firms in technologically sophisticated branches of production. Yet this should not be allowed to obscure the profound dualism of the Chinese economy: the bulk of China's productive structure remains labour-intensive production and processing in which the foremost competitive advantage has been cheap and disciplined labour. As Long Yongtu, former

Chinese Vice-Minister of Foreign Trade and Economic Cooperation, commented with respect to the attributes of Chinese labour: 'Just as water always flows to the lowest point, China is bound to be the first option for foreign capital investment.'[1] One result has been the export of deflation in the form of reduced prices across manufacturing sectors (Blázquez-Lidoy *et al.* 2006), thereby sharpening competitive pressures and forcing enterprises across the international division of labour to restructure their own operations, often generating sharp conflicts between employers and workforces that face intensified labour or redundancies (Lambert and Chan 1999; Bronfenbrenner and Luce 2004; Hart-Landsberg and Burkett 2006).

This raises important questions regarding the particular attributes of Chinese labour forces that are such an attraction for labour-intensive manufacturing. Most accounts of the spatial relocation of productive capital to the Chinese mainland simply assume the presence of 'cheap labour' as an *a priori* factor in productive restructuring. Yet such an assumption ignores the manner in which new Chinese workforces have been created, reproduced, and profitably utilised within global capital circuits through an ongoing revolution in the social conditions of labour within China. This has resulted in the creation of multiple Chinese labour forces, each structured by different social institutions and differentially integrated into Chinese productive structures and, therein, the international division of labour. Two fundamental processes stand out: the formation of migrant labour forces that are central to the expansion of industrial production in China; and the reshaping of workforces located in the state-owned enterprise sector who formerly enjoyed the job security and welfare privileges of the 'iron rice bowl'.

Making workers for the 'workshop of the world'

The processes of creating migrant labour forces and breaking the 'iron rice bowl' of urban workers are part of a wider commodification of labour-power ongoing within reform China. The commodification of labour-power involves 'freeing' workers to contract openly in the market to any willing employer in return for a wage. Concurrently, commodification also 'frees' the worker from any alternative form of subsistence and makes them dependent on repeatedly securing wage labour for survival. This stands in marked contrast to labour conditions in China during the Maoist era, when labour was centrally managed through a range of social institutions that limited mobility in accordance with the designs of the planned economy. In the rural sphere, the collectivised agricultural sector assigned people to work teams at birth and strictly limited their mobility into urban areas through a household registration (*hukou*) and food distribution system. Linking income and consumption to fixed production teams prevented movement into alternative rural occupations. Similarly, urban labour mobility was restricted through a system of bureaucratic job allocation that tied a worker to a particular work unit (*danwei*). The latter functioned not only as a lifelong place of employment, but also as an enterprise-based system of social welfare through which a range of social goods – including housing, healthcare, education, and childcare – was provided (the 'iron rice bowl').

Restructuring these institutions has proved pivotal in China's integration into global capitalism. The expansion of production in areas such as the Pearl River Delta required a dramatic increase in the size of the labour force and – moreover – workforces that could be flexibly incorporated into production processes and made to labour intensively for long hours in order to meet the demands of capital valorisation. Such workforces simply did not exist in China in the late 1970s. They were fashioned over the course of the 1980s and beyond through incremental reforms leading to a profound social and political transformation in the nature of work and employment in contemporary China. As Sally Sargeson emphatically portrays in her seminal work on proletarianisation in China:

> Workers' roles, their public image, and their relations with their employers have been dramatically transformed ... they have become the object of policies, re-education campaigns and new disciplinary systems designed to make their attitudes and behaviour compatible with the needs of the 'socialist market economy'.
>
> (1999: 19)

First and foremost, the de-collectivisation of agriculture carried out as part of the initial reforms in the late-1970s broke the strict connection between the rural population and centrally administered job teams. It facilitated households to contract pieces of land on a familial basis and, in so doing, freed up large quantities of surplus labour that could then seek other employment opportunities. The gap between rural incomes and urban wages provided an obvious incentive for rural-urban migration. Nonetheless, the manner in which migration has been regulated through the *hukou* fixed residence system has aided in the creation of a worker underclass, or *dagongzai*, that is central to the competitiveness of labour-intensive export industry in China. Migrant workers, women in particular, are concentrated in labour-intensive light manufacturing industries such as apparel, electronics, shoes, and toys, as well as low-end service sectors. More than 100 million peasant-workers have worked either in TNCs directly owned or joint-ventured by big, brand-name American and European companies, or for their increasingly giant production contractors and subcontractors. China's processes of industrial restructuring and proletarianisation are unquestionably the largest in human history in terms of the number of people affected. Until the early 1990s, it was consensually agreed that the number of 'floaters' was about 70 million nationwide. The Fifth National Population Census of China, in 2000, estimated that there were actually over 120 million internal migrant workers in cities, while other estimates range from 100 to 200 million persons (Lavely 2001).

This class of internal rural migrant labourers has been constructed as a floating population which, denied formal residence status in the cities, is excluded from the provision of social services and is pushed towards employment in sectors characterised by poor working conditions, stagnant wages, and high insecurity of labour. Despite the establishment of labour markets through commodification, therefore, Chinese migrant workers face a wide range of constraints upon their actions and their lack of formal status has made them vulnerable to the systematic violation of basic labour rights. Ching Kwan Lee (1998), Anita Chan (2001), and Ngai Pun (2005) have highlighted in detail the militaristic and despotic nature of factory discipline, including rigid controls over movement, forced overtime, monetary penalties for missing productivity targets, and frequently delayed or failed payment of wages, all of which have proved fundamental to the profitability of labour-intensive manufacturing. As these authors have detailed, these disciplinary systems revolve around gendered forms of worker control. Indeed, the development of SEZs across China has been predicated on a massive harnessing of young migrant workers, in particular of unmarried women, while male migrants have frequently found work in the construction sector. By 2000, female migrant workers accounted for about 47.5 per cent of China's internal migrant workers and recently made up about 65.6 per cent of all migrants in Shenzhen (Liang and Zhongdong 2004).

Young female migrants leave rural areas for complex reasons, not only in response to economic push-and-pull factors, but also to escape patriarchal power structures, limited freedoms, and the monotony of agricultural work within the villages (Lee 1998; Pun 1999). Female migrant labour thereby occupies a contradictory position in Chinese society: at one and the same time it is part of a subjective struggle for greater freedom and a product of the restrictive contours of state institutions, which extend managerial discipline from the shop floor into the realm of social reproduction. Chinese migrant workers in the export-processing sector – whether they are male or female, single or married – are accommodated in dormitories within or close to factory compounds. The dormitories are not provided to procure labour loyalty or to retain scarce skills. Rather, the 'dormitory labour regime' in China is a modality of domination through which management within the foreign-owned capitalist firms aims to facilitate control over when labour is performed and how labourers act in their non-working day in order to maximise the exploitation of their labouring capacities (Smith and Pun 2006; Pun and Smith 2007).

The results of the dormitory system include an absolute lengthening of the workday and the subsequent compression of a 'worklife' owing to excessive workweeks. In terms of hours worked, migrants surpass the levels set by permanent urban residents, indicating the manner in which Chinese export industries require extensive working days in order to expand the scope of production. As Fang Lee Cooke (2005: 149) has detailed, the employment statistics of 2000 indicate that 56.9 per cent of migrant workers worked more than fifty hours a week, and another 37.6 per cent worked between forty and forty-nine hours. In contrast only 17.8 per cent of urban residents worked over 50 hours a week during the same period. Moreover, with easy access to labour power during the workday, managers are able to implement a 'just-in-time' labour system for 'just-in-time' production by implementing forced overtime at short notice. Given the fixity of labour within dormitories, firms are able to exercise control over workers' accommodation, food, social and leisure pursuits, and travel, facilitating an intensity of labour that can be quickly harnessed according to changing demands of the commodity chain. Au Loong-Yu (2006) has noted examples of US garment buyers abandoning Vietnam to source from China, despite cheaper wages in the former, owing to a notably quicker turnaround of orders.

Low wage rates are, nonetheless, insidious across labour-intensive manufacturing in China. High turnover in the workforce and strict governmental controls make it more difficult for workers to engage in collective bargaining in general and to demand wage increases in particular. As a result, wages have remained depressed despite economic growth. A Ministry of Labour and Social Security report in 2004 stated that: 'Studies show the salary of a migrant worker in the Pearl River Delta area has grown by a mere CNY68 (US$8.20) over the last 12 years, far behind the increase in living expenses, and in real terms, wages are declining' (cited in Tao 2006: 532). In Guangdong, this means that despite yearly double-digit economic growth, real wages for migrants fell over this period. Of course, the two factors are not unrelated, and it may be reasonably asked to what extent such a form of export-oriented growth of foreign-owned or controlled industries, which does not have to rely on local consumption fuelled by rising wages, can bring about all-around development and improvements in the conditions of workers? In addition, migrants are regularly subjected to delayed payment of wages as both a manner of keeping wages lower and of disciplining workers. According to one study cited by Ran Tao, 72.5 per cent of migrant workers had experienced some form of withheld wages (Tao 2006: 537). The situation is endemic within the construction industry, forcing acknowledgement from the central government in 2004 that migrant workers at thousands of construction projects across the country were owed $43 billion in unpaid wages – some of which had remained unpaid for up to ten years, and some of which was for work on government-funded projects. Concurrently, in the export industries the maintenance of a high level of wages in arrears is a common managerial policy used to avoid worker turnover and discipline workers, as leaving the firm would relinquish their claim on unpaid wages. If pressed through legal means to pay wages in arrears, firms usually prefer to close factories down in default and reopen with the slate wiped clean.

While migrant labour forces in China have been central to the expansion of productive activities into global capital circuits, other and more prosperous workforces have been created in an uneven manner. The proliferation of export-orientated industries in coastal zones has facilitated an expansion of localised divisions of labour, with a range of skilled occupations emerging as part of both the management of the labour process and the development of service industries that are essential to the continued operation of the export sector, including everything from financing to machinery maintenance. The movement of workers out of the state sector and into the private sector for skilled positions has been rapid in some areas such as Guangdong and, more recently, Shanghai. This is despite the fact that leaving the state sector is to renounce rights to welfare services worth around 40 per cent of the wage packet (Tao 2006: 533). Within the private sector larger multinationals offer pay and working conditions that surpass those of the state sector, particularly for younger and technically skilled workers. Skilled labour for managerial and technical tasks is in sharp demand and can command relatively high wages and advancement opportunities, particularly in the foreign sector. As Tai-lok Lui has argued 'state administrators, managers, private entrepreneurs, and professionals and technicians have come to constitute those social classes that benefit enormously and disproportionately from marketization and privatization' (Lui 2005: 473).

Conversely, small and medium-sized firms that comprise the labour-intensive manufacturing enterprises and joint ventures operated by overseas capital or locally managed enterprises are characterised by migrant workforces and the kinds of despotic production relations described above. The duality of the Chinese industrial sector thus manifests itself in profound labour market segmentation, characterised by strong urban/rural and gender differentiations that apportion specific jobs to different types of workers. Along these lines, rewards to work are profoundly differentiated. While the effects of the intensification of labour during the 1990s led to labour productivity rising by 170 per cent between 1990 and 1999, real wages increased by less than 80 per cent, helping to push up profit rates at the expense of labour (ILO 2007: 6). Moreover, these wage gains were distributed in a highly unequal fashion, with skilled labour and management taking the lion's share of such increases.

During the late-1990s, the unequal dynamics of labour market formation were intensified, owing to the government's attempt to rationalise employment in the state-owned sector as a means of deepening China's integration into global capitalism. Even at the turn of the millennium, the state sector accounted for 50 per cent of urban employment (Taylor 2002) and, as indicated above, it did not operate according to capitalist principles of labour management and profit maximisation. Rather, within the context of the planned economy, the political functions of linking workers to the state through cradle-to-grave employment and social welfare were paramount. The social transformations involved in the integration of the Chinese economy into global capitalism, however, have profoundly problematised such relationships. The growth of the foreign-funded private sector increased competitive pressures upon state-owned enterprises (SOEs), which were increasingly viewed as performing poorly and a burden on state resources. On the one hand, this intensified pressure on the government to dissolve loss-making SOEs. On the other, it put pressure on state-sector managers to fundamentally restructure workplace relations in line with the 'human resource management' strategies prevalent in the private sector (Cooke 2005).

The results of these pressures were profound. The aforementioned strategy of 'grasping the large, releasing the small' led to the dissolution of a significant segment of the SOE sector, whereas capitalist rationalisation of remaining firms meant the shedding of workers seen as surplus to the profitability of the enterprise. These dynamics are complex, as laid-off workers from enterprises that continue in business typically join the ranks of the *xiagang*; a status that denotes the worker is still tied to the enterprise and will be reemployed if conditions improve. In the meantime, the worker is eligible for a stipend from the enterprise for a period of three years, although this is a fraction of the former wage. As such, detailing the numbers of unemployed is difficult. While the official count of laid-off workers increased from 3 million in 1993 to 17.24 million in 1998 (Cai 2002: 325), this may significantly understate the gravity of the situation. Dorothy Solinger (2002: 304) suggests that, despite the ambiguity of the official numbers, 'it is certain that quite precipitously millions of past renowned, now former workers are comprising a sorry – and terribly sizeable – mass of newborn marginals', or what she refers to as 'downwardly mobile workers' within the context of contemporary China's developing social relations of commodified labour-power. Reinforcing these claims, Hart-Landsberg and Burkett cite an ACFTU survey which established that, among workers who had found employment after being laid off from state enterprises:

> 18.6 percent were odd-job manual workers, 10 percent did various sorts of hourly work (which usually refers to activities such as picking up others' children from school); 5.2 percent had seasonal jobs; 60 percent were retailers operating stalls; and a mere 6.8 percent had obtained formal, contracted employment. A worrisome 45 percent among the stall keepers were discovered to be highly vulnerable, mobile peddlers selling in shifting sites without a license.
>
> (2005a: 610)

In short, the great majority of workers dismissed from state enterprises become members of the 'reserve army' of the unemployed, broadly defined to include those eking out an existence in the informal sector. As for official unemployment figures, they have soared to historic heights, leaping from 7 million in 1993 to 20 million in 1999. The government has predicted an annual addition of 35 million urban jobseekers over the next five years, with perhaps over half joining the ranks of the unemployed. Incidents of strikes and worker protests, hovering around three to four thousand every year since the mid-1990s, have become widespread, especially in interior and north-eastern provinces. As Trini Leung (1998a) and Ching Kwan Lee (2002, 2003) note, during the 1990s the most restive workers were those in loss-making or bankrupt state-owned enterprises, which account for some 50 per cent of all state firms nationwide, and more specifically those workers in traditional, labour-intensive, low technology and mass production manufacturing in the state sector – all of whom bear the brunt of socialism's retreat.

Within the SOEs, the 'iron rice bowl' has been fundamentally broken by a concerted movement towards fixed term contracts, performance-based pay incentives (including penalties for missing production targets), and a restructuring of welfare provision that involves a creeping privatisation of essential services. State-supplied housing, medical care and education have declined in quality and availability, and increased in cost to workers (Blecher 2002). To shore up flagging profitability, SOEs have increasingly hired large numbers of migrant workers at the same time as making redundant higher-paid urban workers who would qualify for numerous social benefits (Unger 2002: 124). The intensification of work alongside the precarisation of employment – and therein the threat of acute downward mobility – has led to an increased number of workplace tensions.

This has raised difficult questions concerning the role of trade unions within China. The All China Federation of Trade Unions (ACFTU) existed into the 1990s as an arm of management and – ultimately – the Party-state. It now occupies an uncomfortable position as an intermediary between the designs of management and the resistance of workers. Meanwhile, the unevenness of China's post-socialist transition for work and employment relations has given rise to asymmetrical outcomes within the labour force. It is perhaps no surprise then that a range of conflicts – including those occurring within the industrial workplace and those targeting the complicity of local government in redundancies, unavailable services, and exploitative conditions within factories – have been rising exponentially. The following section examines the outline of this rising tide of protest and its potential effects.

Worker contestation and industrial relations in the Chinese 'workshop of the world'

We have highlighted above that despite the celebration of China's economic success in attaining the status of the new 'workshop of the world', the impact upon workers has been highly uneven. While the formation of labour markets and enterprise privatisation have subordinated workers to capitalist production relations, political authoritarianism has largely deprived them of formalised collective organisational means to resist oppressive labour conditions and industrial relations. This creates a number of social contradictions in a country where the Party-state still hails workers as the 'masters of society'. Indeed, in terms of the statutes of existing labour law, Chinese workers enjoy a range of rights and protections. Nonetheless, the developmental dynamics unleashed by China's capitalist transition have undermined the existing pro-labour policies and those proposed by the central government since the onset of reforms. The notable feature of these regulations is the provision for important labour protections, including those concerning minimum wage, work hours, and social insurance for internal migrant workers citywide. However, precisely in the course of these government-initiated labour reforms, at least two broad concerns surfaced: first, state and collective workers have been hard hit by industrial restructuring (their mass unemployment further exposing the lip-service that government pays to labour); second, labour policies and labour regulations are unevenly implemented at local levels and hence protection for workers is seldom enforced. As Hart-Landsberg and Burkett explain (2006: 25):

> Poor employment terms and the lack of institutional support for workers seeking to improve them flow directly from the nature of China's capitalist restoration. As part of the reform process, regional and local government officials were freed from central oversight and encouraged to promote private enterprise, especially foreign enterprise, for their mutual profit. Thus, most provincial and local authorities now depend heavily for their own success on attracting and keeping profitable firms in their jurisdiction. In many cases, local government officials have actually become shareholders in these ventures. As a result, workers often find their efforts to improve conditions undermined by the very local governments that are supposed to protect them.

Illegal overtime, illegal wage rates, and below-subsistence income remain endemic grievances, which trade unions are best suited to address. Capitalist development has led to an accumulation of such grievances as enterprise directors sought to ensure the profitability of their enterprises by all and any available means. Moreover, employers sought to avert conflict with their employees by denying responsibility, thereby trying to turn the workers' grievances against the Party-state, so that capitalist development implied not only an increase in the potential for industrial conflict, but also the transformation of such conflict into social contestation with the formulation of political demands, including demands for the enforcement of existing labour laws (Leung 1998a, 1998b; Lee 2002, 2003). As Clarke (2005) explains, the accumulation of grievances and the ensuing industrial and social unrest, almost entirely spontaneous and outside trade union structures, have presented a challenge to the legitimacy of the official trade unions as representatives of the interests of workers, and to their function for the state of neutralising industrial conflict and maintaining social peace. At no other time in its history has the ACFTU been regarded with more disdain by workers than at present, when both the state and the non-state sector workers need help more than ever before.

To date, labour agitation in both sectors remains diffuse and localised, without cross-class or cross-region collaboration. The most significant working-class protests took place in 1989, when state sector workers joined students, intellectuals, and private entrepreneurs in a nationwide anti-corruption, anti-inflation, pro-democracy movement. The government's deadly crackdown, coupled with heavy sentences for worker leaders, resulted in labour acquiescence for the first half of the 1990s. Facing an increasingly volatile labour market since the mid-1990s, however, both migrant and state workers have once again become restive. Nonetheless, protests are usually contained within single enterprises. Plant closure, bankruptcy or relocation cause the most protests, as these are moments of heightened solidarity among workers who find themselves collective victims suffering from unpaid wages and pensions. Both state-owned enterprises and non-state factories share similar features that can be conducive to workers' collective action. For example, despite its role in mobilising intensive labour by migrant workers, the presence of the 'dormitory labour regime' can promote collective action since it fashions intense interaction among workers (almost entirely women) who share harsh living and working conditions and experience constant surveillance (Smith and Pun 2006). The residential quarters of state workers similarly facilitate communications and an aggregation of interests, especially in times of massive layoffs or dismissals. On the other hand, the prevalence of work-unit revolts also means a general lack of laterally organized opposition across firms or regions. Official trade unions are conspicuously absent in autonomous worker protests, making inter-factory mobilisation difficult. The regime's highly repressive stance toward 'organised dissent' also generates self-limiting action among workers in protests. As long as workers remained work-unit-bound in their demands and action, the government responded with moderation and tolerance.[2]

Workers with grievances usually begin their collective action by lodging complaints, requesting local government intervention. In so doing, workers are following a well-established channel of political participation under Chinese Communist rule. Dating back to the 1930s, petitioning to the Letters and Visits Bureau is an institutionalised and legitimate means of making demands and expressing popular discontent toward the government (Luehrmann 2003). Officials handling the petitions usually direct workers to labour-arbitration committees or pressure state enterprises to redress workers' grievances. When repeated visits to the labour bureau fail to deliver owed pensions, or when migrant workers are frustrated by pro-employer decisions of labour arbitrators or judges, petitioners are prone to take their demands from the courtrooms to the streets. There is an important difference in migrant workers' and state sector workers' proclivity to street action. Migrant workers, no matter how marginalised, are indispensable to local economic development whereas laid-off, unemployed, and retired workers in the rust-belt are a liability to the local government. Therefore, regions with more migrant workers also have a more developed legal infrastructure. The result is that migrant workers are more susceptible to bureaucratic processing, routinisation and rationalisation of labour conflicts. Veteran state workers in rustbelts are more inclined toward spontaneous mass and radicalized action. In rare cases, such unconventional and what workers call 'radical' actions can lead to city- or neighbourhood-wide, multi-day confrontations. Violent clashes with police, or even the armed forces sent in by the higher authorities, have also led to arrest and imprisonment of workers' leaders.

The need for floating workers for industrial representation in the new labour regime is greater than that of other worker categories, but is seldom met. Given their precarious, temporary situations working in industrial districts where they are vulnerable outsiders, migrant workers are in a particularly weak position to mount protests. Nevertheless, there are a growing number of wildcat labour actions that are not sanctioned by the government, and other less confrontational forms of resistance have erupted in an increasing number of foreign-funded factories, especially large manufacturing establishments (Appelbaum 2006; Chan 2006). Accounts of labour insurgency in official statistics of arbitrated labour disputes, and other studies about strikes and protests show that migrant workers have been increasingly taking collective action to fight for their legitimate interests. Most working-class protests are still occurring in the northeast rustbelt provinces where layoffs and pension corruption have generated enormous unrest. Still, the full employment and rising wages of coastal China have done little to ameliorate social conflict. Guangzhou City reported nearly 900 protests involving more than 50,000 workers in 2004. One protest in seven involved more than 100 people, indicating that in Guangdong, as in so many other parts of China, resentment, anger, and social conflict lie just beneath the surface (Cody 2004; Tanner 2005).

There is thus a potential for large-scale protest at 'market reforms' and social and political upheaval – a prospect the political elite is anxious to avoid. To this end, they are presently instituting policies that they suggest will improve the condition of disadvantaged social groups in order to build a so-called 'harmonious society'. In 2005, China drew up its own standard of 'corporate social responsibility' (CSR), initially only for the textile industry. The concept of CSR was introduced into China in the mid-1990s. It originated with the anti-sweatshop movement in the developed countries, which accused brand-name Western corporations of turning a blind eye to dangerous, inhumane conditions in factories around the world that made merchandise for them under contract. To ward off the criticism, many Western companies adopted 'corporate codes of conduct', demanding compliance with a minimum set of standards by their sub-contractors. When CSR was first pressed upon China's supplier factories in the 1990s, factory managers came under pressure to have safer and cleaner shopfloors and dormitories, to comply with China's labour law in terms of wages and work hours, and to establish better occupational and health programmes.

But supplier-factory managers soon learned how to resist these impositions and hide transgressions from monitors and auditors. Double bookkeeping, the practice of covering up genuine factory records by faulty ones, is common. The Chinese manager of a large factory that supplies garments to multinational corporations in the Pearl River Delta economic zone in Guangdong confessed to *The Financial Times* (April 21, 2005) that the workers' time cards and salary statements were faked to meet the clients' codes of conduct. A team of six employees were assigned to prepare the forged documents, which are 'a perfect match' for the foreign buyers' requirements. Such strategies clearly indicate the limits of factory audits.[3]

Having invested resources in improving their corporate image but reaping little gain, and still pressured by North American and Asian labour rights activists, some of the Western TNCs turned in frustration to the idea of 'workers' training' and even to democratic elections for workers' committees or workplace trade-union branches. The rationale is that workers are the best monitors of their own conditions. However, such issues raise wider questions regarding the interaction between labour codes of conduct and local labour organisations (see Chapter 4 in this volume). The fundamental failure of the current monitoring system practised by most TNCs is that workers' participation is conspicuously absent throughout the drafting and implementation of codes of conduct. One detailed study of codes and labour conditions in two large Chinese apparel factories concluded that, rather than leading to labour rights in the workplace, the implementation of corporate codes of conduct resulted at best in 'managerial paternalism', with labour rights (if granted) originating from above. The companies devoted huge resources to setting up systems and procedures, but demonstrated little genuine concern for labour rights and less still for workers' representation or participation owing to a deep reluctance to alter prevailing power relations between capital and labour (Pun 2005; see also Sum and Pun 2005; Wells 2007). The real value of these corporate codes of conduct is that they legitimise the idea of a global social standard to accompany global production systems and can provide an impetus to local organising, even as their failures demonstrate that they do not offer a vehicle for the transformation of the exploitive and oppressive labour relations that prevail in China's foreign-funded enterprises.

In this vein, the contradictions afflicting China's official trade union have led to a period of change with uneven and ambiguous outcomes. To a large extent, the ACFTU, with its membership of over 100 million and a workforce of over 500,000 staff, remains dominated by Party authority and, in practical terms at the enterprise level, is a component of management. In disagreements between workers and management, the ACFTU frequently has divided loyalties and generally responds with political caution. To avoid potential conflict in the past, it has tended to concentrate its work in non-industrial areas such as welfare and housing, which have been linked to workers' employment in the ACFTU's main sector of activity – the SOEs.

Such a role was never adequate to ensure worker interests were articulated in the 'patron–client' relations which dominated industrial relations prior to the reforms (Walder 1986). In the context of 'market reforms' and of post-socialist transition, however, the interests of the industrial parties are far more starkly set against each other. Over much of the reform period, official trade unionism has been insufficiently autonomous of management and Party to defend worker interests, and the trade unions and their cadres have acted ineffectually or against workers' interests.

Nonetheless, the changes in Chinese industrial relations have stimulated internal reforms (Ng and Warner 1998; Gallagher 2004). Faced with a financial and membership crisis, the ACFTU has had to establish branches in enterprises from the booming private sector – an effort epitomised by the recent drive to unionise China's Wal-Mart stores (Chan 2007). Given the desire by China's unions to expand membership, if groups of Chinese workers in the coming years use legally-sanctioned means to set up trade union branches and then affiliate them to the ACFTU, it might provide the workforce with representation, bargaining power, and a voice to contest the manner and effects of China's integration into global capitalism. Whether or not this occurs will depend on whether a new union branch is organised in a way that enables it to be representative of workers or, alternatively, whether the ACFTU reverts to the practice that union branches in future are again always to be imposed top-down, through prior management–union agreement, and dominated in their operations by a management–union alliance. Under China's labour laws and the present political situation, they may find this politically feasible and more productive than fighting to set up autonomous trade unions. The recent success of the ACFTU in setting up workplace union branches at Wal-Mart supercentres in China demonstrates that Chinese labour laws are the fulcrum around which the evolution of labour relations and trade unionism is currently anchored. The laws are the tools used by all sides to argue their positions. Wal-Mart used the Chinese trade union law to refuse to let the ACFTU set up unions; and the ACFTU in turn used the procedures stated in the law to set up union branches.

The ACFTU's confrontation with Wal-Mart has opened up a means for reformers to operate in future, and has set a precedent for Chinese workers to move beyond mere resistance by taking on their employers and demanding union branches. Still, it is important to note that although the ACFTU is not the monolithic structure it is often portrayed to be, it has little experience with grassroots initiatives, and many union officials are nervous about activities that are not hierarchically initiated and controlled. Nor are they accustomed to, or comfortable with, having to organise workers themselves, whatever the precedent set by the recent experience with Wal-Mart. Reformers within the ACFTU want to push in that direction, but they are themselves untrained and on unsure ground. There are union officials and local union constituents who understand the principles of organizing and are willing to push the limits. But they are constrained by pro-capital forces within the Communist Party, the government, and the ACFTU on the one hand, and domestic and international anti-union forces on the other.

Still, the more progressive elements of the leadership of the ACFTU are aware of the need to activate the base by encouraging primary trade union organisations to articulate their members' aspirations within the framework of collective bargaining. The alternative is large-scale social upheaval, for if gross social injustice continues to prevail, workers may resort to large-scale protest actions and even violence. This is a possibility that the Communist Party has been forced to take increasingly seriously. Of the two main types of workers, it may be the migrant workers rather than the state workers who will be in the forefront of the struggle. By now, the downsizing of state enterprises has passed its peak. If the government is able to establish a workable social welfare system for the urban poor as part of its 'harmonious society' programme, it may be able to contain urban discontent. Yet the conditions of migrant workers who are still outside the welfare safety net have shown little improvement. The labour rights consciousness of migrant workers is now soaring, ironically developing as a by-product of global capital's CSR movement. To date, the ACFTU has not engaged migrant workers, and this provides an opportunity for the growth of better-organised collective protest action. An independent trade union movement could be sparked by the oft-predicted 'hard landing' of the Chinese economy, which would accentuate the release of migrant workers and the further rationalisation of SOEs.

Conclusion

As a result of the profound transformations of China's productive structures that have occurred in the context of its post-socialist transition, the centre of gravity of China's working class has shifted decisively. The representative model of a Chinese worker as a SOE employee with lifetime guarantees of employment, welfare, housing, health, and education is no longer adequate as a picture of the present and certainly not of the future. The dominant employment form of the future is more likely to involve contracted workers in non-state enterprise employment who will be privately responsible for much of their own and their families' welfare. The new working class in the process of formation does not identify with the interests of their managers, employers, Party, or state to the same extent as in the past, for there is much less that binds them to these bodies. This shift has profound implications for China's political economy since the Communist Party relied for much of its legitimacy on the proclaimed identity of interests it shared with the working class. Social welfare arrangements and industrial relations are also greatly affected by this shift, and the development of acceptable policies in these areas will play a large part in enshrining viable capitalist labour markets.

As elsewhere in East and Southeast Asia where there are large movements of the workforce from agriculture into industry, workers whose employment is precarious, who were previously considered peripheral, and were marginalised by industrial institutions, are now central to the process of capitalist development in China. They do not arrive in these difficult industrial environments with pre-formed understandings of industrial relations, trade union practice, or industrial discipline. Nor do their employers. In the case of much of the rest of Asia, industrial discipline in the global factory is being imposed locally by the state and employers, frequently with coercive mechanisms that are unlikely to be vetted through the TNCs' voluntary codes of conduct. Moreover, while endogenous social forces are playing a part in the remaking of the Chinese working class, they are doing so in and through the integration of China's economy within global capitalism. The only means of industrial representation for this new class is the official trade union (ACFTU), which still owes its primary allegiance to the Party and management. As new capitalist labour market arrangements intensify the work process – increasing control over labour, inter-firm competition, and pressure on wages – there is a growing need for the new working class to be able to articulate its interests autonomously. The globalised nature of the production chains in which Chinese workers are embedded will continue to impact upon forms of collective representation, notably in the contradictory pressures for greater competitiveness alongside those for corporate social responsibility in terms of labour standards. The following two chapters further develop these key issues.

Notes

1 *People's Daily*, 21 December 2002.
2 Interview with Han Dongfang, director of the Hong Kong-based *China Labour Bulletin*, 2 February 2007.
3 See also the report by the Clean Clothes Campaign 'Quick Fix': www.cleanclothes.org/publications/quick_fix.htm

References

Adams, F.G. *et al.* (2006) 'Why is China So Competitive? Measuring and Explaining China's Competitiveness', *World Economy* 29(2): 95–122.

Appelbaum, R. (2006) 'Giant Factories, Militant Labor: The Rise of Fordism in China?', Paper presented at the annual meeting of the American Studies Association Annual Convention, Oakland, CA, Marriott City Center.

Appelbaum, R.P. and Lichtenstein, N. (2006) 'A New World of Retail Supremacy: Supply Chains and Workers' Chains in the Age of Wal-Mart', *International Labor and Working Class History* 70(1): 106–125.

Blázquez-Lidoy, J. *et al.* (2006) *Angel or Devil? China's Trade Impact on Latin American Emerging Markets*, Paris: Overseas Development Centre, OECD.

Blecher, M. (2002) 'Hegemony and Workers' Politics in China', *China Quarterly* 170: 283–303.

Blim, M.L. (1992) 'The Emerging Global Factory and Anthropology', in F.-A. Rothstein and M.L. Blim, *Anthropology and the Global Factory: Studies in the New Industrialization in the Late Twentieth Century*, New York: Bergin & Garvey, pp. 1–33.

Bronfenbrenner, K. and Luce, S. (2004) *The Changing Nature of Corporate Global Restructuring: The Impact of Production Shifts on Jobs in the US, China, and Around the Globe*, Washington, DC: US-China Economic and Security Review Commission.

Burkett, P. and Hart-Landsberg, M. (2000) *Development, Crisis, and Class Struggle: Learning from Japan and East Asia*, New York: St. Martin's Press.

Cai, Y. (2002) 'The Resistance of Chinese Laid-off Workers in the Reform Period', *China Quarterly* 170: 327–344.

Chan, A. (2001) *China's Workers under Assault: The Exploitation of Labor in a Globalizing Economy*, Armonk, NY: M.E. Sharpe.

—— (2007) 'Organizing Wal-Mart in China: Two Steps Forward, One Step Back for China's Unions', *New Labor Forum* 16(2): 87–96.

Chan, J.W. (2006) 'Chinese Women Workers Organize in the Export Zones', *New Labor Forum* 15(1): 19–27.

Clarke, S. (2005) 'Post-Socialist Trade Unions: China and Russia', *Industrial Relations Journal* 36(1): 2–18.

Cody, E. (2004) 'Workers in China Shed Passivity, Spate of Walkouts Shakes Factories', *Washington Post*, 27 November, p. A1.

Cooke, F.L. (2005) *HRM, Work and Employment in China*, London: Routledge.

Enright, M. *et al.* (2005) *Regional Powerhouse: The Greater Pearl River Delta and the Rise of China*, Singapore: John Wiley & Sons, Ltd.

Fröbel, F. *et al.* (1980) *The New International Division of Labour: Structural Unemployment in Industrialised Countries and Industrialisation in Developing Countries*, Cambridge: Cambridge University Press.

Gallagher, M.E. (2004) '"Time is Money, Efficiency is Life": The Transformation of Labour Relations in China', *Studies in Comparative International Development* 39 (2): 11–44.

Hart-Landsberg, M. and Burkett, P. (2005a) 'China and Socialism: Engaging the Issues', *Critical Asian Studies* 37(4): 597–628.

—— (2005b) *China and Socialism: Market Reforms and Class Struggle*, New York: Monthly Review Press.

—— (2006) 'China and the Dynamics of Transnational Accumulation: Causes and Consequences of Global Restructuring', *Historical Materialism* 14(3): 3–43.

Heartfield, J. (2005) 'China's Comprador Capitalism is Coming Home', *Review of Radical Political Economics* 37(2): 196–214.

Henderson, J. (1989) *The Globalisation of High Technology Production: Society, Space, and Semiconductors in the Restructuring of the Modern World*, London: Routledge.

ILO (International Labour Office) (2007) *Global Employment Trends Brief*, Geneva: International Labour Office.

Lall, S. and Albaladejo, M. (2004) 'China's Competitive Performance: A Threat to East Asian Manufactured Exports?', *World Development* 32(9): 1441–1466.

Lambert, R. and Chan, A. (1999) 'Global Dance: Factory Regimes, Asian Labour Standards and Corporate Restructuring', in J. Waddington, *Globalization and Patterns of Labour Resistance*, London: Mansell, pp. 72–104.

Lardy, N.R. (2007) 'Trade Liberalization and Its Role in Chinese Economic Growth', in W. Tseng and D. Cowen, *India's and China's Recent Experience with Reform and Growth*, London: Palgrave, pp. 158–169.

Lavely, W. (2001) 'First Impressions of the 2000 Census of China', *Population and Development Review* 27(4): 755–769.

Lee, C.K. (1998) *Gender and the South China Miracle: Two Worlds of Factory Women*, Berkeley, CA: University of California Press.

—— (2002) 'From the Spectre of Mao to the Spirit of the Law: Labor Insurgency in China', *Theory and Society* 31(2): 189–228.

—— (2003) 'Pathways of Labour Insurgency', in E. Perry and M. Selden, *Chinese Society: Change, Conflict and Resistance*, London: Routledge, pp. 71–92.

Leung, T.W. (1998a) *The Politics of Labour Rebellions in China, 1989–1994*, Hong Kong: Hong Kong University Press.

—— (1998b) 'S'organiser pour défendre ses droits: contestations ouvrières en Chine dans les années 1990', *Perspectives chinoises* 48: 6–21.

Liang, Z. and Zhongdong, M. (2004) 'China's Floating Population: New Evidence from the 2000 Census', *Population and Development Review* 30(3): 467–488.

Lichtenstein, N. (2006) 'Wal-Mart's Tale of Two Cities: From Bentonville to Shenzhen', *New Labor Forum* 15(2): 9–19.

Loong-Yu, A. (2006) 'The Post MFA Era and the Rise of China, Part I', *Against the Current* (125), online. Available at: www.solidarity-us.org/node/185

Luehrmann, L.M. (2003) 'Facing Citizen Complaints in China, 1951–1996', *Asian Survey* 43(5): 845–866.

Lui, T. (2005) 'Bringing Class Back in: China Re-stratified', *Critical Asian Studies* 37 (3): 473–480.

Naughton, B. (1997) 'Economic Policy Reform in the PRC and Taiwan', in B. Naughton, *The China Circle: Economics and Technology in the PRC, Taiwan and Hong Kong*, Washington, DC: Brookings Institution Press, pp. 81–110.

Ng, S.H. and Warner, M. (1998) *China's Trade Unions and Management*, New York: St. Martin's Press.

Pun, N. (1999) 'Becoming Dagongmei: The Politics of Identity and Difference in Reform China', *The China Journal* 42: 1–19.

—— (2005a) 'Global Production, Company Codes of Conduct, and Labor Conditions in China: A Case Study of Two Factories', *The China Journal* 54: 101–113.

—— (2005b) *Made in China: Women Factory Workers in a Global Workplace*, Durham, NC: Duke University Press.

Pun, N. and Smith, C. (2007) 'Putting the Transnational Labour Process in its Place: The Dormitory Labour Regime in Post-Socialist China', *Work, Employment & Society* 21(1): 27–45.

Ross, A. (2006) *Fast Boat to China: Corporate Flight and the Consequences of Free Trade*, New York: Pantheon.

Sargeson, S. (1999) *Reworking China's Proletariat*, Basingstoke: Macmillan Press.

Smart, A. and Smart, J. (1992) 'Capitalist Production in a Socialist Society: The Transfer of Manufacturing from Hong Kong to China', in F.-A. Rothstein and M. L. Blim, *Anthropology and the Global Factory: Studies in the New Industrialization in the Late Twentieth Century*, New York: Bergin & Garvey, pp. 47–61.

Smith, C. and Pun, N. (2006) 'The Dormitory Labour Regime in China as a Site for Control and Resistance', *International Journal of Human Resource Management* 17 (8): 1456–1470.

So, A. (2001) 'The Origins and Transformation of the Chinese Triangle', in A. So, *The Chinese Triangle of Mainland China, Taiwan and Hong Kong*, Westport, CT: Greenwood Press, pp. 1–22.

Solinger, D. (2002) 'Labour Market Reform and the Plight of the Laid-Off Proletariat', *China Quarterly* (170): 304–326.

Steinfeld, E. (2004) 'China's Shallow Integration: Networked Production and the New Challenges for Late Industrialization', *World Development* 32(11): 1971–1987.

Sum, N. and Pun, N. (2005) 'Globalization and Paradoxes of Ethical Transnational Production: Code of Conduct in a Chinese Workplace', *Competition and Change* 9 (2): 181–200.

Sung, Y. (1991) *The China–Hong Kong Connection: The Key to China's Open-Door Policy*, Cambridge: Cambridge University Press.

—— (1997) 'Hong Kong and the Economic Integration of the China Circle', in B. Naughton, *The China Circle: Economics and Technology in the PRC, Taiwan and Hong Kong*, Washington, DC: Brookings Institution Press, pp. 41–80.

Tanner, M. (2005) 'Chinese Government Responses to Rising Social Unrest', Washington, DC, testimony presented to the US-China Economic and Security Review Commission.

Tao, R. (2006) 'The Labor Market in the People's Republic of China: Development and Policy Challenges in Economic Transition', in J. Felipe and R. Hasan, *Labor Markets in Asia: Issues and Perspectives*, London: Palgrave, pp. 503–557.

Taylor, B. (1999) 'Japanese Management Style in China? Production Practices in Japanese Manufacturing Plants', *New Technology, Work and Employment* 14(2): 129–144.

—— (2002) 'Privatization, Markets and Industrial Relations in China', *British Journal of Industrial Relations* 40(2): 249–272.

Tsui-Auch, L.S. (1999) 'Regional Production Relationships and Developmental Impacts: A Comparative Study of Three Production Networks', *International Journal of Urban and Regional Research* 23(2): 345–360.

Unger, J. (2002) *The Transformation of Rural China*, Armonk, NY: M.E. Sharpe.

Walder, A. G. (1986) *Communist Neo-Traditionalism: Work and Authority in Chinese Industry*, Berkeley, CA: University of California Press.

Wells, D. (2007) 'Too Weak for the Job: Corporate Codes of Conduct, Non-Governmental Organizations and the Regulation of International Labour Standards', *Global Social Policy* 7(1): 51–74.

Wong, M. and Chang, D. (2005) 'After the Consumer Movement: Toward a New International Labour Activism in the Global Garment Industry', *Labour, Capital and Society* 38(1–2): 127–156.

Yam, T.K. (1997) 'China and ASEAN: Competitive Industrialization through Foreign Direct Investment', in B. Naughton, *The China Circle: Economics and Technology in the PRC, Taiwan and Hong Kong*, Washington, DC: Brookings Institution Press, pp. 111–138.

Yeung, H.W. (2004) *Chinese Capitalism in a Global Era: Towards Hybrid Capitalism*, London: Routledge.

Part II

Commodity chains, labour standards and corporate social responsibility

4 Restructuring and conflict in the global athletic footwear industry

Nike, Yue Yuen and labour codes of conduct

Jeroen Merk

No other company symbolises the mobilisation of American companies overseas more than Phil Knight's Nike, Inc. *The Washington Post* once argued. '[Nike's] thirty year-anniversary in Asia is as close as any one company's story can be to the history of globalization, to the spread of dollars ... into the poor corners of the earth' (cited in LaFeber 1999). Nike was not only the first to have its shoes sourced in Asia, it was also the first in the marketing and advertising of athletic shoes. The company played an important role in transforming sport shoes and apparel into a fashion statement. For this reason, academics from various disciplines have shown much interest in how Nike organises the production of its commodities (see, e.g. Donaghu and Barff 1990; Korzeniewicz, 1994; Goldman and Papson 1998). Today, moreover, practically every brand-name sportswear company has a business plan similar to that of Nike's strategy of focusing on the branding and marketing of sportswear.

Despite the comprehensible attention placed on Nike, however, this chapter argues that there is another 'success' story to tell about a company that emerged during the same period but at the other end of the earth, namely Yue Yuen Industrial. Yue Yuen is a Taiwanese-owned industrial conglomerate that controls 17 per cent of the world branded footwear market and employs more than 265,000 people. Yue Yuen's factories are located in several countries in Southeast Asia, most importantly mainland China. This company successfully (i.e., profitably) internalised precisely what companies such as Nike sought to externalise: the organisation of the labour-intensive moments of athletic footwear production. Instead of making profits from marketing and distributing branded sportswear, Yue Yuen produces for consumer markets elsewhere. During the past ten years, NGOs and labour organisations have frequently criticised Yue Yuen (often indirectly by blaming Nike, Reebok, Adidas or Puma) for its harsh control of the work force, poor working conditions, low wages, and aggressive attitude towards labour unions (see, e.g. Chan 1996; Kwan 2000; Connor 2002).

More generally, the production and circulation of athletic footwear can be taken as an example how within global capital circuits branded corporations have largely 'freed' themselves from commitments to space-specific investments at least as far as concerns the labour-intensive production of their merchandise. They have organised their businesses around the creation of 'commodity spectacles', while cutting themselves free from actual production. In this process, branded corporations saved on wage costs and social security expenditures, even though a significant part of the cost-saving related to outsourcing are now spent on marketing activities in a battle to control market shares. The management of mass labour processes ends up being outsourced to specialists in the manufacturing who carry out the routine tasks of production. Transnational production implies the growing power of capital to organise and control labour on ever larger geographical scales while *ignoring* the social reproductive needs of labour.

However, the effort of brands to disassociate themselves from the actual production of their commodities has been thwarted by numerous global anti-sweatshop campaigns. During the past fifteen years anti-sweatshop campaigns have pushed branded corporations in a range of industries, including athletic footwear, to implement and monitor their supply chains on labour rights, including freedom of association and collective bargaining. Exposed to anti-sweatshop campaigns attacking their substandard working conditions, and so turned the feel-good logos into symbols of exploitation, many corporations have taken some steps to address the worst forms of exploitation. It has resulted in a wide variety of mainly non-state forms of labour regulation such as codes of conducts, ethical labels and multi-stakeholder initiatives established supposedly to allay the destructive effects of an unfettered market economy.

The first section of this chapter will recall some basic characteristics of how the production of athletic footwear is organised, emphasising the functional split between brands operating at the point of consumption and manufacturers operating at the point of production. The second section will discuss Yue Yuen and provide some basic background information on this giant manufacturer. In the third section, the chapter will turn to issues concerning corporate social responsibility (CSR) and look critically at attempts to encourage nascent forms of worker self-representation in Yue Yuen factories.

The athletic footwear industry: a functional split

Only a limited number of brands dominate the athletic footwear market. Nike alone accounts for 35 per cent and the twenty largest companies represent over 92 per cent of the global wholesale. In the summer of 2005, Reebok was taken over by Adidas. As a result, the sector will now be even more concentrated, with only two companies (Nike and Adidas) controlling over 50 per cent of the market.

The total worth of the athletic footwear market is estimated US $17.012 billion wholesale, while at the retail level, it is valued at some US $25 billion. Table 4.1 shows that most of the sportswear is sold in the USA and EU.

At the same time, as Table 4.2 shows, most athletic footwear is produced in a small number of low-wage countries. The functional split not only

Table 4.1 *International athletic footwear market by region, 2002*

Country	*(%)*
US	47
EU	31
Asia	16
Japan	8
Other	6

Source: Sporting Goods Intelligence (2003)

reflects a division of labour between companies in the footwear chain (like brands and manufacturers) but also between consumption at one location, and production at another.

By cutting themselves free from the labour-intensive production of their merchandise, almost all brand-named sportswear corporations have 'freed' themselves from commitments to space-specific investments. Instead, brands have organised their businesses around the creation of 'commodity spectacles'. Brands like Nike or Adidas focus on conceptualising the shoe (design, research, and innovation) and distribution (marketing, advertising), while the labour-intensive processes are outsourced. In order to control market outlets, Nike alone spent a billion US dollars on marketing per year. Nike has played a large role in transforming sport shoes and apparel into fashion statements (Goldman and Papson 1998). Almost all of the brand-named corporations have copied Nike's strategy of focusing on branding their sportswear. On average, sportswear brands spend 10 per cent of revenues on marketing. This reflects the notion that sportswear brands, like other fashionable products, are not created primarily around the physical product, although this of course is the core precondition of their business, but around the consumption of experience, life-style, attitude, reputation and image.

At the same time, manufacturers operating in low-wage countries are now performing the more routine tasks of production. Particularly Taiwanese and South Korean manufacturers dominate the production of athletic shoes. These companies, which began as suppliers to Western companies in the 1970s, relocated most of their production sites once production costs (wages)

Table 4.2 *Athletic footwear US imports – market share by country, 2002*

Country	*(%)*
China	75.7
Indonesia	13.5
Vietnam	4.0
Thailand	3.7
South Korea	1.3
Other	1.8

Source: UBS Warburg, 19 May 2003

started to increase. Today most of their factories are located in China, Indonesia and Vietnam. Like the brands, therefore, they have internationalised their activities. These manufacturers produce shoes that are distributed and sold under the name of the contractor and little control is exercised over (retail) market outlets in Western countries. Generally speaking, their lack of control over large market outlets renders them dependent. This illustrates the subordinated position of productive capital when inserted into these kinds of global capital circuits. However, as we will discuss shortly, some of these manufacturers, particularly Yue Yuen, are doing remarkably well.

Manufacturers have specialised in organizing the labour-intensive parts of footwear production. They have to handle issues concerning employment, working conditions, skill, and production technology and the circumstances under which labour is reproduced (Henderson *et al.* 2002: 448). Contingent upon specific designs, the production of athletic footwear involves about 150–200 different steps in the manufacture of a single shoe (see Mamic, 2003). In order to generate scale advantages, assembly takes place in large factories that often employ between 5,000–10,000 workers. Most of these workers are young (about 17–24 years old) and female (about 70–90 per cent). The majority of these workers have only recently migrated from rural villages to industrial production zones, and represent the latest influx into the global industrial workforce (see Chapter 3 in this volume).

Transnational outsourcing and shifting capital-labour relations

Outsourcing gives brand-named corporations access to so-called *dual labour markets*, characterised by growing division between 'core' workers and 'marginalised' or 'peripheral' workers. The externalisation of a 'non-core' labour force turns the organisation of this labour force, as Atkinson (1984) notes, into 'somebody else's problem'. Harrison argues in an article that takes Nike as its main example that the principal mechanism at work here 'is intended to capture the continuing dispersal of production, but ultimately under the technical and financial control of managers in a relatively small number of big . . . multinational corporations and their strategic allies' (Harrison 1994: 206).

In this type of dual labour market, a company seeks to capitalise the use value of a small number of highly qualified labourers like managers, technicians, designers, innovators, sometimes called symbolic workers – who have to conceptualise, oversee, manage and reintegrate globally fragmented labourer processes, while the repetitive, monotone or 'simple tasks' are treated (in Marxist parlance) as 'abstract' labour, which can be bought from others. The flexibility of capital accumulation here turns into flexible labour relations as workers are treated as a 'subcontracted component' rather than a fixture internal to employer organisations (Robinson 2004: 19). Only a small group of 'core' workers who are deemed essential for the company are kept in-house and given stable contracts, job security and high wages; the labour-intensive parts of production is done by a 'peripheral' workforce, associated, for instance, with the fast growing number of export processing zones where women workers in particular end up with insecure, labour-intensive and low-paying jobs. In the sportswear industry, the ratio between the number of workers employed by branded corporations and workers employed by (various) subcontractors is estimated at an average of 1 to 20.

By extricating themselves from material production processes and shrinking the workforce, sourcing companies like Nike and Adidas have saved on wage costs and social security expenditures. They have transmitted the burden of labour demands from high-wage organised sectors of the labour market to low-wage and low-organised sectors of the labour market. It has led to a production system in which sourcing companies do not need to pay attention to the reproductive requirements of labour power. This lack of attention is symbolised by wages that fail to meet basic needs (housing, energy, nutrition, clothing, health care, education, potable water, child care, transportation, and savings), or provide additional discretionary income, or take into consideration the number of dependants. It makes it possible to exploit labour through short-term contracts, long working hours, forced and unpaid overtime, unsafe working conditions, payment tied to unrealistic production targets or piece-rate systems, and redundancy policies that offer no or highly inadequate severance pay compensation. In other words, production costs are divested – ideally entirely – of reproduction costs. The authoritarian and repressive political conditions in which production typically takes place raise various – often legal – barriers to the right to organise, and these exacerbate the problem because employees are prohibited or restricted from demanding basic workers rights.

The abstract formality of exchange relations makes it possible for sourcing companies to ignore the overall conditions in which (mass) production processes are embedded. At least in the first instance: labour struggles in the factories and countries of production as well as public discontent in areas of consumption concerning substandard labour conditions brings the issue back to the various corporate headquarters in New York, London, Tokyo, Amsterdam, or Paris. These protests against sweatshop conditions are part of a broader, societal response to limit the disintegrating and alienating aspects of commodification. The global anti-sweatshop movement has contributed to the condition that a growing number of sourcing companies, particularly those with well-known brand-names, can no longer afford to distance themselves from some form of responsibility for the conditions under which their goods are made. We return to this topic later, first I shortly discuss another key relation: the relation between brands and manufacturers.

Transnational outsourcing and inter-capitalist relations

The functional split between branded companies and manufacturers causes each of them to concentrate on a different aspect of the production process. For brands, this inter-organisational division of labour has made it possible to combine 'inflexible means of production with flexible and dynamic forms of company organization' (Donaghu and Barff 1990: 538). The flexible forms derive from the relations brands have built up with production networks in low-wage countries. The inflexible means are associated with the assembly of athletic footwear production, which remains a very labour-intensive process. Thus, buyers often steer or control production processes even if they have little relation to the actual production of goods made on their behalf. Control over end-markets, which either takes place directly in the case of large retailers like Wal-Mart, Carrefour, or Metro, or indirectly in the case of international brand-named companies like Nike or Gap, places them in a powerful position vis-à-vis manufacturers (suppliers). The control over end-markets puts them in a position to control transnational, decentralised and competitive sourcing networks.

It is therefore often argued, for example, in the global commodity chain approach (Gereffi 1994, 1999; Kaplinsky and Morris 2001), that manufacturing (e.g., the labour-intensive, or assembling moment of production) represents a rather 'lower order' or 'dead end' factor in competitiveness for the supplier, which remains subordinated to agents that control 'higher-order' factors like proprietary technology, product differentiation, brand reputation, consumer relations and constant industrial upgrading (see Raikes *et al.* 2000: 5–6). It is assumed that most of the profits are made – *appropriated* might be a better term – by companies controlling consumer markets either through control over the technological innovative processes of production or through branding and marketing. Thus, with regard to the sportswear industry, Korzeniewicz has argued that Nike's commercial success is based on retaining 'control over highly profitable nodes in the athletic footwear commodity chain, while avoiding the rigidity and pressures that characterize the more competitive nodes of the chain' (1994: 251). Goldman and Papson argue that it 'is very difficult to compete in today's footwear industry without engaging in the outsourcing of labour to relatively unskilled labourers in impoverished countries' (1998: 11).

While this picture is often correct, the global restructuring of production processes is also accompanied by the emergence of an East Asian fraction of capital that specialises in the organisation of predominantly export-orientated, low-skill, low-wage, labour-intensive, and high-volume manufacturing across a range of industries. Instead of being 'prisoners of the OEM sourcers', these companies have turned the tapping of the world's reservoirs of cheap labour supplies into a highly profitable activity. Departing from the vantage point of production, these companies have become focused on producing either high quality components or finished products often for several (competing) brand-named corporations of either Western or Japanese origin. This is especially true for companies of Taiwanese, South Korean and Hong Kong origin that have successfully upgraded into first-class original equipment manufacturers. There is little (and almost no academic) research available on this emergence of this type of companies and their role in reshaping global production (but see SOMO 2003; Appelbaum 2004; AMRC 2005). However, these corporations not only play an increasingly important role in organizing these supply chains, but many of them have set up production sites in Asia and particularly mainland China, Latin America and Africa. The biggest firms employ tens of thousands of workers. Henry Cornell, a Goldman Sachs executive, put it this way: 'These types of businesses are not very sexy ... but it is a superb economic model for northern Asia. They can make significant profits being manufacturers for research and development-oriented companies in the United States' (*The Wall Street Journal*, 10 March 2000).

Without easy access to end-consumer markets, squeezing profit out of organising mass-production processes is for these companies the most profitable route to follow. These companies play a particular role in 'mediating commercial capital from the West and workers in Asia', as Dae-oup Chang of Asia Monitor Resource Centre (AMRC) puts it (2005: 18). It is particularly this capital fraction that organises, manages, disciplines and exploits the insertion of the world's new workers into factories.

Take, for example, the Taiwanese-owned Foxconn, a world-leading manufacturer of connectors and cable assemblies in the world. The company has a market capitalisation of over $6 billion and employs over 200,000 employees at its Longhua facility in China. Besides the electronics equipment it produces for a variety of IT companies, it also produces the highly popular iPods, Nanos and Shuffles sold by Apple. The company came under public scrutiny after a journalist reported on its militaristic treatment of workers, long working hours and crowed dormitories. Another example is Nien Hsing Textile Co., which is the world's largest jeans producer. Its clients include well-known retailers and branded companies such as Kmart, Sears, and Gap. While its plants in Taiwan only employ 700 people, its facilities in Lesotho and Central America employ thousands of workers. Union repression and illegal dismissal of union members turned the company into a target of a year-long transnationally organised solidarity campaign with protest actions taking place in Europe, the United States, Lesotho and Taiwan. Eventually, these protests were successful when the company and the union signed an accord and the union leaders and workers were reinstated (SOMO 2003: 5).

Now we will take a closer look Yue Yuen which, even though it is the largest shoe manufacturer in the world, is unknown to the consuming public because it does not brand shoes but only produces and assembles them.

Pou Chen/Yue Yuen

The Pou Chen Group was founded by the Tsai family, who established a family business in Taiwan in 1969 that produced rubber shoes including PVC sandals and indoor slippers. From the beginning, Pou Chen generated enough profits to ensure its rapid expansion. One family member recalls its development: 'From slippers, we made sandals. From sandals we made shoes. From shoes we made sports shoes' (*Wall Street Journal*, 7 March 2000). During the 1970s and 1980s, it developed into a more diversified and technically advanced original equipment manufacturer (OEM) and eventually as an original design manufacturer (ODM). As a result, Pou Chen started to receive orders from Japanese and US companies such as Sears Roebuck and Mitsubishi. In 1979, Adidas started to order shoes from Pou Chen and their relationship continues to this day. These kinds of contracts motivated Pou Chen to specialise even further in the production of athletic footwear. Reebok designated Pou Chen as its most important producer in 1985, Nike followed suit in the beginning of the 1990s.

Labour shortages, wage increases and currency appreciation made Pou Chen disperse production sites from Taiwan into China (1988), Indonesia (1993) and Vietnam (1995). The main vehicle for this overseas expansion, *Yue Yuen Industrial Holdings*, was established by Tsai Chi Jen – the brother of Pou Chen's founder – in order to facilitate expansion in China in 1988. Despite the difficult political relationship between Taiwan and Mainland China, Pou Chen boasts about its ability to maintain friendly relations with leaders from both countries. An introductory videotape shows Yue Yuen's Chairman Tsai Chi-jui giving a pair of sneakers to Taiwan President Lee Teng-hui, immediately followed by a warm handshake with China's President Jiang Zemin (*Indian Express*, 27 August 1997). To have personal connections is an essential feature of doing business in China.

The Yue Yuen Corporation listed itself on the Hong Kong stock exchange in 1992. It is also worth noting that Yue Yuen even operates a few production lines in the USA (Los Angeles) where it produces shoes for New Balance, a brand which emblazons its shoes as 'Made in the USA'.

Yue Yuen currently has an estimated 17 per cent share of the world athletic footwear market and an estimated 11–12 per cent in the more fragmented casual footwear market (Morgan Stanley, 8 October 2003). The company receives orders from over thirty different sport shoe brands such as Nike, Reebok, Adidas, New Balance, Asics, Lotto, and Puma, but also from important casual or brown shoe brands like Timberland, Rockport, Clarks, and Dr. Marten's. The number of shoes produced rose sharply from 57 million pairs in 1996 to 130 million pairs in 2002. Yue Yuen continues to take over more and more of its competitors' business. For each of the last ten years, Yue Yuen's sales have grown an average of 19 per cent, while expansion in the total (athletic) shoe market itself was less than half that.

Economies of scale

Using economies of scale, Yue Yuen has succeeded in lowering its average production costs. Direct costs are reduced by utilising a more detailed division of labour. Indirect costs are spread across a larger revenue base. Another source of comparative advantage is that Yue Yuen has more production capacity enabling it to react swiftly to rush orders or to accelerate changes to production line configurations, and to the manufacturing and delivery processes of a new shoe. The actual production process of shoe manufacturing takes only one day for an entire batch of shoes, and the assembly time of a particular shoe can be measured in minutes. It is the lead time of the delivery of materials that takes the most time. For example, in 2000, the inventory turnover was 40 days, down from 45 days in 1998. The average for Yue Yuen's competitors was, according to one investment report 45–60 days in 2001 (Morgan Stanley, 7 September 2001). Yue Yuen's size makes it possible to order materials in advance, which offers time advantages. Yue Yuen's plants in China, Vietnam and Indonesia are equipped with the latest technologies for footwear manufacturing including CAD-CAM systems and highly efficient automated machinery. This powerful production base and advanced equipment give them the flexibility to respond rapidly to customer demands for quicker delivery and shorter lead times to the major consumer markets of the world.

Moreover, while brand-named corporations externalise more and more of their business tasks, Yue Yuen internalises them, for example, through the in-house supply of shoe components (such as shoe pads, midsoles, counters, etc.) and raw materials (glue hardeners, rubber, coatings, chemical materials, etc.) and production tools. As a fully integrated operation, Yue Yuen offers 'one-stop' shopping to merchandisers (Miller 2004: 231). The company treats each brand as an individual cost centre. There is a high level of brand management involvement with virtually constant presence on site of Nike, Reebok and Adidas managers (ITGLWF 2002: 6). In addition, Yue Yuen has also invested in its logistical abilities to shorten lead times for inbound materials and outbound products. This has provided Yue Yuen with control over quality standards and has reduced delivery and transport times. It has also served to increase the cost-effective procurement of raw materials. Again, this has helped shorten the inventory turnover time. In addition, the company established on-site design teams to foster closer ties with its main customers. This is particularly important since, due to falling profit margins, brand-named corporations have sought to reduce indirect costs related to production and to speed up lead times. As a result, the company plays, as one investment report puts it, 'a key part in the whole supply chain for its key customers. Smaller players without sufficient resources will find it difficult to match Yue Yuen's services to its customers' (Morgan Stanley, 8 October 2003).

At the same time, competition between Yue Yuen and its customers takes place around the distribution of profits. All relationships between corporations, even if mediated through the market, are structured by different degrees of power and influence. Most analysts and researchers assume that athletic footwear suppliers are automatically less powerful than the branded corporations in the chain (see, e.g. Korzeniewicz 1994; Goldman and Papson 1998).

There is no doubt that branded companies generally have more bargaining power. Their sourcing networks are designed to prevent suppliers from obtaining too much bargaining power. Branded corporations can relatively easily switch to other suppliers, while suppliers often rely perilously on a single buyer. However, compared to these manufacturers, Yue Yuen's customer portfolio is very diversified, as it supplies goods to some forty different brands. Nike, Reebok, and Adidas represent 60 per cent of Yue Yuen's turnover, while the five largest customers accounted for a total of 68 per cent. Still, in 2002, Yue Yuen sold 28 per cent of its shoes to Nike, whereas Nike receives only about 15 per cent of its shoes from Yue Yuen. Although this power-relation is unequal, it cannot be said that Yue Yuen is dependent on Nike. According to Daniel Chan, finance director of Kingmaker Footwear Holdings, a Hong Kong shoe supplier: 'If Yue Yuen said today, "I won't supply anymore to Nike," then Nike would be scared' (*The Wall Street Journal*, 7 March 2000). Moreover, Yue Yuen has proven to be a profitable company. In 2002, its net profits were higher in absolute terms than those of Reebok and Adidas, and surpassed only by Nike.

Managing mass labour processes

Although Yue Yuen has upgraded many of its business tasks, managing large numbers of workers located in low-wage countries *remains* their core activity. Like any other workplace, management is here confronted with three inter-related questions with regard to management control over labour. First, management has to ensure an efficient allocation of tasks with respect to the technical nature of the production process (e.g., maintaining a technical division of labour). Second, management has to impose discipline on workers related to the speed and quality of work. Third, since the labour process is not an autonomous area of management, it has to formulate a strategy to deal with the individual or collective resistance of workers to this discipline (Gough 2003: 31). While management can follow an array of different control strategies with regard to this set of questions, from a co-operative stance on one end of the continuum to a coercive stance on the other, the division of labour between brands and manufacturers in the footwear industry implies that it is the manufacturer who has to formulate a strategy on how to control the biggest share of its workers.

Departing from the point of production, Yue Yuen's expansion in the 1980s and 1990s is underpinned by a repressive labour strategy based on preventing workers from organising and exercising collective bargaining power. Its high productivity rates are the result of long hours and forced overtime, for example, through its use of a piece-rate quota system in which quotas are set very high and are difficult to meet. Further, it enforces a strategy of strict discipline and punishment in a military-style factory regime, sometimes described as 'management by terror and browbeating' (Katz 1994). Over the past ten years, many labour advocates and researchers have criticised the company and its buyers for substandard labour conditions in its factories (see, e.g. Chan, 1996; AMRC and HKCIC 1997; Kwan 2000; Connor 2002).

Although it is likely that the news of most workers' rights violations never gets beyond the factory walls, some violations have been widely reported in the international press. In 1996, a floor manager in one of the Vietnam factories forced 56 women to run a 4-km circuit around the plant as punishment for wearing non-regulation shoes. Twelve workers fainted and were taken to hospital. David Tsai, Pou Chen's group president, responded by saying that it was an isolated error of judgment that 'could happen to any company in the process of internationalisation' (*Indian Express*, 27 August 1997). Another Pou Chen supervisor, also in Vietnam, was given a six-month jail term when 100 workers were forced to stand in the sun because one worker had spilled a fruit tray on an altar. When one employee walked away after 18 minutes of standing in the heat, he was fired. After local union officials and Nike management intervened, the worker was reinstated.

Yue Yuen and codes of conduct

However, Yue Yuen has not been immune to outside pressure from brand-named companies who fear 'reputational risk'. Substandard labour conditions and extreme forms of exploitation in the athletic footwear industry became a public issue in the early 1990s when anti-sweatshop groups started to target branded corporations over labour conditions in the factories that produced their wares. Nike, Reebok, Adidas, and occasionally, smaller brand-name corporations like Fila, Puma or Lotto, became targets of these campaigns, which gained momentum over the course of the decade. The central aim of these transnationally organised campaigns was to improve working conditions and 'to bring back to the TNC level some responsibility for workers no matter in whose employment they are or in what part of the world they live' (*Clean Clothes Newsletter* 2000). Working conditions were publicised through 'name and shame' campaigns. Research has shown that numerous basic workers' rights are regularly violated in factories and workplaces that supply these brands. Numerous reports, scandals and campaigns have revealed violations of the ILO core conventions. In response to global anti-sweatshop campaigns, the targeted companies instituted some small labour rights improvements. For example, they declared their commitment to the principle of respecting a worker's right to organise and they began to co-operate with various international monitoring and verification initiatives, such as the Fair Labour Association (see, for discussion, O'Rourke 2003; Merk 2007).

For Yue Yuen, the interest that brand-name corporations like Nike and Reebok now show in labour and employment conditions is a trend that first surfaced in the mid-1990s. 'In the past', Thomas Shih, a deputy Yue Yuen manager in a Chinese factory told a *Financial Times* journalist cynically: 'it was all about whether you could hit the workers or slap them. Now we talk about how we celebrate their birthdays' (4 February 2003). After the public relations disasters in Vietnam, the company started to co-operate with various brands on the improvement of workplace conditions, although reluctantly. Discussions with various corporate social responsibility (CSR) managers from branded companies indicate that they had significantly more difficulties in shaping Yue Yuen's social policy when compared to smaller footwear manufacturers. One Adidas manager describes Yue Yuen's approach on CSR as mainly 'customer driven'. He adds that Yue Yuen is a very hierarchical company and 'communication goes very slow' (Anderson, personal communication). In 1999, Reebok even decided to withdraw $40 million in annual sneaker contracts from the Zhongshan plant because of slow progress (Collier 2000).

Nonetheless, pressure seems to have softened Yue Yuen's disciplinary methods. It has reportedly resulted in some improvements in areas such as terms and conditions, particularly in relation to 'levels of overtime and dormitory accommodations for migrant labour' (Miller 2004: 226). In its 2000 Annual Report, the company reports that staff costs increased as a result of the hiring of additional workers to compensate for stricter rules on employees' working hours. It has also been pointed out that Yue Yuen has changed its system of fining workers for misbehaviour and its practice of paying wages based mainly on piece rates. The company also switched to less toxic, water-based glues used on its production lines.

When I interviewed two Yue Yuen managers in 2003, the company had seven years of experience in working with codes of conduct and it had hired 152 employees to work on CSR-related issues in its factories (Ip, personal communication, 2003). When asked how Yue Yuen works with the various management systems of its customers related to the implementation and monitoring of codes of conduct, the company responded by saying that it considers the various codes of conduct as 'similar affairs' (ibid.). Yue Yuen has strictly assigned different production lines to different buyers in order to comply with the various codes of conduct. It is notable that within the Yue Yuen organisation, these employees are given positions in the customer relations department (instead of the human resources or production departments). Doug Miller of the International Textile Garment Leather Workers' Federation (ITGLWF) argues that Yue Yuen has succeeded in maintaining a fragmented set of commercial relationships by maintaining discrete profit centres and production lines with each merchandiser client, which makes a more integrated approach towards labour issues difficult. One CSR manager for one of Yue Yuen's buyers has observed that raising labour issues at Yue Yuen remains difficult and researchers visiting Yue Yuen factories still notice that workers are very obedient and are generally afraid to speak up (Wells, personal communication,10 Feb. 2006). On the other hand, Yue Yuen commands larger financial resources for the implementation of the sometimes costly procedures related to codes than most of its competitors.

In 2001, Yue Yuen even developed its own code which includes the following set of standards: (1) no forced labour; (2) no child labour; (3) no discrimination; (4) compensation and welfare; (5) working hours; (6) reward/disciplinary practices and complaints systems; (7) freedom of association; and (8) environmental protection and occupational safety. While these standards are roughly similar to an average labour code of conduct, the document does not make reference to ILO standards. The right to freedom of association is described by Yue Yuen as follows:

> Based on the right of personal freedom, the company complies with free association policies [when] permitted by the local government. The company can neither prohibit labourers from joining free associations by any excuses, nor inhibit them from participating in any assembly permitted by the local government.
>
> (Yue Yuen 2001)

In other words, the company allows freedom of association if permitted by national law, which it has to anyway. The document does not elaborate on Yue Yuen's policy in cases where freedom of association is restricted by law as in China and Vietnam where the majority of its production sites are located.

Worker committees at Yue Yuen facilities

Labour advocates generally consider current approaches on monitoring and implementing labour standards sub-optimal because workers and their organisations at the production level have generally been excluded from the mechanisms set up to implement, monitor or verify code compliance (see, e.g. CCC 2005). As a result, workers in the affected factories often have no idea that these codes even exist or that they have not been trained in how to properly utilise them. In general, compliance programmes seldom focus on the workers themselves or prioritise the right to organise and workers and their representative organisations are excluded from the mechanisms set up to implement, monitor, and verify codes of conduct.

Labour advocates have therefore stressed the central importance of the *right to organise* (freedom of association and the right to collective bargaining) as a fundamental for workers to create and sustain a change in their conditions. The importance of the right to organise lies predominantly in the fact that it constitutes the basic conditions through which workers can demand that their rights are respected. These rights are sometimes described as 'enabling rights', meaning that full implementation would provide mechanisms through which trade unions can ensure that other labour standards are observed as well. As noted previously, when workers can form independent trade unions and bargain collectively, there may be little need for a code of conduct. These rights are enshrined in various ILO Conventions (nos 87, 98 and 135 respectively) and they are closely related to other civil and political rights, including freedom of expression, freedom of the media, and universal suffrage (ILO 2004: 8).

Labour rights are therefore more accurately described as *workers' human rights* or *human rights at work*. This means that *trade union rights* flow from human rights. If workers have freedom of association, they must be allowed to form genuinely independent organisations that have rights too. This means, for example, that they must have the right to legal personality, to own property, issue publications, and so on. Freedom of association is therefore indispensable to the enjoyment of other human rights; it is a bed-rock human right that is essential for, among other things, a democracy (Justice 2005). In other words, the right to form or join trade unions is bound up with the ability of society as a whole to exercise a wide range of civil rights such as free speech and the like (ibid.). From this it follows that freedom of association cannot be ensured or respected by business enterprises, alone or together with other multi-stakeholder initiatives, through codes of conduct, in situations where the government does not permit the exercise of other civil and political rights. Overall, the implications of this have not been adequately addressed in the code of conduct debate. Most code auditing and implementation activities are based on the idea that a supplier can ensure respect for human rights (ibid.). It is questionable, therefore, whether these privatised forms of labour regulation will work in the long run without a more interventionist role by states (Chan and Wang 2003), particularly in the context of states that limit restrict freedom of association.

Parallel means

In places where freedom of association is legally restricted, many codes of conduct have called for the establishment of workers' representatives mechanisms as so called 'parallel means'. These state that where a country's laws restrict freedom of association, the employer 'shall facilitate' or 'not obstruct' parallel means of association and bargaining.

Opinions on the value of these statements differ: according to some, they provide a loophole which allows companies to operate in countries where human rights are violated. In addition, there is a risk that worker representation mechanisms are used to prevent real trade unions from being established. The very real danger is that codes of conduct inadvertently contribute to this by relying on monitoring schemes in which auditors conclude that, for example, a health and safety committee counts as compliance with freedom of association. In countries where workers are legally allowed to join and form their own trade unions, auditors should be careful not to treat any clearly undemocratic mechanism as 'a step in the right direction'. Others believe that the parallel means provision might encourage nascent forms of worker self-representation in countries where independent unions are prohibited. In factories with no formal union recognition, such councils or committees might grant workers a voice or establish an alternative representation system. For that reason and in the context of the garment and sportswear industry where formal trade union representation is marginal, these mechanisms can be considered as potentially contributing to the establishment of trade unions.

The idea of 'parallel means' is loosely based on experiences in apartheid-era South Africa, when opponents of the apartheid regime encouraged transnational companies to engage with independent trade unions of black workers that operated outside the legal framework. These illegal trade unions played a central role in bringing down the apartheid regime. One can, however, seriously question to what extent these experiences can actually be applied to countries like China or Vietnam, where, unlike South Africa, no independent trade unions exist outside the official government controlled system of labour regulation (Justice and Kearney 2003; see also Chapter 3 of this volume).

In today's practice, the notion of 'parallel means' refers to activities that aim to elicit workers' views or increase their involvement with the enterprise through the establishment of worker representation mechanisms. Companies are encouraged, in other words, to help create an environment where these rights are respected. A number of Yue Yuen's key customers – Nike, Reebok, Adidas and Puma – have been involved in facilitating worker training programmes and/or establishing worker representation mechanisms. In 2001–2002, Yue Yuen was one of the three Chinese footwear factories that agreed to participate in China Capacity Building Project – Occupational Health and Safety. This project aimed at setting up plant-wide health and safety committees involving production workers as full, active committee members. Yet, the organisers of the training observe that in the Yue Yuen factories, management supported the establishment of health and safety committees but in a top-down manner. A negative consequence of this approach is a 'lack of democratic processes within the committee and generally weak participation from line-level workers' (Szudy *et al.* 2003: 365). These kinds of committees clearly run the danger of becoming a management-driven substitute for unions.

Since this project, various brands have conducted health and safety training sessions in Yue Yuen factories. Adidas has noted that the health, safety and environment (HSE) Committee has been running 'very effectively', providing benefits to factory management and their production workers. Most of the committee members were elected directly by production line workers through factory election campaigns. It has provided mechanisms for training workers in basic HSE, and for promoting effective communications between management and workers with regard to health and safety management, control of workplace hazards and promotion of safe work practices. According to Adidas' manager Frank Henke, the factory has now 'broadened the role of committee members to include responsibility for managing labour disputes and related employment practices' (Henke,

2005). Now the workers are able to raise a wider variety of issues related to their workplace concerns' (ibid.). This committee, together with the welfare committee, began to 'develop a more serious agenda addressing workplace concerns' (ibid.). Adidas also notes that all Yue Yuen facilities have welfare committees, but that these typically do not deal with social activities and support services for workers in the factory (canteen, postal facilities, entertainment, counselling, etc.). These committees act more 'as a bridge between management and production line workers' (ibid.). It is, however, the intention that other committees 'will follow such a pattern and to the point where industrial relations issues – both HSE and employment matters – are being discussed between factory management and elected worker representatives' (ibid.). Nike and Puma have set up similar systems.

Despite these efforts, the relation between codes of labour practice and accompanying implementation schemes concerning freedom of association and collective bargaining remains a problematic one. While freedom of association is considered to be the key to ensuring sustainable improvements at the workplace, the relocation of production to countries that restrict these rights highly complicates attempts to address worker rights' violations. In addition, freedom of association and collective bargaining are generally seen as difficult standards to monitor compared to other codes of conduct obligations. It is anything but clear whether the parallel means vehicles will promote genuine representation. At best, it is an intermediate solution for situations in which no independent trade unions exist or are allowed to exist. In addition, such activities are presently more of a sideshow than the main act and the scale of existing training programmes does not match the complexity of today's sourcing networks. Furthermore, Yue Yuen's high labour turnover – over 30 per cent annually – greatly complicates the establishment of independent worker organisations.

Conclusion

The athletic footwear industry can be considered an archetypal global sector, with clear and sharp functional differences between branded companies and manufacturers, each operating in different geographical areas and specialising in different functions. In this regard, Nike and Yue Yuen represent mirror images of each other within the athletic footwear industry. Both have successfully specialised in a particular moment of the production and circulation process. But while most of the attention has focused on branded corporations like Nike who seek to control market outlets, we have in this chapter underlined the role of Yue Yuen in the actual production of athletic footwear.

Yue Yuen successfully internalised what branded companies sought to externalise, namely the labour-intensive moments of footwear production. Departing from the vantage point of production, Yue Yuen now specialises in producing high-quality finished products for several competing brand-named companies. The company operates factory sites on scales unprecedented in the footwear industry. Yue Yuen has followed various strategies to strengthen its hold on the production of shoes. It has diversified its customer base, relocated production sites, improved the internal supply of raw materials, and reduced overall delivery time. This allows Yue Yuen to offer a fully integrated package of services related to shoe production. It has probably been achieved via cost saving in these areas that have positioned Yue Yuen ahead of many of its direct competitors who concentrate solely on taking advantage of cheap labour resources. But, despite its size, Yue Yuen still has no control over end-consumer markets. In that regard, the company remains dependent upon brand-named corporations. This also seems to have influenced its participation in the implementation of ethical standards and seems to have softened some its disciplinary methods. However, the critical question remains to what extent these CSR programmes will encourage labour self-organising at sites of production.

References

AMRC (2005) *Asian Transnational Corporation Outlook 2004: Asian TNCs, Workers and the Movement of Capital*, Hong Kong: Asian Monitor Resource Centre.

AMRC and HKCIC (1997) 'Blood, Sweat & Shears; Working Conditions in Sports Shoe Factories', in *China Making Shoes for Nike and Reebok*, Hong Kong, September.

Appelbaum, R. (2004) 'Commodity Chains and Economic Development: One and a Half Proposals for Spatially-Oriented Research', working paper prepared for CSISSS/IROWS Specialist Meeting, Globalization in the World System: Mapping Change over Time, University of California at Tiverside, 7– 8 February.

Atkinson, J. (1984) 'Flexibility: Planning for an Uncertain Future', *Manpower Policy and Practice* 1(summer): 26–29.

Chan, A. (1996) 'Boot Camp at the Shoe Factory: Where Taiwanese Bosses Drill Chinese Workers to Make Sneakers for American Joggers', *The Washington Post*, November.

Chan, A. and Wang, H. (2004) 'The Impact of the State on Workers' Conditions: Comparing Taiwanese Factories in China and Vietnam', *Pacific Affairs* 77(4) Winter.

Clean Clothes Campaign (2005) 'Looking for a Quick Fix: How Weak Social Auditing Is Keeping Workers in Sweatshops', report, October.

Collier, R. (2000) 'Labour Rights and Wrongs: Some U.S. Firms Work to Cut Abuses in Chinese Factories' *The San Francisco Chronicle*, 17 May.

Collins, J.L. (2003) *Threads: Gender, Labour, and Power in the Global Apparel Industry*, Chicago: The University of Chicago Press.

Connor, T. (2002) 'We Are Not Machines: Despite Some Small Steps Forward, Poverty and Fear Still Dominate the Lives of Nike and Adidas Workers in Indonesia', www.cleanclothes.org (accessed 16 July, 2003).

Donaghu, M.T. and Barff, R. (1990) 'Nike Just Did It: International Subcontracting and Flexibility in Athletic Footwear Production', *Regional Studies*, 24(6): 531–562.

Financial Times (2003) 'How Cheap Labour, Foreign Investment and Rapid Industrialization Are Creating a New Workshop of the World', 4 February.

Gereffi, G. (1994) 'The Organization of Buyer-Driven Global Commodity Chains: How US Retailers Shape Overseas Production', in G. Gereffi and M. Korzeniewicz (eds) *Commodity Chains and Global Capitalism*, Westport, CT: Praeger Publishers, pp. 95–122.

—— (1999) 'International Trade and Industrial Upgrading in the Apparel Commodity Chain', *Journal of International Economics*, 48(1): 37–70.

Goldman, R. and Papson, S. (1998) *Nike Culture, the Sign of the Swoosh*, London: Sage Publications.

Gough, J. (2003) *Work, Locality and the Rhythms of Capital*, London: Continuum.

Harrison, B. (1994) *Lean & Mean; Why Large Companies Will Continue to Dominate the Global Economy* New York: Guildford.

Henderson, J., Dicken, P., Hess, M., Coe, N. and Yeung H.W.C. (2002) 'Global Production Networks and the Analysis of Economic Development', *Review of International Political Economy* 9(3): 436–464.

Hengstmann, R. (2005) e-mail, 23 August (on file).

Henke, F. (2005) e-mail, 30 August (on file).

ITGLWF (2002) 'First Global Workshop for Worker Representatives within the Pou Chen Group', 15–17 January, Pasir Ris, Singapore (document on file).

ILO (2004) *Organizing for Social Justice: Global Report under the Follow-up to the ILO Declaration on Fundamental Principles and Rights at Work*. Geneva: ILO

Justice, D. (2005) e-mail (on file).

Justice, D. and Kearney, N. (2003) 'The New Codes of Conduct; Some Questions and Answers for Trade Unionists', in I. Wick, *Workers' Tool or PR Ploy? A Guide to Codes of International Labour Practice*, Bonn: Friedrich Ebert Stiftung, pp. 92–114.

Kaplinsky R. and Morris, M. (2001) *A Handbook for Value Chain Research. Prepared for the ICRC*, www.ides.ac.uk/ids/global/pdfs/VchNov01.pdf (accessed 18 May 2002).

Katz, D. (1994) *Just Do It: The Nike Spirit in the Corporate World*, Holbrook: Adams Media Corporation.

Korzeniewicz, M. (1994) 'Commodity Chains and Marketing Strategies: Nike and the Global Athletic Footwear Chain', in G. Gereffi and M. Korzeniewicz (eds) *Commodity Chains and Global Capitalism*, Westport, CT: Praeger Publishers.

Kwan, A. (2000) *Producing for Nike and Reebok*, Hong Kong: Christian Industrial Committee.

LaFeber, W. (1999) *Michael Jordan and the New Global Capitalism*, New York: W.W. Norton.

Mamic, I. (2003) *Business and Code of Conduct Implementation: How Firms Use Management Systems for Social Performance*, Geneva: International Labour Organisation.

Merk, J. (2004) 'Regulating the Global Athletic Footwear Industry: The Collective Worker in the Product Chain', in L. Assassi, D. Wigan and K. van Der Pijl (eds) *Global Regulation: Managing Crises After the Imperial Turn*, New York: Palgrave Macmillan, pp. 128–141.

—— (2007) 'The Private Regulation of Labour Standards: The Case of the Apparel and Footwear Industries', in J.C. Graz and A. Nölke (eds) *Transnational Private Governance and its Limits.*

Miller, D. (2004) 'Preparing for the Long Haul: Negotiating International Framework Areements in the Global Textile, Garment and Footwear Sector', *Global Social Policy* 4(2): 215–239.

Morgan Stanley (2001) 'Athletic Footwear and Apparel: Everything You Always Wanted to Know about Sports', Hong Kong, 7 September.

—— (2003) 'Yue Yuen Industrial', Hong Kong, 8 October.

O'Rourke, D. (2003) 'Outsourcing Regulation: Analysing Non-Governmental Systems of Labour Standards and Monitoring', *Policy Studies Journal* 31(1): 417–437.

Raikes, P., Jensen, M.F. and Ponte, S. (2000) 'Global Commodity Chain Analysis and the French Filière Approach: Comparison and Critique', CDR Working Paper 00.3, Brighton: Centre for Development Research, University of Sussex.

Robinson, W.I (2004) *A Theory of Global Capitalism: Production, Class, and State in a Transnational World*, Baltimore, MD: Johns Hopkins University Press.

SOMO (2003) 'Asian TNCs', SOMO Bulletin on Issues in Garments & Textiles', Amsterdam, available at: www.cleanclothes.org/publications/03–07–somo.htm

Sporting Goods Intelligence (2003) *Market Fact: Athletic Footwear and Apparel*, Glen Mills: SPI.

Szudy, B., O'Rourke, D. and Brown, G.D. (2003) 'Developing an Action-based Health and Safety Training Project in Southern China', *International Journal of Occupational and Environmental Health* 9(4): 357–367.

The Wall Street Journal (2000) 'Asian Firms Grab Rewards in the Global Supply Chain', 7 March.

UBS Warburg (2003) 'Athletic Footwear: Running at a Slower Pace', New York, 19 May.

WWW (2003) 'Action Research on Garment Industry Supply Chains: Some Guidelines for Activists', Manchester: Women Working Worldwide.

Yue Yuen (2001) 'Corporate Social Responsibility', document on file.

5 Offshore production, labour standards and collective organisation in the globalising US apparel industry

Étienne Cantin

> Perhaps the now widespread recognition that an old form of exploitation has reappeared in the new sweatshops will occasion a new willingness to encounter global capitalism as a new form of capitalist political economy. In particular, it is one in which workers' strategic resources are challenged by new advantages for their employers. But as in each previous era of capitalism, these are not forces to which it is necessary to acquiesce. Knowledge creates opportunity to act but responsibility as well.
>
> (Robert J. S. Ross 2002: 117)

The increasing transnationalisation of apparel production through foreign direct investment, production contracting and other production linkages established by transnational corporations (TNCs) has contributed to a growing unevenness of labour standards and industrial relations institutions across global production networks. As capital seeks out the cheapest possible workers for labour-intensive industries, it establishes the foundations for both a 'global race to the bottom' and an intensification of uneven capitalist development (Bonacich and Appelbaum 2000: 54; Chan and Ross 2003; Kiely 2003). It is widely argued that this leads to a decline of labour standards and unionised industrial relations, as employers use lower labour standards as a source of comparative advantage, and TNCs use capital mobility – or simply the threat of it – to change the power relations between capital and labour across multiple jurisdictions within global capitalism. In this manner, the formation of transnational production chains in apparel manufacturing has fostered the 'sweating' of low-wage manufacturing workers in the United States and abroad and a crisis of trade-union action (Bonacich and Appelbaum 2000; Bronfenbrenner 2000; Appelbaum 2005; Appelbaum and Lichtenstein 2006).

The US apparel industry is particularly advanced in terms of outsourcing and offshore production shifts, but others are rapidly moving along a similar path (Bronfenbrenner and Luce 2004). Moreover, apparel is one of the industries where some the most forward-looking experiments in trade-union revitalisation are tried out amidst the struggles of garment workers, their organisations, and their allies within the anti-sweatshop movement to strengthen organisation, mobilisation and collective action in resistance to the sweating of low-wage manufacturing workers both in the United States and offshore. As Miriam Ching Yoon Louie puts it (2001: 13), the goal of this social movement has been to change 'sweatshop industry workers [into] sweatshop warriors ... who clearly understood where they fit into the "big picture"'. Within this context, the current chapter seeks to understand global productive restructuring as a contested process. It examines how low-wage manufacturing workers and their unions have fought back against 'sweating' and other oppressive and exploitative conditions amidst the globalisation of the US apparel industry. To do so it addresses the following questions: (1) amidst the historical process of 'globalisation' of the US apparel industry, what has weakened garment-worker unionising? (2) How has the union responded to these challenges? What has been tried? What has succeeded, what has failed, and why? These questions and their answers are important not only for the apparel industry but also for most low-wage manufacturing and some service industries.

The first section of this chapter describes the 'big picture' – the 'globalisation' of the US apparel industry – and assesses the impact of contracting out and of the formation of transnational capitalist production chains on US garment workers and their unions. It explores the processes that have transformed the US apparel and retail complex into a network of TNCs that rely on a vast network of low-wage, female-dominated production sites around the world. The second section examines how garment workers and their unions have understood and responded to the causes of job loss, declining wages, and the re-emergence of apparel sweatshops in the United States and developing countries, with a special emphasis on collective struggles through which a significant part of the new and emerging global labour force, apparel workers, might become 'sweatshop warriors' empowered to earn a living wage and to contest the modes, if not the very logic, of today's global capitalism.

The 'big picture': contracting out, offshore production shifts, and the crisis of organised labour

A growing number of TNCs in apparel manufacturing exhibit the characteristic organisation of 'buyer-driven' commodity chains, in which control resides with brand-name retailers that place wholesale orders with manufacturers, who in turn rely on independently-owned contractors/factories around the world to employ the labour necessary to fill those orders (see Chapter 4 in this volume). In searching out these factories, manufacturers and retailers scour the planet for the lowest-cost production, as well as places that are relatively freer from government regulation, environmental constraints, and pressure from independent labour movements. Theorists such as Richard Appelbaum, Gary Gereffi and Gary Hamilton have emphasised the market-making potential of the contemporary 'buyer-driven' supply networks in order to more clearly evaluate the hierarchy of power and profitability that characterises contemporary global trade in apparel and other manufactures. At the crux of transnational production chains in apparel and other consumer-goods industries now stand the giant retailers that increasingly make the markets, set the prices, and determine the worldwide distribution of labour for that gigantic stream of commodities that flows across their counters.

During the past two decades or so, retailing in the United States has indeed become increasingly concentrated as a handful of giant but 'lean' retailers have developed overwhelming market power and truly transnational production networks (Appelbaum 2005). The buying power of Wal-Mart and other retail giants gives them the upper hand in dealing with manufacturers, since they are often able to dictate wholesale prices, especially for less well-known firms that lack loyal consumers (Petrovic and Hamilton 2006). What the formation of buyer-driven and transnational production chains in apparel manufacturing actually means for low-wage garment workers is increasingly obvious. Since profits are taken out at each level of the supply chain, labour costs are reduced to a tiny fraction of the retail price. As Edna Bonacich and Richard P. Appelbaum argue: 'The movement offshore ratchets down wages in the industrial world, while the workers in poor countries find that they must operate under regimes in which their efforts to raise wages are crushed' (2000: 79). This has only been exacerbated over time by what Nelson Lichtenstein and Richard P. Appelbaum describe as

> [a] shift of power within the structures of world capitalism from manufacturing to a retail sector that today commands the supply chains which girdle the earth and directs the labour power of a working class whose condition replicates much that we once thought characteristic of only the most desperate, early stages of capitalist growth.
>
> (2006: 106)

Contracting out and the capital mobility are not new to the US apparel industry. Indeed, garment workers and their unions have had to cope with a fragmented and unstable working situation since the nineteenth century. From the earliest stages of mass production of apparel in New York City, work was contracted out from 'inside shops' to smaller contracting factories and to 'sweated' home workers who were predominantly women and immigrants. As John R. Commons explained in 1901:

> [The] sweating system originally denoted a system of subcontract, wherein the work is let out to the contractors to be done in small shops or homes ... The system to be contrasted with the sweating system is the 'factory system,' wherein the manufacturer employs his own workmen ... The position of the contractor or sweater now in the business in American cities is peculiarly that of an organizer and

> employer of immigrants ... The contractor can increase the number of people employed in the trade at a very short notice. During the busy season, when the work doubles, the number of people employed increases in the same proportion.
>
> (Commons [1901] 1977: 44–45)

Under this definition, which remains largely accurate to this day, the origins of the sweatshop turn specifically and concretely on a unique system of decentralised capitalist production via contracting out, and not simply the conditions it engenders. Early in the twentieth century, New York garment workers went on strike on several occasions to secure an end to the subcontracting system as well as higher wages, shorter hours, and union recognition. Apparel-industry unions such as the International Ladies' Garment Workers' Union (ILGWU) and the Amalgamated Clothing Workers' Union (ACWU, in the men's clothing industry) developed from garment workers' protests against the sweatshop conditions encouraged by the subcontracting system as well as the capitalist restructuring of work, which replaced craft control by section work and increasingly reduced skill to speed as the apparel industries were mechanised. The ILGWU was able to build itself into a powerful union by using the general strike across entire sectors of apparel manufacturing and by signing 'jobbers' agreements that bound manufacturers who contracted to use only union contracts. Under the historic settlement with employers that became known as the Protocols of Peace, much of the north-eastern apparel industry was able to become unionised during the early decades of the twentieth century, and for a time the number of sweatshops diminished greatly, although they persisted at the fringes of the industry. Just as the hard-won labour–management contract in the US apparel industries seemed most successful, the Protocols of Peace began to disintegrate and the union's bargaining power began to erode as a result of contracting out, capital movement, and the expansion of nonunion, 'runaway shops'.

Clearly, sweated labour and the runaway or 'out-of-town' shops were connected as manufacturers continually sought out cheap labour and nonunion environments – first within the United States and then offshore. It was relatively easy to establish a runaway factory since apparel manufacturing has traditionally required very little capital investment. The essentials of such a business have historically consisted of sewing machines, a location, workers, and a contract. Labour has remained the largest proportion of ongoing capital outlay. To secure work, contractors engaged in fierce bidding wars where employee wages were a key factor as costs for other capital outlays – such as rent and equipment – remained relatively constant. The migration of the industry from unionised, relatively high-wage centres of production such as New York, Chicago and Philadelphia to rural Pennsylvania and later to the South proved devastating to garment workers and their unions during the 1920s. Among the four hundred hosiery plants scattered up and down the East Coast, union organisation dropped from higher than 90 per cent just after World War I to about 25 per cent in 1929. Piece rates were slashed by a quarter and total wages, which peaked in 1927, declined by more than 60 per cent over the next six years of the Depression. Such grim statistics might well forecast the destruction of the union, but the Full Fashioned Hosiery Workers turned this economic and organisational catastrophe into a well-managed retreat. The key to their survival was collaboration with unionised hosiery firms and a programme of wage concessions that would assure the competitiveness of the organised segment of the industry. That highly defensive solution proved short-lived. By the time David Dubinsky assumed the presidency of the ILGWU in 1932, contracting 'out of town' to runaway shops had grown to be a major problem for city-based apparel unions. As the nation's economy stalled with the onset of the Great Depression, competition among garment manufacturers – sometimes referred to as 'jobbers' – placed tremendous pressure on contractors who were played against one another for even the smallest margins. Contractors responded by ignoring union agreements, paying substandard wages, breaking local unions altogether, and seeking the cheapest labour possible by 'running away' to remote areas.

'Out of town' meant anywhere outside New York City and other centres of garment manufacturing like Chicago where the unions had been fairly successful in securing better wages and working conditions for the bulk of the garment workers. At first, it meant New Jersey and rural communities in upstate New York, south-eastern Massachusetts, and in western Pennsylvania, where the decline of anthracite coal mining led wives and daughters of jobless miners to take jobs at any wage they could. Increasingly, it also meant the American South, where many small towns were looking for new investment and offered apparel manufacturers and textile producers tax breaks, cheap financing, and a rural, low-wage, largely female labour force was socialised to the conditions of hard work and compliance to factory discipline. A large part of the advantage of moving from New York to New Jersey in the 1920s, or from the North-east to the South and West from the 1930s was union avoidance. Indeed, it was the move 'out of town' that helped end unionisation in both textiles and apparel as companies moved outside the union's jurisdiction, to the South. By the 1950s, manufacturers started moving production to southern regions where unions did not have a strong presence, and where sixteen states had passed 'right-to-work' laws after the enactment of the 1947 Taft–Hartley Act, which severely weakened the power of organised labour to maintain and increase wages and improve working conditions. The unions' strategy aimed at organising these regional workers, if only to protect the centres of production. The union, however, put greater faith in efforts to expand government regulation, repeatedly calling on Congress to stop the capital flight, connecting it with cheap regional labour and 'right-to-work' law through references to the sweatshop. Inveighing against the owners of 'runaway shops,' the ILGWU argued that 'the right to work they are trying to get is for low, sweatshop wages' (ILGWU 1959: 145).

In November 1958, a strike was called in seven North-eastern states where the ILGWU had a large concentration of organised workers by workers demanding a 15 per cent wage increase. But the employers of many western Pennsylvania locals, where wages were low and dresses were made for the low end of the market, claimed they could not sustain a wage increase in the face of the slow growth of demand and the wage competition from the lower-wage South. The strike was finally settled by arbitration, with the union winning an increase of 8 per cent – basically an increase to match the cost of living. The settlement of the strike appeared to restore the power of the ILGWU, but after that the union's hold over the labour force began to slip away as the labour contract was challenged by 'runaway' shops. Whereas in 1949, there were over 339,000 apparel workers employed in the New York metropolitan area alone, by 1960, the number of workers in the state had already declined to about 271,200 as clothing production moved out of town. Thus, North-eastern apparel workers, like the unionised textile-industry workers before them, began to see job losses and wage reductions even before the industry started to move offshore to developing regions of the Americas and later to the Asian-Pacific Rim. The years between 1949 and 1960 indeed saw a major decline in the earnings of apparel workers compared to those of workers in other manufacturing industries. Apparel wages in the New York City region, which was already beginning to lose its prominence as the centre of American apparel production, declined even more in the face of competition from the low-wage US South. By 1960, however, the threat to garment unions was no longer regional; it was international and global.

Offshore production, in which US entrepreneurs contracted foreign-based textile and apparel factories that assembled low-wage apparel for purchase by US retailers, was an immediate post-World War II development – an era often overlooked in many studies of the globalisation of the US garment industry. Yet, as Carmen Teresa Whalen has shown (2002), in the immediate post-war era, Puerto Rico became the first of what would later be known as export processing zones. The political ties between the United States and Puerto Rico facilitated the emergence of patterns of investment and migration that would be repeated in other countries. Puerto Rico's policy-makers crafted an economic development strategy based on industrialisation by invitation, and the US garment industry relocated to Puerto Rico to take advantage of low wages for women, as well as tax exemptions and other incentives. Puerto Rico became the model for a particular strategy of economic development that was based on foreign investment and export-oriented industrialisation, and that was accompanied by massive out-migration. The globalisation of the garment industry shaped the pattern of labour migration to the US. It was predominantly women who left Puerto Rico for the United States, where they took up low-wage jobs in the garment industries in New York and elsewhere.

Puerto Rico illustrates key elements of the export-oriented process of capitalist industrialisation that proliferated later in Japan and East Asia, along the US–Mexico border, in the Caribbean, and in Central America. The push by US apparel companies to produce abroad was welcomed by governments of many developing countries seeking to industrialise. Apparel is relatively labour-intensive, requiring little start-up capital. It has thus been one of the first industries that newly industrialising countries entered. Their governments welcomed the orders from US firms, which boosted their exports and therefore, their foreign exchange earnings. In exchange, they offered US TNCs a controlled labour force typically composed of young women who were seen as preferable because of highly gendered assumptions about their 'nimble fingers' and their supposed reluctance to join unions. In many cases, the offer had been backed by repressive regimes that provided guarantees against labour unrest. TNCs relocated the labour-intensive, lower wage work of assembling lower-value-added goods (no longer only textiles and apparel but now toys, jewellery and electronics as well) to export-processing zones where low-paid women workers make up about 80 per cent of the workforce (Safa 1986; Collins 2003). Without a doubt, the move offshore has intensified competition amongst the countries of the South and to a lesser degree, between the North and South. As more and more developing countries were drawn into export-led development, they competed among themselves for foreign investment, outbidding each other to offer concessions to investors designed to reduce the cost of production (London and Ross 1995).

As more apparel producers moved their assembly operations to low-wage regions, the competitive pressure for domestic manufacturers to move offshore also intensified, even when they were producing profitably in the United States or for other reasons preferred to produce domestically. As America's apparel industry became more and more globalised, the competitive pressures to open new markets in lower and lower wage regions of the world have led to a race to the bottom. The result of this intensification of competition within the apparel industry's increasingly global capitalist production chains for American garment workers was not only job losses and wage reductions, but also a reemergence of apparel sweatshops. 'Let us not make a distinction between sweatshop products,' stated the ACWU, 'whether they come from the South or from Japan or Hong Kong' (ACWU 1960: 283). Worried about imports as early as 1959, the ILGWU kicked off a 'Look for the Label' campaign that relied upon economic nationalism to prod the consumer to 'Buy American'. While US apparel unions responded to the construction of transnational capitalist production chains with a 'Buy American' campaign, US corporations eagerly sought to boost their profit margins by exploiting cheap labour in new investor friendly export processing zones, accelerating disinvestments from US-based apparel manufacture. ILGWU membership began to plummet as domestic apparel manufacturers closed up shop or shifted production offshore. 'The competitive advantage of imported apparel is based primarily on the exploitation of sweatshop labour,' said the ACWU as early as 1960:

> The men's and boy's apparel industry was historically a sweatshop industry in this country. Our union was born out of rebellion against the misery and degradation of the sweatshop. The courage and self-sacrifice of our members in the early struggle against sweatshop conditions laid the foundation for the labour and welfare standards which workers in the men's and boy's apparel industry enjoy today. Those standards, in fact, the continued existence of the industry and the jobs of hundreds of thousands of workers, are now in grave jeopardy as a result of the rising tide of apparel imports. We must not permit the evils which we fought against at home destroy us from abroad.
>
> (ACWU 1960: 279)

The proliferation of sweatshops in industrialising regions of the global South has coincided with the increasing number and declining conditions of such workplaces in the United States, or as one commentator put it, 'the resurgence of so-called sweatshops in metropolitan countries' (Fernández-Kelly 1983: 80; cf. Ross 2001, 2002; Rosen 2002; Whalen 2002; Collins 2003: 1–2). While giant apparel retailers and manufacturers have established connections with as many as a thousand factories around the globe, giving them enormous flexibility (and leverage) in weathering the frequent ups and downs of the fashion industry, US garment workers have become contingent labourers, employed and paid only when their work has been needed, never knowing if their factory will be getting work, or – if it does – whether there will be enough for them to be hired. Where there has been work, highly competitive bidding – or worse, price dictation – has driven down contract prices so low that the contractors, despite whatever ethnic or other ties they may have with their workers, often simply have not been capable to pay decent, or even minimum, wages. The contractors have therefore 'sweated' their earnings straight out of a largely female and immigrant apparel workforce by circumventing regulations, operating unsafe workplaces, and, increasingly, shifting production offshore in order to recreate the conditions necessary for their survival.

Already in the 1970s, many manufacturers with union contracts found it cheaper to pay 'liquidated damages' to the ILGWU (a fee to compensate for removing work from union shops) than continue production in unionised US shops. By the early 1990s, as historian Dana Frank has charged, the ILGWU's 'rate of liquidated damages sank below the level at which it was punitive and prevented a shift overseas, and became merely a payoff'. With less power, the union entered the 'Crafted with Pride in the USA' coalition dominated by textile manufacturers, which sought to block cheaper imports (Frank 1999: 146–147, 187–192). All too often, however, 'Made in the USA' labels hid the presence of sweatshops, both in the United

States and in export-processing zones such as those of where offshore production was taking place. Indeed, if Leon Stein's classic book, *Out of the Sweatshop* (1977), stood as a testament to the historic victory over the problem a generation ago, by then the rapid decline of conditions of work and employment in US-based apparel manufacturing made clear that the victory was short-lived. Many of the predominantly female and migrant workers who account for the majority of garment workers in contemporary US apparel production both on the mainland and offshore are indeed employed in sweatshops that compete for retail contracts against the declining unionised sector (Ross 2001, 2004; Appelbaum 2005). The resulting wage competition has caused a vicious cycle of spiralling cost-cutting, as union shops in New York and elsewhere lowered their prices to compete for work against non-union workers, while attempts to organise these workers in Los Angeles and other non-union areas by ILGWU and its successor UNITE! were largely unsuccessful (cf. Bonacich and Appelbaum 2000: esp. Chap. 9; Ness 2003, 2005).

Guess?'s move to Mexico illustrates the problem of organising workers and combating sweatshops in a global economy increasingly dominated by buyer-driven commodity chains. In 1997, faced with a union organising drive, Labor Department pressures, and large doses of bad publicity, Guess? moved much of its production out of Los Angeles entirely, to Tehuacán, Mexico, 1,700 miles away. Tehuacán's garment workers, whose wages average $25–50 for a 48-hour workweek, with forced and unpaid overtime often used to meet production quotas, toil in giant windowless factories protected by armed guards. As a result, neither independent unions nor US Labor Department officials can create embarrassing publicity for the growing number of American jeans manufacturers who have flocked to a city where a delegation of human rights observers found

> that workers' rights are not respected and codes of conducts are not enforced; instead they are subordinated to the global search for cheap labour. Humane treatment of *maquiladora* workers and respect for their rights are traded off for the mass production of on-time and high-quality clothing.
>
> (quoted from Bonacich and Appelbaum 2000: 67)

Manufacturers are likely to respond to union organising drives or increased government scrutiny by contracting with distant factories. Organising workers at the point of production, the century-old strategy which served to build the power of labour in Europe and North America, is best suited to production processes which are controlled by manufacturers and where most of the work goes on in-house. Not all industries are equally mobile, but in those in which production can easily be shifted almost anywhere on the planet – along with the ever-present threat of such mobility – the effectiveness of point-of-production organising is severely compromised (Bonacich 2001; Bonacich and Gapasin 2002).

The once well-paid, highly unionised apparel industry is a case in point: the number of unionised American garment workers has declined drastically over the past three decades or so. The US apparel industry has lost thousands more jobs than the textile industry jobs since its peak in 1973, and every month brings reports of new job losses. In the decade of the 1980s alone, over 850,000 apparel manufacturing jobs were lost in the industrial North, most of which occurred in the US while a roughly equivalent number of apparel sector jobs were created in the developing world, mostly in Asia, Latin America and the Caribbean. By 1995, after the first wave of jobs losses related to the North American Free Trade Agreement (NAFTA), there were only 846,000 domestic apparel jobs left in the US and only 523,000 by April 2002. The growing ability of US apparel retailers and manufacturers to move their production operations offshore not only leads to job losses but also allows firms to pit workers in different locations against each other, dampening wage negotiations, undermining unionisation, and fostering concessionary bargaining in which remaining employees must give up benefits in order to retain their jobs. While large numbers of apparel workers are losing their jobs, those still employed have suffered deeper wage losses than workers in any other US manufacturing industry, a growth in unemployment, degraded and contingent employment, an intensification and deterioration of work, a crisis of organised labour and increased income, gender, and racial polarisation – as women and people of colour have faced a disproportionate impact from all these developments. Starting out at the low end of the wage distribution, apparel workers lost more in wages than did manufacturing workers in any other industry. In 2000, the average garment worker in the US earned less in real wages than in 1955. The old apparel unions, the ILGWU and the ACTWU, have faced huge losses in membership. They have lost members at an even faster rate than jobs have declined, as employers have turned increasingly to non-union shops. Loss of membership has inevitably been accompanied by a loss of power, and the unions have had a hard time protecting those members who remain.

Advancing low-wage workers' interests in the era of global capitalism

In an effort to recover some lost ground, the ILGWU and ACTWU decided to merge in 1995 to form UNITE!, the Union of Needletrades, Industrial, and Textile Employees. Faced with what appears to be a dying industry, UNITE! has expanded its organising efforts to include industrial workers who are linked somewhat or not at all to its old, core jurisdiction. The Guess? campaign was a turning point for UNITE!'s role in the US apparel industry. For one thing, the union became disillusioned with trying to organise the apparel industry in Los Angeles. The union still had a large membership base in New York sewing factories that it had to maintain, but the leadership did not seem interested in opening new fronts in organising immigrant garment workers. The union decided to take two approaches. First, it shifted its new organising efforts to industries that were outside its traditional jurisdiction but related to the apparel industry, including industrial laundries and distribution centres. In neither case was the industry likely to leave the United States. The women's wear production factories, in contrast, were seen as too fragile to organise. They would simply go out of business or move offshore, leaving impoverished immigrant workers even worse off than they had been. It seems safe to say that the union is barely holding on to its garment-worker membership and is continually losing ground in this industry, even as it is moving into other areas. Obviously, not all manufacturing firms are as globally mobile as apparel manufacturing; some industries and industrial sectors are more regionally tied. These less mobile sectors may afford easier organising opportunities for trade unions. Nevertheless, the challenge remains: how do workers organise in those industries that can flee? Globally mobile industries and sectors are a growing component of advanced capitalism in the United States and elsewhere. They cannot be set aside as unorganisable.

Apparel-industry unions, of course, have not altogether abandoned garment-worker organising. In 1990, Jeffrey Hermanson, a talented organiser and brilliant strategist, became head of the ILGWU's Organizing Department. During the 1990s, he made a number of serious attempts to revive the union, including the Leslie Fay strike. Leslie Fay was a large union jobber (manufacturer) that tried to break its contract by shifting production to nonunion contractors on the grounds that all their competition was doing it. The ILGWU decided to draw a line in the sand and fight the company. A strike was called, and the union won. Shortly thereafter, however, Leslie Fay declared bankruptcy. Hermanson saw the need for the union to develop an international strategy. It had to help workers in other countries organise themselves so that the industry could not pit First World workers against Third World workers – a strategy that 'drives wages down on both sides, and allows businesspeople to portray labour-rights advocates as domestic protectionists bent on depriving *maquila* workers of their industrial wage ticket out of poverty' (Ross 2003: 233). Hermanson helped organise the first unionised factory in an export-processing zone in the Dominican Republic and contributed to a legacy of militant unionism there (Armbruster-Sandoval 2005). He also developed the idea of Garment Worker Justice Centers. These centres could serve as places where workers could come to deal with grievances concerning their jobs and could develop their capacity to fight back. Although these workers were not covered by collective-bargaining agreements and did not become full-fledged union members, the hope was what they would develop union consciousness and contribute to the struggle in their own factories.

Over the 1990s justice centres were developed in New York, Texas and California. In the face of a loss of proactive organising by UNITE! in the Los Angeles garment industry, a group of organisations concerned with the sweating of immigrant workers came together to form the Garment Workers Center (GWC). One of the GWC's key tenets is that it be multiracial, bringing together Latino and Asian garment workers. Perhaps this is the best model for organising workers under the extremely repressive labour regime in the Los Angeles apparel industry. Given the ability of capital in the apparel industry to shift location through outsourcing, the fight to win a contract with a particular employer at a particular worksite seems almost futile. Workers may win a skirmish in the battle, but lose the war as the major (sometimes indirect) employer shifts production away from that site. An alternative approach is to organise workers regardless of where they are employed, instead of organising a particular firm, waging a campaign against that firm, and trying to win a contract for the employees of that particular employer. The GWC adopts such a worker-centred approach to organise where workers live, and regardless of where they work, with the aim of defending the rights of the unorganised and building solidarity among workers in the hope that one day they can be unionised. Before it merged to form UNITE! in 1995, the ILGWU also ran a number of these centres, including one in Los Angeles (Hermanson 1993; Ness 1998; Bonacich 2000). Unfortunately, the LA centre suffered from changing staff at the top, and inconsistent support for the concept from UNITE!'s top leadership. In Los Angeles, other unions have targeted key areas with high immigrant populations and have combined aggressive, political efforts (e.g., get out to vote campaigns and particular candidate elections) with highly visible and militant union campaigns, like Justice for Janitors. Their purpose has been to create a power-base for traditional unions within the immigrant communities, linking broader political issues with the bread and butter concerns of workers. One advantage of this approach is that employers find it harder to engage in retaliations against activists, especially in the form of shifting production away from their plant. On the other hand, there is always the danger that the entire sector will decide to leave the region.

UNITE!'s second approach has been to support, join, and develop the growing anti-sweatshop movement, including the important student movement. As is widely recognised, globalised capitalism demands a global response from workers. But as the above discussion has suggested, it is difficult to organise local workers who are employed in the globalised manufacturing sector and even more difficult to organise across borders and among even more oppressed workers in the global South. Some day, perhaps, a truly international labour movement will confront global capital, but such a day seems a long way off. In the meantime, efforts by organised labour to mobilise factory workers at the bottom of the retail-driven production chain must be matched with efforts at community-based organising and international solidarity work by unions, consumer groups, and labour rights activists. Some promising efforts are occurring in this arena, most notably, the development of an anti-sweatshop movement in the United States and other countries. The anti-sweatshop movement aims to mobilise constituencies in the United States, including students, consumers and religious organisations to protest the effects of globalisation and flexible production on workers and their families around the world, and to demand that these industries take responsibility and change their practices. Shortly after its formation UNITE! initiated the Stop Sweatshops Campaign, with the National Consumers' League (NCL) as co-chair, which sought to mobilise middle-class consumers, especially religious groups and women's clubs, to demand that local retail stores reject sweatshop-made goods. Increasingly, UNITE! has been relying on consumer politics as a lever to pry open space for organising. The discovery in August of 1995 of the El Monte, California, 'slaveshop' – where seventy-two Thai women bent over machines behind barbed wire producing clothes for Nordstrom, Sears, Montgomery Ward, and other brand-name stores – stimulated an end-of-the-century campaign against the sweatshop orchestrated by trade unions and nongovernmental organisations (NGOs) that relied on public scrutiny to force corporate compliance with 'human rights' and labour standards. Dependence on mass marketing and reliance on logos and corporate image had made business vulnerable to reformer appeals to ethical consumption in ways only dreamed of by the NCL in the past (Ross 2003).

Consequently, in the 1980s and early 1990s, some brands, like Levi-Strauss and Nike, sought to ward off exposure of the conditions under which their goods were made by establishing firm-based codes of conduct monitored by their own employees or accounting agencies. As a result of the growing public pressure from the anti-sweatshop movement, a number of corporations have adopted their own codes of conduct, some as a result of government initiative (for example, the Fair Labor Association and its predecessor, the White House Apparel Industry Partnership), and some on their own (for example, The Gap). Adopting a code turns out to be relatively easy; implementing it is another story (see Chapter 4 by Jeroen Merk in this volume and Esbenshade 2004). The real value of corporate codes of conduct, even at the best companies, lies in the realm of ideology, for they 'legitimize the idea of a worldwide social standard, even as their chronic failures demonstrate that any real transformation of the global supply chains must come from other sources' (Appelbaum and Lichtenstein 2006: 121; see also Wells 2007). Despite their obvious limitations, corporate codes of conduct have been used as a framework for advancing the goal of empowering workers to advance their own interests, a goal taken up by the second wave of anti-sweatshop activists that emerged in the late 1990s.

This approach involves the formation of partnerships between unions and non-governmental organisations in the US as well as in the producing country that aim to strengthen the workers' bargaining power on the shop floor. Numerous NGOs such as United Students Against Sweatshops (USAS) and the Workers' Rights Consortium (WRC), which formed around these issues in the late 1990s, are now working with unions and NGOs in southern countries. A national network of campus organisations was built and

USAS, which has had affiliates on 180 different campuses, emerged as a major force in the anti-sweatshop movement (Featherstone 2002). Student activists wanted to help the labour movement fight sweatshop conditions that violated basic human dignity. The character of the 'commodity chain' connecting universities and the sweatshops actually gave students power to change working conditions. As large institutional buyers, universities could influence producing companies, and collectively their advantage was substantial. The anti-sweatshop movement spread to Canada, where activists formed the Maquila Solidarity Network, while Europeans formed the Clean Clothes Campaign, which has its headquarters in The Netherlands. The combination of North–South and union–NGO alliances produced several success campaigns in the 1990s and early 2000s, including the Kukdong case in Mexico (discussed below). The movement also successfully organised workers and improved conditions in several plants in the Dominican Republic and in the Kimi plant in Honduras, the Phillips–Van Heusen plant in Guatemala, and the Mandarin plant in El Salvador (Armbruster-Sandoval 2005).

On 21 September 2001, the first-ever collective bargaining agreement ever between an independent union and a Mexican *maquiladora* manufacturing apparel was signed on behalf of the 400 workers at the Kukdong (renamed Mexmode) *maquiladora* in Atlixco, Mexico. Kukdong International/Mexmode is a Korean-owned factory in Puebla, Mexico, that makes logo-ed apparel under contract with Nike, Reebok, and other suppliers for the US college market. Kukdong-made apparel sells in numerous college bookstores, including Purdue, Georgetown, the University of Michigan, and the University of California at Berkeley. In early January 2001, five workers were fired from the factory, protesting low pay, abusive supervisors, rancid food, and lack of representation by a company union that was imposed on them by factory management. As is typical in Mexico, workers were forced to pay dues to an official union, the Confederación Revolucionario de Obreros y Campesinos (CROC) with ties to the ruling party in Puebla, the Partido Revolucionario Institucional (PRI). Some 800 (out of 900) workers then went on strike, initiating a protracted and occasionally violent struggle that ended the following September with the formation of an independent union – the Sindicato de los Trabajadores de la Empresa Kukdong International de Mexico (SITEKIM), which is the first in a Mexican garment *maquila*. Early in the strike period both the WRC and an FLA affiliate (Verité) had conducted independent audits that confirmed the workers' complaints, reports that were made public (by the WRC as a matter of policy; by Verité under public pressure), resulting in demonstrations at Niketown retail outlets and coverage in the mainstream US press. Students, US organised labour (UNITE!, the AFL-CIO) and university administrators put direct pressure on Nike, as well as on the Mexican government, to accept the workers' demands. Nike at one point even cancelled its contracts with the factory, reducing its income to a fifth that of previous levels, but once the factory agreed to the workers' demands, Nike rewarded it with a new $2.5 million contract. The Kukdong/Mexmode struggle is evidence of the success can occur when pressure is brought to bear on the manufacturer, government, and contractor simultaneously – what Esbenshade (2004) calls the 'triangle of resistance'. Ultimately, however, only independent local unions are situated to tap into what the workers themselves want, and to remain ever-vigilant once changes are instituted. Effective resistance by organising apparel workers at the local level and their allies within the anti-sweatshop movement led to an agreement in April 2002 to increase wages and benefits. According to the Clean Clothes Campaign (2002), the total increase, including benefits and bonuses, could reach 40 per cent, and workers appear to have kept their advances so far (Wells and Knight 2007).

Conclusion

Garment workers' best hope in the era of global lean production is a 'coordinative unionism' which combines the local mobilisation capacity of the workplace and community with the scope of national and transnational strategies (Wells 1998). This model extends unionism horizontally while deepening its democratic roots through renewed mechanisms of working-class mobilisation, communication, representation, and participation. UNITE!'s Garment Worker Justice Centers and other forms of local labour bodies that are working with their communities to build local economies that are more democratically accountable are examples of this model. Coordinative unionism also entails that 'rank and file' unionists continuously bargain with managers and use direct action tactics as well as official strikes to build solidarity, participation and bargaining leverage. It means that unionised workers help unorganised workers to organise themselves across transnational capitalist production chains. High priority must also be given to the horizontal coordination of strategies among union locals in the same sector, and among workplaces and communities in which workers are dealing with the same employers in order to weaken divide and conquer tactics of corporations which cause unions to react defensively and attend to the immediate survival needs of 'their' individual workplaces. This coordination among unions, community groups and social movements is critical to building mass working-class power against the TNCs' capacity to 'race' towards the bottom of the supply chain in the search for the cheapest product, which poses enormous problems for labour standards and conditions as well as for workers' right to organise. This right is the most effective weapon of low-wage manufacturing workers against sweating and other oppressive and exploitative conditions they confront in today's global capitalism for the global 'race to the bottom' has turned the weapon of unionising into a double-edged sword: If workers organise, they are likely to lose their jobs, as corporations will move to factories where unions are forbidden and therefore labour is cheaper. This dynamic has on several occasions discouraged efforts by workers to form independent trade unions, since unionised shops are vulnerable to losing their contracts. Global competition between contractors competing for the orders of these 'big buyers' has been a key factor in keeping labour costs down, since any factory that could not meet the price requirements of its clients risked losing business to another factory down the street or around the globe. But if workers do not organise, their rights will continue to be violated.

These conditions pose a significant challenge for the anti-sweatshop movement – a challenge that has increased with the end of apparel quotas on 1 January 2005 and the integration of China in global production chains under the WTO. The elimination of quotas now allows garment retailers and manufacturers to move their production to those countries offering the lowest labour costs and the most vulnerable workers. Most analysts have concluded that China will be the principal beneficiary (Appelbaum and UNCTAD 2005). As discussed in Chapter 3, the workforce in Chinese coastal provinces such as Guangdong is overwhelmingly composed of migrants from inland villages who do not have access to social services or adequate housing so long as they are without residence permits. They work and reside on the sufferance of their employer, who often holds their identity papers until they complete their labour 'contract'. It is these and other features of the Chinese system of labour and industrial relations that, together with the broader socio-political dynamics and struggles that underpin contemporary shifts in the international division of labour, allow China 'to lead in . . . [the] race to the bottom in labour standards' in apparel manufacturing and other labour-intensive industries (Chan 2003: 41).

For all the challenges 'Chinese competition' poses, the best guarantee for an amelioration of labour standards and industrial relations in metropolitan low-wage manufacturing is that a strong labour movement will emerge in China amidst current processes of industrialisation and proletarianisation. As Beverly J. Silver and Giovanni Arrighi point out, '[g]iven the size and growing centrality of the Chinese working classes in world society, a strong Chinese labour movement would have a major invigorating impact on the world labour movement as a whole' (Silver and Arrighi 2001: 73). As discussed in Chapter 3, resentment, anger and social conflict lie just beneath the surface as workers seek to pressure factory managers and provincial officials to live up to Chinese labour and environmental laws, as well as to the specific employment contracts and working condition promises which brought so many to China's coastal factory districts in the first place. As they push back against this system, they begin to crack the chains – supply chain as well as others – that have given Wal-Mart and its retail competitors such overweening power in the global economy, and that have tied down apparel and other low-wage manufacturing workers here and there in a subordinate and exploited position in today's contested global capitalism. Building the capacity for the unfettered organising of low-wage workers worldwide must therefore necessarily be a long-term strategy for union organisers and anti-sweatshop activists worldwide (Chang and Wong 2005). There is, in other words, no straightforward solution to the sweatshop problem which does not point to the need for international worker solidarity to contest the modes, if not the very logic, of the globalisation of industrial capitalism. But – as discussed in the final chapter of this volume – the problem is how to achieve it.

References

ACWU (1960) *Proceedings of the 22nd Convention of the Amalgamated Clothing Workers Union*, New York: n.p.

Appelbaum, R.P. (2005) 'Fighting Sweatshops: The Changing Terrain of Global Apparel Production', in R.P. Appelbaum and W.I. Robinson (eds) *Critical Globalization Studies*, New York: Routledge, pp. 369–378.

Appelbaum, R.P. and Lichtenstein, N. (2006) 'Supply-Chains, Workers' Chains and the New World of Retail Supremacy', *International Labour and Working Class History* 69(2): 106–125.

Appelbaum, R.P. and UNCTAD (2005) 'TNCs and the Removal of Textiles and Clothing Quotas', Geneva: United Nations Conference on Trade and Development (UNCTAD).

Armbruster-Sandoval, R. (2005) *Globalization and Cross-Border Labour Solidarity in the Americas: The Anti-Sweatshop Movement and the Struggle for Social Justice*, New York: Routledge.

Bonacich, E. (2000) 'Intense Challenges, Tentative Possibilities: Organizing Immigrant Garment Workers in Los Angeles', in R. Milkman (ed.) *Organizing Immigrants: The Challenges for Unions in Contemporary California*, Ithaca, NY: ILR Press, pp. 130–149.

—— (2001) 'The Challenge of Organizing in a Globalized/Flexible Industry: The Case of the Apparel Industry in Los Angeles', in R. Baldoz, C. Koeber and P. Kraft (eds) *The Critical Study of Work: Labor, Technology, and Global Production*, Philadelphia, PA: Temple University Press.

Bonacich, E. and Appelbaum, R.P. (2000) *Behind the Label: Inequality in the Los Angeles Apparel Industry*, Berkeley, CA: University of California Press.

Bonacich, E. and Gapasin, F. (2002) 'The Strategic Challenge of Organizing Manufacturing Workers in Global/Flexible Capitalism', in B. Nissen (ed.) *Unions in a Globalized Environment: Changing Borders, Organizational Boundaries, and Social Roles*, Armonk, NY: M.E. Sharpe, pp. 163–188.

Bronfenbrenner, K. (2000) 'Uneasy Terrain: The Impact of Capital Mobility on Workers, Wages and Union Organizing', Report to the U.S. Trade Deficit Review Commission. Washington, DC: U.S. Congress.

Bronfenbrenner, K. and Luce, S. (2004) *The Changing Nature of Corporate Global Restructuring: The Impact of Production Shifts on Jobs in the US, China, and Around the Globe*, Washington, DC: US-China Economic and Security Review Commission.

Chan, A. (2003) 'A "Race to the Bottom": Globalisation and China's Labour Standards', *China Perspectives* 46(2): 41–49.

Chan, A. and Ross, R.J.S. (2003) 'Racing to the Bottom: International Trade without a Social Clause', *Third World Quarterly* 24(6): 1011–1028.

Chang, D.-O. and Wong, M. (2005) 'After the Consumer Movement: Toward a New International Labour Activism in the Global Garment Industry', *Labour, Capital & Society* 38 (1–2): 127–155.

Clean Clothes Campaign (2002) 'Update on Mexmode (Kukdong)', (April 18), Clean Clothes Campaign.

Collins, J.L. (2003) *Threads: Gender, Labour, and Power in the Global Apparel Industry*, Chicago: University of Chicago Press.

Commons, J.R. ([1901] 1977) 'The Sweating System', in L. Stein (ed.) *Out of the Sweatshop: The Struggle for Industrial Democracy*, New York: Quadrangle/New York Times Book Co.

Esbenshade, J.L. (2004) *Monitoring Sweatshops: Workers, Consumers, and the Global Apparel Industry*, Philadelphia, PA: Temple University Press.

Featherstone, L. (2002) *Students Against Sweatshops: The Making of a Movement*, London: Verso.

Fernández-Kelly, M.P. (1983) *For We Are Sold, I and My People: Women and Industry in Mexico's Frontier*, Albany, NY: State University of New York Press.

Frank, D. (1999) *Buy American: The Untold Story of Economic Nationalism*, Boston: Beacon Press.

Hermanson, J. (1993) 'Organizing for Justice: ILGWU Returns to Social Unionism to Organize Immigrant Workers', *Labour Research Review* 12(1): 52–61.

ILGWU (1959) *Proceedings of the 30th Convention of the International Ladies' Garment Workers' Union*, New York: n.p.

Kiely, R. (2003) 'Global Uneven Development, the Race to the Bottom and International Labour Solidarity', *Review: A Journal of the Fernand Braudel Center* 26 (1): 67–88.

London, B. and Ross, R.J.S. (1995) 'The Political Sociology of Foreign Direct Investment: Global Capitalism and Capital Mobility, 1965–1980', *International Journal of Comparative Sociology* 36(3–4): 198–121.

Louie, M.C.Y. (2001) *Sweatshop Warriors: Immigrant Women Workers Take on the Global Factory*, Boston: South End Press.

Ness, I. (1998) 'Organizing Immigrant Communities: UNITE's Workers Center Strategy', in K. Bronfenbrenner (ed.) *Organizing to Win: New Research on Union Strategies*, Ithaca, NY: ILR Press, pp. 87–107.

—— (2003) 'Globalization and Worker Organization in New York City's Garment Industry', in D.E. Bender and R.A. Greenwald (eds) *Sweatshop USA: The American Sweatshop in Historical and Global Perspective*, London: Routledge, pp. 169–184.

—— (2005) *Immigrants, Unions and the New U.S. Labor Market*, Philadelphia, PA: Temple University Press.

Petrovic, M. and Hamilton, G.G. (2006) 'Making Global Markets: Wal-Mart and Its Suppliers', in N. Lichtenstein (ed.) *Wal-Mart: The Face of Twenty-First-Century Capitalism*, New York: New Press, pp. 107–142.

Rosen, E.I. (2002) *Making Sweatshops: The Globalization of the U.S. Apparel Industry*, Berkeley, CA: University of California Press.

Ross, A. (2003) 'The Rise of the Second Antisweatshop Movement', in D.E. Bender and R.A. Greenwald (eds) *Sweatshop USA: The American Sweatshop in Historical and Global Perspective*, London: Routledge, pp. 225–246.

Ross, R.J.S. (2001) 'The Decline of Labour Standards in the U.S. Apparel Industry', in G. Kohler and E.J. Chaves (eds) *Globalization: Critical Perspectives*, New York: Nova Science, pp. 277–294.

—— (2002) 'The New Sweatshops in the United States: How New, How Real, How Many, and Why?', in G. Gereffi, D. Spencer and J. Bair (eds) *Free Trade and Uneven Development: The North American Apparel Industry after NAFTA*, Philadelphia, PA: Temple University Press, pp. 100–122.

—— (2004) *Slaves to Fashion: Poverty and Abuse in the New Sweatshops*, Ann Arbor, MI: University of Michigan Press.

Safa, H. (1986) 'Runaway Shops and Female Employment: The Search for Cheap Labour', in E. Leacock and H. Safa (eds) *Women's Work*, South Hadley, MA: Bergin & Garvey, pp. 122–135.

Silver, B.J. and Arrighi, G. (2001) 'Workers North and South', in L. Panitch (ed.) *Working Classes: Global Realities. Socialist Register 2001*, London: Merlin, pp. 53–76.

Stein, L. (ed.) (1977) *Out of the Sweatshop: The Struggle for Industrial Democracy*, New York: Quadrangle/New York Times Book Co.

Wells, D.M. (1998) 'Building Transnational Coordinative Unionism', in S. Babson and H. J. Nunez (eds) *Confronting Change: Auto Labor and Lean Production in North America*, Detroit: Wayne State University Press, pp. 487–505.

—— (2007) 'Too Weak for the Job: Corporate Codes of Conduct, Non Governmental Organizations and the Regulation of International Labour Standards', *Global Social Policy* 7(1): 51–74.

Wells, D.M. and Knight, G. (2007) 'Bringing the Local Back In: Trajectory of Contention and the Union Struggle at Kukdong/Mexmode', *Social Movement Studies*, 6(1): 83–103.

Whalen, C. T. (2002) 'Sweatshops Here and There: The Garment Industry, Latinas, and Labour Migrations', *International Labour and Working-Class History* 61: 45–68.

6 Corporate social responsibility and labour market discipline

Contesting social reproduction in low-wage America

Ryan Foster

This chapter is concerned with two intersecting historical phenomena that are rooted in the rise of neoliberalism as the dominant economic and social order in the United States over the past twenty-five years: (1) the increasing dependency of workers employed in low-wage labour markets on community non-profit agencies such as food banks in order to meet their daily basic needs; and (2) a corollary rise in corporate philanthropy directed towards these same agencies as a demonstration of 'corporate social responsibility' (CSR). Why are multinational corporations in the retail industry, such as Wal-Mart, Home Depot, Target, and Best Buy, which – as discussed in the previous two chapters – have been at the leading edge of cost-saving strategies, such as flexible supply chains, outsourcing, and labour-saving technologies now dramatically expanding the amount of money they are giving to community charities through their CSR programmes? More importantly, what were the economic, social, and political circumstances in which low-wage workers became dependent on such charities, and hence corporate philanthropy, for their very survival?

In answering these questions, this chapter argues that corporate philanthropy directed at the working poor has been made possible as an act of 'social responsibility' by the class-based assault on the welfare state and rise of resistance to neoliberalism in the United States. By 'made possible', I understand two interlocking historical processes. First, I am referring to the increasing necessity of corporate philanthropy to ensure the social reproduction of workers in low-wage labour markets that has come as a consequence of the cutbacks to and privatisation of social welfare. Second, I am referring to the crisis of legitimacy of neoliberal corporate rule that has been generated by a wide range of resistance movements who, lacking effective legal and traditional political means to curb corporate behaviour, have increasingly turned to attacking the corporate brand image. Corporations have countered with elaborate public relations strategies to counter this threat to their bottom line, CSR being one of them.

However, more is at stake here than the individual corporate brand image and bottom line. This struggle involves the strategy of 'divide and sponsor', a phrase I use to describe the contemporary historical process in which capital has stripped labour of its bargaining power on the one hand, and then reinforced its dependency on corporate philanthropy for social reproduction, on the other. Thus, it is at the intersection of this corporate crisis of legitimacy which damages public perception and hence profits, and the growing demand for basic social welfare in the United States, that the process of 'divide and sponsor' can be understood both as a technique to defend the legitimacy of the corporation as a dominant social institution, and as a project to regulate the social reproduction of low-wage workforces. The chapter proceeds in three sections: first, it charts the relationship between neoliberal social policy reforms and the rising dependency of the working poor on community charities. Second, it offers a brief overview of the material and symbolic terrain of CSR as a reaction to anti-corporate movements, before mapping corporate philanthropy as a particular strand of this movement. Third, it weaves together arguments forwarded in the previous two sections through a case study of corporate philanthropy as CSR in the retail industry, focusing on the community-giving programmes of 'Big Box' stores.

Neoliberal social policy reform and the enforcement of low-wage work

In comparison to the thirty years after World War II, the past twenty-five years have witnessed a dramatic reversal of the process and ideology of social policy making in the United States (Blau and Abramovitz 2004; Fox Piven 2004a, 2005b; Simmons 2004). Neoliberal social policy reform is understood here as a set of retrenchments and market reforms to the welfare state that began with the Reagan administration (1981–1989). These reforms have resulted in the reformulation of programmes such as welfare, unemployment insurance, social security, and state-subsidised medical assistance that reduced economic insecurity and provided workers with a degree of independence from their employer. Through funding cutbacks and welfare-to-work programmes designed to promote 'individual responsibility' and an end to 'dependency' on the state, neoliberal reforms have sought to reduce the independence of workers from the labour market. In conjunction with an assault on organised labour and an increase in low-wage temporary work created by corporate restructuring in the service sector, neoliberal reform has broken down systematically important elements of independence and solidarity previously employed by labour to resist the discipline of capital. Alongside the rising cost of living and the decline of real wages endemic to the post-Fordist era (cf. Pollin 2002), these developments have impacted heavily on low-wage workers and their families, leaving them compelled to sell their labour-power to the highest bidder and hostage to highly exploitative work environments owing to fear of unemployment.

As Frances Fox Piven (2004a; 2004b) has argued, the replacement of Aid to Families with Dependent Children (AFDC) with Temporary Aid to Needy Families (TANF) (both referred to as 'welfare') under the Personal

Responsibility and Work Opportunity Reconciliation Act (PRWORA) of 1996, is one of the most visible examples of a much larger campaign to enforce the logic of low-wage work in the United States. Although 'welfare reform' (as the PRWORA is known) began under successive Republican administrations in the 1980s and early 1990s, it was Bill Clinton's administration in 1996 that signed the PRWORA into existence – a bill designed by a Republican-controlled House and Senate, which sought to 'end welfare as we know it'. Among other things, the bill added the requirement to work a minimum of 30 hours a week to receive benefits ('welfare to work'), imposed a 60-month lifetime limit on benefits, and the requirement to establish the paternity of the child before receiving assistance, all of which was aimed towards preventing 'out of wedlock pregnancies', the promotion of two-parent families, job preparation and work, and an end to 'welfare dependency'. Such goals reflected the spirit of the decades-long, multifaceted discursive campaign headed by conservative elites such as Charles Murray and Newt Gingrich to reverse the social policy doctrine of the Fordist era (Peck 2001).

Notwithstanding arguments by its proponents that 'welfare reform' has proved wildly successful due to the dramatic drop in welfare rolls across the United States following its implementation, the socio-economic implications of welfare to work participants have been anything but promising. The majority of participants become trapped in dead end, low-wage positions in the service sector (Fox-Piven 2004a; Simmons 2004; Robinson 2004). For example, between 1996 and 2000, the retail trade (including eating and drinking establishments) employed the highest number of former TANF recipients, at 32 per cent as well as the highest number of employees receiving Earned Income Tax Credit (EITC), a tax credit subsidy for low-wage workers (Boushey 2001). Not only do firms in the retail industry pay lower wages than other service industry jobs (e.g. health care, leisure and hospitality, education, see Bureau of Labor Statistics 2007), but they also provide fewer benefits on average than other industries in the service sector, and often are enticed by competing state and municipal governments to locate in a particular locality in exchange for tax breaks or other forms of subsidy such as the Work Opportunity Tax Credit (WOTC) and the Welfare to Work Tax Credit (WtWTC), which grant these firms access to a reserve army of welfare-to-work participants and further underwrite their labour costs (Zabin *et al.* 2004). Such practices have generated growing criticism of major retail firms such as Wal-Mart, which some scholars have dubbed 'parasitic industries' (Duggan 2001; Robinson 2004) As Tony Robinson (2004: 257) defines them, parasitic industries are those businesses that 'achieve capital gains by paying wages so low that they sap the vitality of workers, depress a community's productive capacity, and require expanded poverty relief expenditures' to subsidise the social costs of labour. Thus, despite their location at the opposite end of the transnational commodity chain from the production workers who make the majority of products sold in retail stores (see Chapters 3–5 of this volume), we find correlate systems of discipline and marginalisation.

The impacts of neoliberal social policy reform on the working poor

In the enforcement of low-wage work through social policy reform, there have been three major processes that reflect the neoliberal re-commodification of labour in comparison to the relative 'decommodification' (i.e. full employment policies coupled with an expanding social safety net) that prevailed during the height of the Fordist era (Esping-Anderson 1990). First, numerous studies have shown that of workers employed through welfare-to-work programmes, only a very small minority will ever achieve enough upward mobility to leave the ranks of the working poor (Boushey 2001; Goldberg and Collins 2001; Boushey and Rosnick 2004), thus challenging a fundamental pillar of the much vaunted 'American dream'.

Second, many employers in the service industry either do not offer benefits packages, do not offer employees enough working hours each week to qualify for existing packages, or require expensive premiums that only a minority of employees can afford (Zabin *et al.* 2004). This is exacerbated by the fact that continuing cuts to Medicaid and state health care systems under the Bush II administration (2001–present) have made it increasingly difficult for the working poor to rely on state assistance, as well as the fact that the costs of private health insurance have skyrocketed (Blau and Abramovitz 2004). This reality of social policy reform is best exemplified by the fact that, at present, 44 million Americans are without health insurance (ibid.).

Third, the combination of low wages and the increasing inaccessibility of social assistance from employers, the government, and the market has made the working poor increasingly reliant on services delivered by community non-profit social services organisations which, in the period of 1994–2004, expanded their giving operations by 231 per cent (Foundation Center 2005).

The study conducted by Sommerfeld and Reisch (2003) of the impact of welfare reform on the non-profit sector demonstrates a sharp increase in demand among TANF recipients for non-profit services while government budget cuts have left these organisations increasingly desperate for donations. One significant consequence of this process is the growing importance of food banks to the working poor. Basic nutrition is the very bottom line of social reproduction and the inability of full-time workers in low-wage labour markets to meet this precondition for survival through their wages illustrates the crisis of social reproduction among the working poor. America's Second Harvest, the nation's largest food bank network, reports that over the past decade, hunger relief agencies found that the greatest increase in hungry Americans was among the working poor in which 37 per cent of people requesting emergency food assistance in American cities in 2001 were employed (America's Second Harvest 2005a, 2005b, 2006). Peter Eisinger's (1999) study of food pantries and soup kitchens in Detroit led him to estimate that as many as 20 per cent of clients were there because of the 1996 welfare reforms – most because the reduced food stamp allotment didn't meet basic needs. As he argues, 'welfare reform, in its assault on dependency, may simply have had the ironic consequence of replacing dependency on food stamps with dependency on private charity' (ibid.). It is in this light, that food banks have seen a shift in their role as an emergency source of food for the unemployed and the homeless, to a 'part of [a] regular calculation for the family budget' to quote Helen Kozlowski, head of Michigan's Oakland County food bank (Watson 2002). The increasing demand at food banks across the country has been met equally with an increasing demand for donations from cash strapped non-profit agencies. As Second Harvest reports in its 2006 hunger study, over 60 per cent of food banks in America are currently experiencing threats to the stability of their programmes, citing problems related to funding as the most significant reason (Second Harvest 2006).

As food banks and a wide array of other non-profit organisations which serve the working poor have seen an increased demand, these agencies have been desperately searching for new sources of funding, particularly from corporations who are looking to enhance their marketing campaigns (Young 1998). In 1998, Dennis Young of the National Center on Nonprofit Enterprise suggested that

> historically, funding from for-profit corporations has been a relatively small fraction of the support base of private, nonprofit organisations in the United States – approximately 5 per cent of overall charitable contributions to nonprofits and less than 1 per cent of nonprofits' overall revenues.

He proceeded to argue, however, that these statistics were misleading indicators of the importance of corporations to the future support of non-profit organisations, owing to the rise of 'strategic philanthropy' and the 'marketing power of charitable causes' (i.e. the rising amount of corporate giving illustrated in Figure 6.1) (ibid.). It is within this moment that we witness the dual nature of the strategy of 'divide and sponsor': corporate philanthropy is necessary to ensure a minimum level of social reproduction for low-wage workforces, thus preventing social disintegration, violence and revolt, while at the same time it serves to enhance the brand image and marketing power of the corporation. We turn now to the second part of the chapter, in which we discuss the appearance of 'corporate social responsibility' as a reaction to anti-corporate activism, and the emergence of corporate philanthropy as one particular technique by which corporations are defending themselves from resistance movements.

Corporate social responsibility and the crisis of legitimacy

Public trust and investor confidence in corporations, business leaders, and the capitalist system in the United States are at a low not seen since the

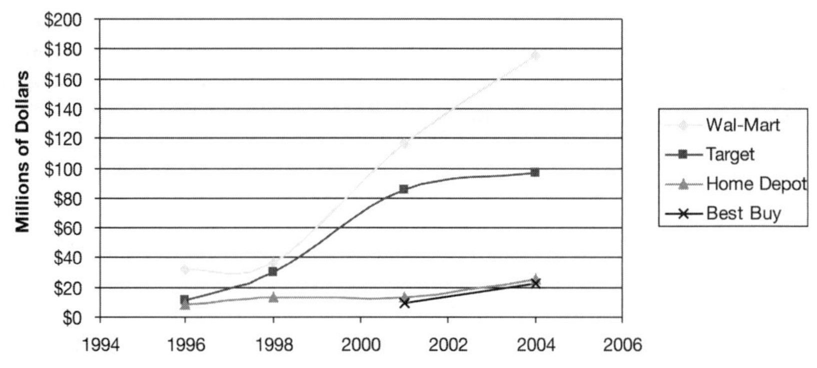

Figure 6.1 Expansion of big-box retailers' philanthropic giving, 1996–2004.
Sources: Corporate Giving Directory (1998, 1997); Foundation Center (2001, 2004).

days of the Great Depression (Jackson and Nelson 2004: 1) The growing public awareness of the exploitation of sweatshop labour in the developing world, major corporate scandals such as Enron and WorldCom, environmental degradation, corporate political lobbying, and anti-corporate protests such as those that occurred in Seattle, Prague, and Davos, are a few among many reasons cited for this growing distrust in which, as polls released by *Business Week* in 2000 and the *New York Times* in 2005 indicated, the majority of Americans now believe that corporations have too much power (Bernstein, 11 September 2000; Jackson and Nelson 2004; Deutsch 9 December 2005). This has prompted calls from many different quarters that American corporations are now facing a major 'crisis of legitimacy' (e.g. Bello 2001; Simons *et al.* 2002; Greenwood 2003; Rayman-Bacchus 2004; Jackson and Nelson 2004; Varney 2004; Bakan 2004). This crisis has been exacerbated by a multiplicity of movements from all sides of the political spectrum which, although representing different causes, are united in their challenge to the neoliberal reformulation of the state, the subordination of social priorities for the sake of 'international competitiveness', and the privatisation and commodification of every aspect of social life that has come to be characterised by the term 'corporate rule' (Starr 2000: 45; see also Klein 2000; Berg 2003). This movement of movements is often congealed by news media into one mass under such buzzwords as 'the anti-globalisation movement', 'the global justice movement' or 'the anti-corporate movement'. The latter term will be used here to characterise the resistance movements illustrated below, following Amory Starr (2000), whose 'three modes of anti-corporatism' offer a useful categorical framework.

As the intensity of these challenges against neoliberalism have grown, so too have corporate-led initiatives to regain social legitimacy, which are largely conducted under the banner of 'corporate social responsibility' (CSR). The latter has popularised the idea of a 'triple bottom line' whereby corporations incorporate social and environmental priorities with their primary responsibility of maximising shareholder value (Elkington 1998). Business-led CSR initiatives have included the adoption of voluntary codes of conduct such as the UN's Global Compact (www.unglobalcompact.org) and the OECD's Corporate Codes of Conduct (www.oecd.org), participation in fair trade movements led by groups such as Oxfam, and partnerships with NGOs such as United Students Against Sweatshops. One pervasive CSR trend is the demonstration of 'social responsibility' through the expansion of corporate philanthropy and community involvement. To reiterate the question posed at the beginning of this chapter, why are multinational corporations in the retail industry, such as Wal-Mart, Home Depot, Target and Best Buy, who have been at the leading edge of cost saving strategies, such as flexible supply chains, outsourcing, and labour-saving technologies now dramatically expanding the amount of money they are giving to communities? Furthermore, why have these corporations, who take advantage of welfare to work programmes, pay poverty-line wages, and actively encourage their employees to rely on social assistance and charity, become so eager to become a beacon of social redistribution? These questions are interrogated through a case study of community-based resistance to big box retailers, and the corresponding emergence of community based corporate philanthropy programmes as a response to defend the corporation's brand image. However, first let us consider the historical emergence of both the theory and practice of CSR.

Corporate social responsibility as a contested concept

The first difficulty in offering an analysis of CSR is that there is a great variety of interpretations on what exactly 'social responsibility' entails, the way to achieve greater social responsibility, or indeed, the issues that are of importance in such a discussion. The huge variety of competing and often contradictory interpretations is also compounded by the encroachment of other terms such as corporate sustainability, corporate citizenship, and corporate governance, all of which promote different agendas for the reform of corporate business practice (Shamir 2004a). In light of the variety of interpretations, the issues involved, the best way forward (i.e. legal regulation vs voluntary altruism) CSR will be preliminarily defined here, following Shamir (2004b), as a contested concept in which there is a struggle over the symbolic meaning of 'social responsibility' between a variety of actors who are divided by their stance on binding legal regulations as a means of reforming corporate business practice. Therefore, an act of 'social responsibility' is defined by its contested nature, wherein part of the audience that the act is marketed to will accept it as a demonstration of morality and an appropriate social role for the corporation, while another part will reject it. Thus, the struggle over defining what 'acts' qualify as 'social responsibility' is constantly evolving according to the individual symbolic battles between corporations and those who seek to regulate them.

However, it is important to note briefly that in light of the massive wave of deregulation and decriminalisation that has been a characteristic of the capitalist state's relationship with corporations in the neoliberal era (Saad-Filho 2005), struggles to regulate corporate behaviour occur in the context of large power imbalances between corporations and the individuals, groups and institutions which seek to sanction them. Given this fact, I am inclined to agree with Naomi Klein (2000) that the brand image of corporations has become a central site of struggle in movements that seek to regulate corporate behaviour, as it is far more vulnerable site of attack than the legal apparatus – a point we will return to momentarily.

Although CSR has been gaining momentum since the early 1990s, since 2000 there has been a virtual explosion of literature, international fora, voluntary codes of conduct, business associations, corporate consultancies, grassroots movements, transnational protest groups, NGOs, and government agencies who all proclaim to be dedicated to making corporations more responsible to society. By way of brief illustration, there are now over 15,500 awards given every year to model corporate citizens, CSR stock market indexes, such as the Domini 400, rating systems which list the 100 most socially responsible corporations developed by business journals such as *Business Week*, and almost every major corporation now publishes an annual social responsibility report, typically detailing its 'good works' (Hopkins 2003; e.g. Ford 2005; Pfizer Inc. 2005; Wal-Mart Stores Inc. 2005a).

The question that must be posed is, why now? Why has CSR become such a growth industry since 2000, and why are US multinational corporations collectively spending billions of dollars to become ostensibly more responsive and accountable to civil society in a time when they are more powerful than ever? In the following section, I critically evaluate these questions by juxtaposing abuses of corporate power that engender anti-corporate action, and corresponding CSR initiatives which seek to defend brand image.

Anti-corporate dissent and CSR – two growth industries, 2000–2005

In the five years that followed the WTO protests in Seattle, CSR initiatives moved from being a relatively unheard of position in Nike's PR department to the standard operating practice for every major corporation in the world. There are four mutually reciprocating trends that have been responsible for driving this growth, and thus intensifying the crisis of corporate legitimacy (cf. Rampton 2002). First, the anti-corporate movement against neoliberal globalisation has intensified since Seattle in 1999 (i.e. Juris 2005), exemplified by the protests in Davos (2001), Quebec City (2001), Genoa (2001), Cancun, (2003), and Edinburgh (2005). It has focused negative media attention on the powerful international institutions the IMF, the World Bank, the G8, the WTO, etc.) that facilitate global capitalism, thus drawing the issue of corporate power more fully into public discourse and engendering institutional responses such as the UN's Global Compact.

Second, drawing on the successes of highly visible 'shaming campaigns' such as those carried out by the National Labour Committee (NLC) in the 1990s, which targeted the Gap, Kathy Lee Gifford's clothing line, and Nike for sweatshop production, anti-corporate activists have stepped up focused attacks on corporations to draw negative media attention to the corporate brand name. In her examination of the international boycott that was successfully organised against Nike in the late 1990s, Naomi Klein points out that what had ironically made the campaign possible was the widespread recognition of Nike's 'swoosh' logo, leading Klein to coin the phrase 'the brand boomerang' (Klein 2000). Amid the boycott, Nike created a theretofore unheard of executive position in the corporate world: 'Vice President for Corporate Responsibility' and involved itself in developing voluntary codes of conduct specifically to do with labour practices (ibid.). Other examples of this phenomenon are campaigns against pharmaceutical company Pfizer by HIV/AIDS activists who allege the company makes life-saving drugs unaffordable for the poor in both developed and developing nations (e.g. Aids Coalition to Unleash Power: www.actupny.org/) as well as campaigns against Royal Dutch Shell, for both alleged environmental degradation and for its complicity in the murders of dissidents in Nigeria (e. g. Amnesty International: www.amnesty.org). Like Nike before them, both Pfizer and Shell have responded with CSR programmes that address the negative attention, with Pfizer developing an access to medicines programme (Pfizer Inc. 2005), and Shell developing an extensive philanthropic interest in environmental causes (Shell 2006).

Third, the fall-out from recent corporate scandals involving Enron, WorldCom, K-Mart, in combination with growing public distrust concerning the connection between big oil companies and the Bush administration's 2003 invasion of Iraq has invigorated anti-corporate debate in popular discourse and has generated a large array of best sellers, journalistic exposes, and forms of artistic expression that have turned criticism of corporate rule into a major growth industry. This has been embodied in popular documentary films such as Mark Achbar and Jennifer Abbot's *The Corporation* (2004), and Michael Moore's *Fahrenheit 9/11* (2004) (now the highest grossing documentary film of all time) which, among other things, challenge the legitimacy of the corporation as a legal 'person', highlight historic and ongoing corporate abuses of human rights and the environment, and take aim at the complicity of the corporate media in selling the invasion of Iraq to the American public.

Fourth, is the increasing tendency for consumers and investors to avoid companies who are perceived as unethical, which has been a direct result of the above trends (Rampton 2002). Marketing literature in particular has focused on changing consumer demand for more 'ethical' products and companies, which in the past decade has dramatically changed from being just the purview of upper class professionals to being prevalent across classes – survey data indicated in 2005 that more than a third of consumers worldwide boycott at least one brand, the most frequent reason given being unfair labour practices (GMI 2005). The most boycotted brands were Nike, Coca-Cola, McDonald's, and Nestlé, each of which has had concerted anti-corporate campaigns directed against it (ibid.). Therefore, it is in the combination of the rise in demand for more ethical products, and the already value-centred brand marketing approach of corporations that we witness cause-related marketing becoming an effective tool by which to address this threat to profit margins. In what follows, I examine the rise of corporate philanthropy/CSR initiatives as a moment of this crisis of legitimacy in which the struggle between anti-corporate activists and corporations is now being most fervently played out over corporate brand image.

Corporate philanthropy as social responsibility

One particular method by which American corporations are engaging their rising crisis of legitimacy is by mobilising corporate philanthropy as a symbol of social consciousness. By corporate philanthropy, I am referring to a particular strand of the CSR discourse in the US in which 'strategic philanthropy' or 'cause-related marketing' has become intertwined with the notion of social responsibility via corporate contributions to the non-profit sector and their subsequent entrance into the public consciousness through marketing campaigns (Silver 2001; King 2001). As the Foundation Center reported in 2005, since 1994, corporate foundations have increased their giving by 74 per cent. Companies such as Wal-Mart and Ford, who gave US$176 million and US$120 million respectively in 2004, set a historical precedent by climbing into the ranks of the top twenty philanthropists in the United States, a club that has historically been the territory of wealthy shareholders, not corporations (Ostrower 1995; Foundation Center 2004; Slate online 2005).

In addition to the growing amount of money multinational corporations are directing to charities, NGOs, community groups, universities, and self-directed social initiatives, is a concerted effort to imprint an image of corporate civic responsibility. In other words, the corporation is to be seen as a 'good citizen', doing its part for the betterment of society. This image is generated by activities such as employee volunteerism, disaster relief, support for the military and other nationalist projects, building low income housing, and environmental protection to name a few. These 'good works', now a popular signifier of this combination of philanthropy and civic initiative (e.g. Wal-Mart and Ford's programmes) are, in turn, publicly reported via commercials and advertisements, the corporate webpage, annual 'social responsibility' reports, the site of sponsorship, and other context-specific mediums as a material and symbolic representation of social consciousness. According to the business literature that promotes such cause-related marketing, it is a highly effective strategy for improving brand loyalty (e.g. Heath

1997; Himmelstein 1997; Werther and Chandler 2005) and also has a demonstrated effect on revenue growth (Lev *et al.* 2006). On the other side of the coin, it also is an effective method to address bad public relations. Miami business professors Werther and Chandler's (2005) recent contribution, entitled 'Strategic Corporate Social Responsibility as Global Brand Insurance', perhaps says it best: 'corporate actions that violate societal expectations damage, even destroy brand image among networked stakeholders who are affluent enough to buy branded products and services. The premiums for CSR brand insurance are paid by leaders who create an organisation-wide commitment to CSR as a means of redefining "profit maximization"' (ibid., p. 317).

In this light, I would submit that these corporate philanthropy/CSR programmes serve two functions. The first is to engage in the ongoing ethical marketing war between competitors that has been a response to the more general increase in ethical consumer and investor demand, and likewise, shore up the brand image against potential attacks, by aggressively marketing the company as socially responsible. The second is to engage the specific criticism directed at the brand from anti-corporate activists that has the potential to generate negative media attention, damage corporate reputation and possibly incite new activist threats against the corporation in other localities (cf. Werther and Chandler 2005). It is to the latter function that we turn our attention to now, in an examination of the retail industry.

Corporate philanthropy: the case of the retail industry

'Big box retailers' or 'category killers', such as Wal-Mart, Home Depot, Target, and Best Buy, have dramatically expanded their community philanthropy programmes in the past decade (Figure 6.1). In combination with rising cash donations, retailers also organise elaborate employee volunteer programmes, in which they arrange to have the low-wage workers they employ 'lend a hand' to non-profit agencies by, in the case of Home Depot for example, building playgrounds in working poor neighbourhoods, or low income housing for teen mothers (Home Depot 2005a).

What is particularly striking about this expansion is that in the period of 2000–2004, in the cases of Wal-Mart, Target, and Best Buy such philanthropy has not only grown as a percentage of net profits (Figures 6.3, 6.4, 6.5), but also rose in terms of the average amount donated by each branch to the community in which it operates (Figure 6.2). In other words, the expansion of these big box retailers' community philanthropy programmes is being carried out at a pace faster than the expansion of profit or geographical expansion of the company.

The expansion of community-giving programmes in the retail industry can be explained, in part, by the rising crisis of legitimacy engendered by anti-corporate challenges to corporate rule. It is within the specific imperative for big box retailers to continually expand into new communities, and the crisis of legitimacy engendered by the expansion of their parasitic busi-

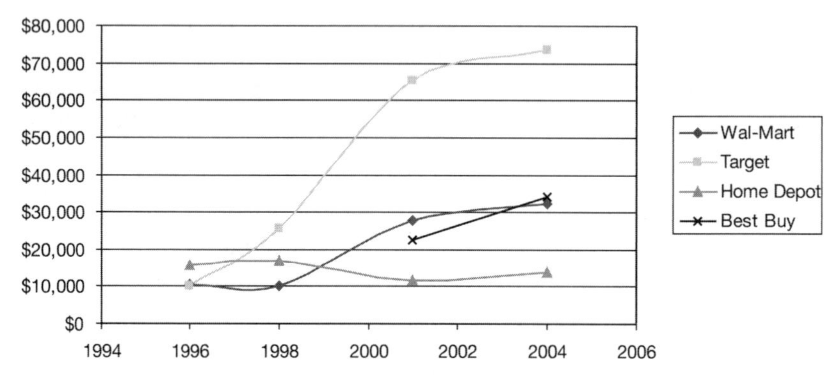

Figure 6.2 "Big box philanthropy – yearly per store average, 1996–2004.

Sources: Corporate Giving Directory (1998, 1997); Foundation Center (2001, 2004); Valueline (2004).

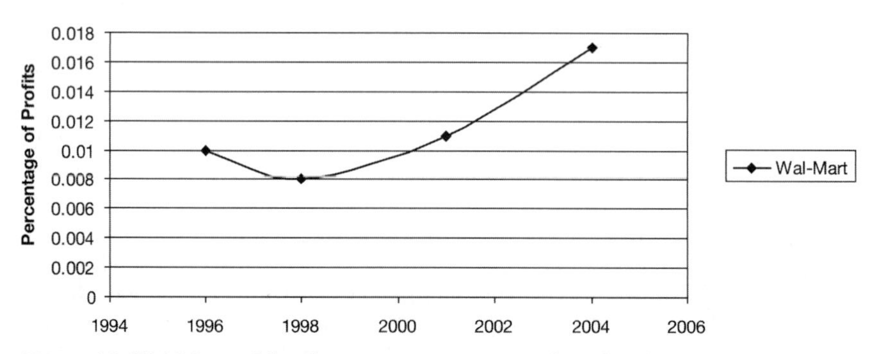

Figure 6.3 Wal-Mart: philanthropy as a percentage of profits,1996–2004.

Sources: Corporate Giving Directory (1998; Foundation Center (2001, 2004); Valueline (2004).

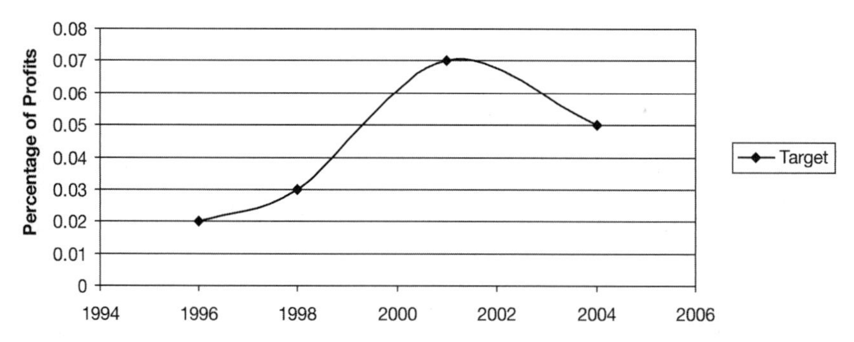

Figure 6.4 Target: philanthropy as a percentage of profits: 1996–2004.

Sources: Corporate Giving Directory (1998, 1997); Foundation Center (2001, 2004); Valueline (2004).

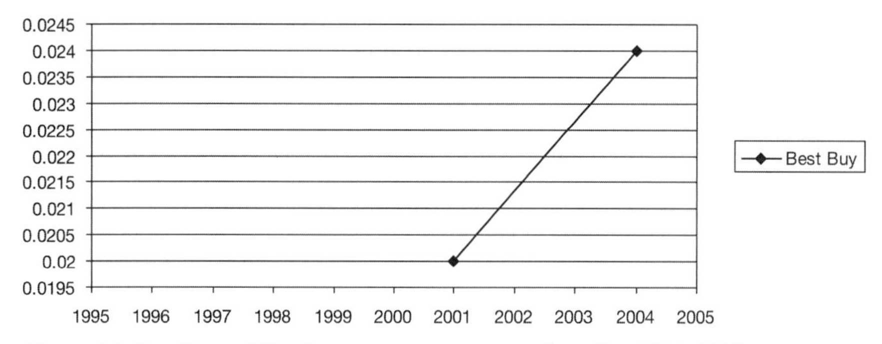

Figure 6.5 Best Buy: philanthropy as a percentage of profits, 2001–2004.

Sources: Corporate Giving Directory (1998, 1997); Foundation Center (2001, 2004); Valueline (2004).

ness practices, that the symbolic struggle over brand image is localised. First, I will review the rise in community-based dissent against retailers, and, second, demonstrate how community philanthropy programmes have been mobilised to defend the company.

The crisis of legitimacy for big box retailers: community activism

The form of resistance to big box retailers that has been the most pervasive has been organised community groups that engage in struggles to prevent the entrance of these corporations into their communities. A study of big box retailers in 2004 by Bernstein Investment and Management has demonstrated that the rise of community activism has the potential to jeopardise the increased expansion, profit margins, and stock value of these corporations (Kozloff *et al.* 2005). The study showed, among other things, that:

> Communities successfully blocked 35 large retail stores openings in 2004, a 60 percent increase compared to 2000. The retailers affected included Bed Bath and Beyond, Best Buy, Circuit City, Costco, Home Depot, Kohl's, Linens n' Things, Target, and Wal-Mart ... [S]uccessful attempts to block new stores grew 21 percent annually from 2002–2004. If this trend continues through 2009 ... community opposition to store siting could impact retailers' annual square footage growth. Even a modest slowing of annual square footage growth in turn, could lead both to lower earnings and lower valuations of big-box retailers' stock.
>
> (Tanner and Gladman 2005: 2)

The study further showed that even in those cases where the attempt to block the opening of big box store had been unsuccessful, the corporation had often faced very costly delays where, in a few cases, store opening had been delayed up to three years (ibid.). According to Al Norman (1999), author of *Slam Dunking Wal-Mart* and head of the activist consulting firm 'Sprawl Busters' which offers technical assistance to community groups fighting retail expansion, 280 communities have successfully beaten back big box stores at least once, or have pressured a developer to withdraw (Sprawl Busters 2005). Such protests have taken place all across the United States over the past decade, but have grown particularly concentrated in

> those regions in the US that have been least saturated by big box retail and that represent the most attractive growth market for future retail development due to their population size, density, and income levels. These regions include California, Texas, Florida, and the Northeast.
> (Tanner and Gladman 2005: 3)

Why have these groups engaged in these protests, and what has the impact on these corporations been?

Norman argues that 'citizens opposed to sprawl generally cite two major reasons for fighting companies like Wal-Mart': (1) Negative impact on the local economy; (2) Negative impact on their quality of life (Norman 1999: 28). With regard to the first point, a growing number of studies have demonstrated that the entrance of big box retailers into local economies drives smaller retailers out of business, depresses wages, and harms unions through predatory competition (e.g. Stone 2001; Los Angeles City Council 2003; Bay Area Economic Forum 2004). With regard to the second point, 'quality of life' refers to diverse issues such as increased traffic, the negative effects on the aesthetics of the community, the destruction of 'main-street', but overall, to quote Norman, these criticisms are directed at 'a loss of community' and a 'loss of sense of place' (ibid., p. 37). Thus, I would submit that the growing number of these campaigns well represents Starr's third mode of anti-corporatism, 'delinking, re-localization, and sovereignty' in which localities contest the broadening and deepening of neoliberal market relations and attempt to protect economic and political autonomy (Starr 2000).

So-called 'anti-sprawl' groups have mobilised a wide variety of tactics in fighting the entrance of big box retailers into their towns, such as contesting rezoning applications, protesting wetland destruction, commissioning economic impact studies, holding referenda, and conducting 'sprawl' education campaigns, to name a few (Norman 1999). The tactics have been responded to in kind by Big Box developers, and the two opposed groups have engaged in an evolutionary form of struggle in which retailers now either attempt to conceal their entrance into town altogether, or if discovered, begin an elaborate community-focused public relations campaign (ibid.). One particular tactic that retailers have employed has been to distribute a 'community resource' guide to local leaders and officials, in which the company outlines its philanthropic commitment to communities, wherein cash donations are implicitly promised to civic institutions, such as the police and fire departments, school scholarship programmes, and non-profit organisations that target needy members of the community. (ibid.). And so, it is in the context of the neoliberal reformulation of the state and the need for basic forms of funding for services such as police, education, and social assistance, on the one hand, and the crisis of legitimacy big box retailers face in communities on the other, that the logic of corporate community-giving programmes becomes clear. It is also worth reiterating that, as I argued in earlier, retailers also have a material stake in the social reproduction of their low-wage labour forces or, in other words, corporate philanthropy mediates the survival of the labour force in a privatised and ad-hoc way without providing any degree of independence from the market.

Retail foundations, community non-profit partnerships, and the working Poor

All four of the retail giants, Wal-Mart, Home Depot, Target, and Best Buy, have developed national partnerships with highly recognised non-profit institutions that are associated with community giving that in particular targets working poor families, such as United Way, the Red Cross, Children's Hospitals, and the United Negro College Fund (Best Buy 2005; Home Depot 2005; Target 2005a; Wal-Mart 2005a). Beyond these national partnerships, there also exists a substantial congruency in the specific targets or themes of the giving programmes. The theme of 'community giving' is the most centrally emphasised, with Target's and Best Buy's programmes actually featuring the word in the title (i.e. Target Community Giving, Best Buy Community Relations), Home Depot's is simply 'Corporate Responsibility' dedicated to 'balancing the needs of communities', while Wal-Mart has adopted the quasi-Christian 'Good Works' community giving programme.

The second most emphasised theme is offering assistance, to quote the Target Foundation's website, which addresses 'the basic needs of individuals or families at risk by providing shelter, food, and clothing' (Target 2005b). Thus, in contrast to the charge from activists that big box retailing is having a severe social, political, economic, and environmental impact on communities, community-giving programmes emphasise the corporation as a moral entity, invested in the betterment of the community and social redistribution, especially to those that are among the needy and disadvantaged. As community-based non-profit human service agencies such as food banks and family support services have increasingly looked to corporations for support since the 1996 PRWORA reforms, and big box retailers have come under fire from community activism, so too have visible community-giving efforts increased. It is also worth noting that part of the evaluative criteria for selection is based on the non-profit organisation's proximity to a local branch, for example, Wal-Mart directly excludes those proposals which are either 'used for benefit outside the local community' or are 'programs outside Wal-Mart communities', while Home Depot offers an online 'eligibility test' in which the applicant must input their proximity in miles from the nearest branch (Home Depot 2005; Wal-Mart 2005a). Thus, the corporation becomes a *de facto* social welfare distribution agency, evaluating the proposals of local non-profit agencies alongside their usefulness in marketing the corporate brand image.

However, as mentioned above, major non-profit organisations such as United Way are active partners in the promotion of cause-related marketing through programmes such as the NCL, as opposed to simply functionaries of corporate strategy. United Way actively seeks out corporate partnerships, advertises corporate donations on its websites, and participates as a partner in corporate-led community fundraising initiatives. For example, the most consistent trend is for each of these corporations is to be a 'pacesetter' for the annual United Way campaign with typically runs from September through November. 'Pacesetters' are 'community leaders' who initiate an 'in-store' contribution drive, or simply donate a sum of money in the months prior to the actual United Way campaign beginning, with the ostensible purpose of 'setting the pace' for the campaign. Corporations, local businesses, and non-profit agencies who are involved, are recognised in local media both at the start of the campaign for their contributions, as well as at the end, when the local United Way typically takes out an advertisement in the local paper to thank the participants (e.g. United Way of Greater New Orleans 2005; Darrow 2004). Perhaps the saddest and most ironic part of such campaigns, and emblematic of the 'divide and sponsor' strategy, is that typically half of what is donated by each corporation comes directly out of the pockets of workers, through voluntary employee paycheque deductions, which Wal-Mart, for example, meets dollar for dollar with a 'matching grant program' (Wal-Mart 2005b). Such is the logic of Big Box philanthropy, which makes its employees rely on charity to supplement their wages on the one hand, while asking them to donate money to the same charities as a symbol of the corporation's benevolence on the other.

In another vein, Wal-Mart and Best Buy, the two retailers of the five expanding the most rapidly geographically across the United States, employ a strategy whereby they donate a sum of money to the local United Way upon opening a new store in a highly visible media event (e.g. Stafford 2004; Smeath 2005) Typically, this involves a grand opening celebration in which local community leaders are present, a pop singer performs, and the local media are invited to report on the charitable contributions given the community, in which the store manager presents a cheque to the United Way campaign manager (ibid.).

Finally, beyond direct donations of both money and materials to non-profit human service agencies are the 'volunteerism' programmes of the big box retailers. By this, I mean that each retailer has adopted a strategy whereby they encourage their employees to become involved in local non-profit organisations, particularly by guaranteeing funding for employees' chosen organisation. These events typically receive favourable local media coverage. For example, on July 31, 2005, an article entitled 'Wal-Mart's Day of Caring "greatest thing" to disabled workers', in the *Decatur Daily*, detailed the participation of Wal-Mart employees in a cookout party for a local agency that employed peopled with physical and mental disabilities (Huggins 2005). Such events are not just common in the South, but across the United States where Wal-Mart has been gaining an increased foothold, with Wal-Mart employees participating in annual 'Day[s] of Caring', for example, in Connecticut (United Way of Meriden and Wallingford 2005), and Washington State (United Way of Snohomish Country 2004).

To return to the two functions of corporate philanthropy/CSR I suggested above, it is with the enlistment of the time and money of their low-wage workforces, that big box retailers seek to both compete in an ethical marketing war with competitors and limit the impact of anti-corporate attacks. To fully illustrate the contradictions inherent to the professed aims of such philanthropic and 'socially responsible' endeavours, and highlight the strategy of 'divide and sponsor', it is worth closing with a quote from a PBS interview with Jon Lehman, a former Wal-Mart manager of 17 years experience:

> I had a Rolodex on my desk, and I still have the Rolodex; I took it home with me. But it's full of business cards of social service outfits in the local city that I was running a store: indigent health care organizations that provided indigent health care, soup kitchens, everything, the United Way – all these people that I had lined up that I would call in the event that an associate came into my office and said, 'I can't afford to take my child to the doctor,' 'I can't afford groceries,' or 'I'm getting kicked out of my house,' or whatever. And I would actually call these places. Many times, I would take the worker down to the United Way in my truck. They didn't know what to do. I'd take them down, help them make [an] application and get some help, you know.
>
> (PBS 2004)

Conclusion

While the creation of global supply chains through the outsourcing of production has frequently been highlighted as a central pillar in the restructuring of the US retail industry (see Chapters 4 and 5), this chapter has examined the other end of the commodity chain: namely, the dynamics of domination and resistance that surround the production and reproduction of low-wage workers who are integrated into the US service sector. Neoliberal reforms to welfare institutions in conjunction with corporate restructuring has served to remake low-wage workforces in the US, who are caught between the discipline of the labour market and dependence on charitable sources to supplement poverty-level incomes. The contradictions of this process have led to the emergence of what I term the 'divide and sponsor' strategy among retailing corporations. Two facets of 'divide and sponsor' are evident: first, the increasing dependence of low-wage workers on corporate philanthropy/CSR for social reproduction; and, second, the increasing need for corporations to employ corporate philanthropy as a method by which to defend their brand image from anti-corporate activism. Voluntary initiatives by corporations cannot address the structural inequalities created by neoliberal capitalism, however. Nor can they reconcile the growing anti-corporate challenges that reject the expansion of corporate rule over every aspect of social life. Consequently, CSR, in general, and corporate philanthropy, in particular, appear to be tenuous features of contemporary capitalism that have the potential to give way to a more coercive forms of corporate rule in the event that they no longer viably regulate these contradictions.

References

America's Second Harvest (2005a) 'Hunger and the Working Poor'. Available at: www.secondharvest.org/learn_about_hunger/fact_sheet/working_poor.html

—— (2005b) 'Hunger Study 2001'. Available at: www.secondharvest.org/learn_about_hunger/Hunger_Study_2001/

—— (2006) 'Hunger Study 2006'. Available at: www.hungerinamerica.org/

Bakan, J. (2004) *The Corporation: The Pathological Pursuit of Profit and Power*, New York: Free Press.

Bay Area Economic Forum (2004) 'Super Centers and the Transformation of the Bay Area Grocery Industry: Issues, Trends, and Impacts', Randolph, Sean R. Project Supervisor. Available at: www.bayeconfor.org/pdf/PPRSCscreen11.2.pdf

Bello, W. (2001) 'Crisis of Legitimacy: The Revolt Against Corporate-Driven Globalization', talk delivered to the Boston Research Center for the 21st Century, Boston, MA, February. Available at: www.tni.org/archives/bello/revolt.htm

Berg, J.C. (2003) *Teamsters and Turtles? U.S. Progressive Political Movements in the 21st Century*, Oxford: Rowman & Littlefield.

Bernstein, A. (2000) 'Too Much Corporate Power?', *Business Week Online*, 11 September. Available at: www.businessweek.com/2000/00_37/b3698001.htm

Best Buy Co. Inc (2005) 'Best Buy Community Relations'. Available at: www.communications.bestbuy.com/communityrelations/philanthropy.asp

Blau, J. and Abramovitz, M. (2004) *The Dynamics of Social Welfare Policy*, New York: Oxford University Press.

Boushey, H. (2001) 'Last Hired First Fired: Job Losses Plague Former TANF Recipients', Economic Policy Institute Online. Available at: www.epi.org/Issuebriefs/ib171/ib171.pdf

Boushey, H. and Rosnick D. (2004) 'For Welfare Reform to Work, Jobs Must Be Available', Center for Economic and Policy Research. Available at: www.65.181.187.63/documents/publications/welfare_reform_2004_04.pdf

Bureau of Labor Statistics (2007) 'National Compensation Survey: Occupational Wages in the United States', United States Bureau of Labor Statistics. Available at: www.bls.gov/ncs/ocs/sp/ncbl0910.pdf

Corporate Giving Directory 1998 (1997) 'Taft Corporate Giving Directory, 19th ed', Taft Group.

CSR Wire (2005) 'CSRWire.com The Corporate Social Responsibility Newswire Service'. Available at: www.csrwire.com/

Darrow, D. (2004) 'Pacesetter Campaign on Target for United Way', *Pueblo Chieftain* 14, July.

Deutsch, C. (2005) 'New Surveys Show that Big Business has a P.R. Problem', *New York Timer*, 9th December, New York.

Duggan, L. (2001) 'Retail on the "Dole": Parasitic Employers and Women Workers', *NWSA Journal* 13(3): 95–115.

Eisinger, P. (1999) 'Food Pantries and Welfare Reform: Estimating the Effect', *Focus* 20(3): 23–28.

Elkington, J. (1998) *Cannibals with Forks: The Triple Bottom Line of 21st Century Business*, Stony Creek, CT: New Society Publishers.

Esping-Andeson, G. S. (1990) *The Three Worlds of Welfare Capitalism*, Princeton, NJ: Princeton University Press.

Ethical Consumer (2005) 'The Rise and Rise of Ethical Consumerism', Ethical Consumer Online. Available at: www.ethicalconsumer.org/philosophy/riserise.htm

Ford Motor Company Inc. (2005) 'Good Works – Responsible, Sustainable, Involved'. Available at: www.ford.com/en/goodWorks/default.htm?referrer=home

Foundation Center (2001) *Foundation Directory*, New York: Columbia University Press.

—— (2004) *Foundation Directory*, New York: Columbia University Press.

—— (2005) 'Foundation Growth and Giving Estimates 2005', Foundation Today Series – Foundation Center Online. Available at: www.foundationcenter.org/gainknowledge/research/pdf/fgge05.pdf

Fox Piven, F. (2004a) 'Neoliberal Social Policy and Labor Market Discipline', in M? Zweig (Ed.) *What's Class Got to Do With It? American Society in the Twenty-First Century*, Ithaca, NY: Cornell University Press, pp. 113–124.

—— (2004b) 'Discipline and Seduction: The Campaign to Regulate American Workers', in L. Simmon (ed.) *Welfare, the Working Poor, and Labor*, Armonk, NY: M.E. Sharpe, pp. 3–10.

GMI (2005) 'More Than a Third of Consumers Boycott at Least One Brand', GMI poll, 29 Aug. Available at: www.gmi-mr.com/gmipoll/release.php?p=20050829

Goldberg, G.S. and Collins, S.D. (2001) *Washington's New Poor Law: Welfare Reform and the Roads Not Taken – 1935 to the Present*, New York: Apex Press.

Greenwood, J. (2003) 'Trade Associations, Change, and the New Activism', in S. John and S. Thomson (eds) *New Activism and the Corporate Response*, Basingstoke: Palgrave Macmillan, pp. 49–66.

Harris Interactive Inc. (2005) 'Reputation Quotient 2004', Harris Interactive Online. Available at: www.harrisinteractive.com/services/reputation.asp

Heath, R.L. (1997) *Strategic Issues Management: Organizations and Public Policy Challenges*, Thousand Oaks, CA: Sage Publications.

Himmelstein, J.L. (1997) *Looking Good and Doing Good: Corporate Philanthropy and Corporate Power*, Bloomington, IN: Indiana University Press.

Home Depot Inc. (2005a) 'Home Depot Inc.: Social Responsibility'. Available at: corporate.homedepot.com/wps/portal/!ut/p/.cmd/cs/.ce/7_0_A/.s/7_0_11N/_s.7_0_A/7_0_11N

Hopkins, M. (2003) *The Planetary Bargain: Corporate Social Responsibility Matters*, Sterling, VA: Earthscan Publications.

Huggins, P (2005) 'Wal-Mart's Day of Caring "greatest thing" to Disabled Workers', *Decatur Daily*, 31 July, Decatur

Jackson, I.A. and Nelson, J. (2004) *Profits with Principles: Seven Strategies for Delivering Value with Values*, New York: Doubleday.

Juris, J. (2005) 'Violence Performed and Imagined: Militant Action, the Black Bloc, and the Mass Media in Genoa', *Critique of Anthropology* 24(4): 413–432

Kotler, P. and Lee, N. (2005) *Corporate Social Responsibility: Doing the Most Good for Your Company and Your Cause*, Hoboken, NJ: Wiley.

Kozloff, E.P., Gordon, I.J. and Higgenbotham, R. (2005) *Not in My Backyard: An Analysis of Community Opposition to Big Box Retail*, Bernstein Research Call, 25 April.

King, S. (2001) 'An All Consuming Cause: Breast Cancer, Corporate Philanthropy, and the Market for Generosity', *Social Text* 19(4): 115–143.

Klein, N. (2000) *No Logo: Taking Aim at the Brand Bullies*, Toronto: Knopf Canada.

Lev, B., Petrovits, C. and Radhakrishnan, S. (2006) 'Is Doing Good Good for You? Yes, Charitable Contributions Enhance Revenue Growth', Social Sciences Research Network, Working Paper. Available at: www.ssrn.com/

Los Angeles City Council (2003) 'Options for Regulating the Development of Superstores, Housing, Community, and Economic Development Committee'. Available at: www.wakeupwalmart.com/facts/regulating-development.pdf

Norman, A. (1999) *Slam Dunking Wal-Mart*, Atlantic City, NJ: Raphel Marketing.

Ostrower, F. (1995) *Why the Wealthy Give: The Culture of Elite Philanthropy*, Princeton, NJ: Princeton University Press.

PBS Frontline (2004) *Is Wal-Mart Good for America? Interview: Jon Lehman*, PBS Frontline Online, Available at: www.pbs.org/wgbh/pages/frontline/shows/walmart/interviews/lehman.html

Peck, J. (2001) *Workfare States*, New York: Guilford Press.

Pfizer Inc. (2005) 'Caring for Community – Partnerships for a Healthier World', Pfizer Inc. Available at: www.pfizer.com/pfizer/subsites/philanthropy/caring/index.jsp

Pollin, R. (2002) *Contours of Descent: U.S. Economic Fractures and the Landscape of Global Austerity*, London: Verso.

Rampton, S. (2002) 'Corporate Social Responsibility and the Crisis of Globalization', *PR Watch Newsletter* Third Quarter, 9(3). Available at: www.prwatch.org/prwissues/2002Q3/csr.html

Rayman-Bacchus, L. (2004) 'Assessing Trust in, and Legitimacy of, the Corporate', in D. Crowther and L. Rayman-Bacchus (eds) *Perspectives on Corporate Social Responsibility*, Burlington, VT: Ashgate, pp. 21–41.

Robinson, T. (2004) 'Hunger, Discipline and Social Parasites: The Political Economy of the Living Wage', *Urban Affairs Review* 40(2): 246–268.

Saad-Filho, A. and Johnston, D. (2005) *Neoliberalism: A Critical Reader*, Ann Arbor, MI: Pluto Press.

Shamir, R. (2004a) 'The De-Radicalization of Corporate Social Responsibility', *Critical Sociology* 30(3): 669–689.

—— (2004b) 'Between Self-Regulation and the Alien Tort Claims Act: On the Contested Concept of Corporate Social Responsibility', *Law and Society Review* 38(4): 635–664.

Shell Inc. (2006) 'Environment and Society Shell'. Online. Available at: www.shell.com/home/content/envirosoc-en/welcome.html

Silver, I. (2001) 'Strategically Legitimizing Philanthropists' Identity Claims: Community Organizations as Key Players in the Making of Corporate Social Responsibility', *Sociological Perspectives* 44(2): 233–252.

Simmons, L. (2004) 'Labor-Welfare Linkages and the Imperative of Organizing Low-Wage Women Workers', in L. Simmons (ed.) *Welfare, the Working Poor, and Labor*, Armonk, NY: M.E. Sharpe, pp. 132–150.

Simons, R., Mintzberg, H. and Basu, K. (2002) 'Memo to: CEOs', *Fast Company Online* May (59). Available at: www.fastcompany.com/online/59/ceo.html

Slate (2005) 'The 2004 Slate 60: The 60 Largest American Charitable Contributions', Slate Online. Available at: www.specials.slate.com/slate60/2004/

Smeath, D. (2005) 'Taylorsville Gives New Wal-Mart a Warm Welcome', *Deseret Morning News* 25 August, Salt Lake City, Utah.

Sommerfeld, D. and Reisch, M. (2003) 'The 'Other America' After Welfare Reform: A View from the Nonprofit Sector', *Journal of Poverty* 7(1/2): 69–95

Sprawl Busters (2005) 'Sprawl Busters – International Clearinghouse for Anti-Sprawl Information'. Available at: www.sprawl-busters.com/

Stafford, J. (2004) 'Electronics retailer Best Buy to Open Fourth Store in Oklahoma City Metro Area', *The Daily Oklahoman*, 16 November, Oklahoma.

Starr, A. (2000) *Naming the Enemy: Anti-corporate Movements Confront Globalization*, London: Zed.

Stone, K. (2001) 'The Impact of "Big-Box" Building Materials Stores on Host Towns and Surrounding Counties in a Midwestern State', paper presented at 2001 Annual Meeting of the AAEA, Chicago, Illinois, August 5–8. Available at: amiba.net/pdf/stone_home_improvement_center_study.pdf

Tanner, J. and Gladman, K. (2005) 'Outside the Box: Guidelines for Retail Store Siting', Christian Brothers Investment Services, Inc. and Domini Social Investments. Available at: www.cbisonline.com/file/StoreSitingGuidelines.pdf

Target Stores Inc. (2005a) 'Target: Community Giving'. Available at: target.com/target_group/community_giving/index.jhtml

—— (2005b) 'The Target Foundation'. Available at: www.targetcorp.com/targetcorp_group/community/mission.jhtml

United Way of America (2005a) 'NCL Top Ten List, United Way of America Online'. Available at: www.national.unitedway.org/ncl/topten.cfm

—— (2005b) 'United Way of America: National Corporate Leaders', United Way of America, Available at: www.national.unitedway.org/ncl/aboutncl.cfm

United Way of Greater New Orleans Area (2005) '2005 Pacesetter Companies' www.unitedwaynola.org/for_companies/companies_that_care/pacesetter.htm

United Way of Meriden and Wallingford (2005) 'Day of Caring', United Way. Available at: www.unitedwaymw.org/CMSLite/default.asp?CMSLite_Page=83&Info=Day+of+Caring

United Way of Snohomish County (2004) 'United Way Mobilizes Volunteers for Day of Caring', United Way. Available at: www.uwsc.org/6_1_9.php

Valueline (2005) 'Wal-Mart; Target; Home Depot; Best Buy', Value-Line: Investment Research. Available at: www.valueline.com/

Varney, D. (2004) "A Crisis of Legitimacy': A Response to the Corporate Social Responsibility Index', published in the *Sunday Times*, 14 March 2004, *CSR Quest Point of View* (5). Available at: www.bitc.org.uk/resources/viewpoint/index varney.html

Wal-Mart Stores Inc. (2005a) 'Good.Works: The Wal-Mart Foundation'. Available at: www.walmartfoundation.org

—— (2005b) 'Wal-Mart and United Way Offer Support', Wal-Mart Foundation. Available at: www.walmartfoundation.org

Watson, D. (2002) 'Recession and Welfare Reform Increase Hunger in US', *World Socialist Web Site*, 11 May. Available at: www.wsws.org/articles/2002/may2002/food-m11.shtml

Werther, W. and Chandler, D. (2005) 'Strategic Corporate Social Responsibility as Global Brand Insurance', *Business Horizons* 48(4): 317–324.

Young, D.R. (1998) 'Corporate Partnerships: A Guide for the Nonprofit Manager', National Center on Nonprofit Enterprise. Available at: www.nationalcne.org/

Zabin, C., Dube, A. and Jacobs, K. (2004) 'The Hidden Cost of Low-wage Jobs in California', Center for Labor Research and Education, UC Berkeley. Available at: repositories.cdlib.org/ile/scl2004/01/

Part III

Global finance and socially responsible investing

7 Pension fund capitalism, pension fund socialism, and dissent from investment

Paul Langley

> [F]financial markets are cutting our throats with our own money, and it has to stop.
>
> (Leo W. Gerard, International President, United Steel Workers of America, 2001)

My focus in this chapter is on the place of the financial markets in funding retirement in the US and UK. I want to concentrate, in particular, on the political contestation of occupational pension fund investment practices. The sheer scale of the financial holdings of pension funds has led commentators to characterise contemporary Anglo-American capitalism as 'pension fund capitalism' (Clark 2000; Toporowski 2000). By way of general illustration, US pension funds hold in excess of one-third of all US bonds and one-quarter of all US equities. The market value of the assets of many occupational pension funds is higher than that of their sponsoring employer. For international organisations and economists, the funds provide a highly significant pool of capital that furthers the efficiency and dynamic restructuring of the 'real' or productive economy (e.g. OECD 1998; Clowes 2000). For critics and labour activists such as Leo W. Gerard, however, the investment relationships between pension funds and the productive economy are far from virtuous. Workers' pension savings are controlled through investment practices that maximise short-term financial returns at the expense of workers' jobs, pay, and long-term welfare. Indeed, this has been widely accepted amongst organised labour in the US since the work of Rifkin and Barber (1978) nearly three decades ago. A class-based politics of resistance tends to follow from this critique, as 'pension fund activists' in US multi-employer and public pension schemes in particular seek to inscribe the interests and values of labour into investment practices. Put differently, the move towards what management doyen Peter Drucker (1976/1995) calls 'pension fund socialism' is held to rest not only on workers' ownership of the means of production through their retirement saving, but also on wresting control over fund investment from the grip of finance capital. Writing worker's interests into investment practices has included channelling capital to directly support unionised employment in the productive economy. But pension fund activism has increasingly come to focus on the 'screening' of investments on the basis of a range of 'ethical' criteria, and shareholder resolutions and campaigns that promote corporate governance reform.

What follows is divided into three sections. The first two sections provide, respectively, a brief overview of the rise of pension fund capitalism, and an examination of the intellectual and political currents of pension fund socialism. The final part of the chapter reflects on the politics of dissent over pension fund investment. As recent contributions to the social theory of finance stress, the power of finance turns on its constitution as highly rational, technical and scientific practices that are specific to 'finance' as a separable domain of more or less discrete actor-networks (de Goede 2005a; Leyshon and Thrift 1997; McKenzie 2006). Viewed in these terms, pension fund activism is of particular significance as it potentially re-politicises finance and poses a challenge to the legitimacy and rationality of existing investment practices. Nevertheless, I argue that dissent from investment is far more uncertain and ambiguous than tends to be assumed by advocates of pension fund socialism.

Pension fund socialism calls for a politics of resistance that opposes a clearly defined enemy – that is, finance capital, or what Leo W. Gerard calls the 'financial markets'. The grounds for this opposition, and the activism that follows, are that finance is 'cutting our throats'. While the collective 'our' that is summoned up here refers in the first instance to unionised labour, pension fund socialism tends to claim to be operating in the name of the working class understood as a cohesive set of interests. 'Our own money' is to be used, then, to secure a very different economy in which 'our' interests are to be privileged through transformed investment practices. This is typical of calls for financial resistance more broadly, where only united opposition to realise a logical and coherent alternative appears capable of resisting financial power. As the course of activist campaigns for corporate governance reform illustrates, the simple juxtaposition of the interests of finance capital against the interests of working-class pension fund members cannot be maintained. Furthermore, such a clear and unequivocal representation of the 'subjects' of dissent is especially problematic during a period in which the vast majority of workers either continue to be excluded from occupational pensions, or are members of defined-contribution single-employer pension funds. As I argue by way of my concluding remarks, however, recognising the presence of such ambiguities within the politics of pension fund socialism should not be taken as a sign of weakness. Rather, the tendency to assume that resisting financial power requires united working-class opposition to realise a consistent and coherent alternative actually limits and devalues the wider and multiple forms of dissent from investment.

Pension fund capitalism

The notion of 'pension fund capitalism' (Clark 2000; Toporowski 2000) draws our attention to the sheer scale of the interdependencies that bind

Anglo-American occupational pension funds and the financial markets. For Minns (2001: 31, 33), for example, contemporary financial markets have come to 'rely substantially on the structure of social security provision' such that '"social security capital" is now as important as other sources of capital . . . It is a key element in fueling the expansion of financial markets'. Blackburn (2002: 6) reckons that in 1999, prior to the bursting of the 'new economy' stock market bubble, the global assets of pension funds were valued at US$13,000 billion. Around 60 per cent of these assets ($7,800 billion) belonged to US savers, with those of UK savers worth US$1,400 billion. He places these figures in perspective by noting that, according to OECD calculations, the world-wide value of stock markets at the time stood at $23,000 billion. Occupational pension funds built up their holdings of financial market instruments gradually in the twentieth century, expanding significantly during the post-1945 era through the Fordist compact between the major employers and their largely male workforce (Cutler and Waine 2001).

'Pension fund capitalism' also directs us to consider a subtle but highly significant change in the interdependencies between the funds and the financial markets. As I have argued elsewhere, since the early 1980s, the discourse and institutions of asset management have come to frame the marshalling of collective retirement savings (Langley 2004a). While the formerly dominant place of sovereign and corporate bonds within pension funds' portfolios had already been eroded during the 1960s and 1970s as relatively high rates of inflation undermined the returns from these fixed-interest instruments, it was the rise of asset management that ensured that 'investment' took on new meanings and that equity holdings were further consolidated.

Advocates of pension fund capitalism not only stress the importance of financial market investment to funding retirement, but also trumpet the contribution of fund investment practices to economic growth and competitiveness. Such views inform, for example, agendas for the reform of continental European pension arrangements (see, for example, OECD 1998). Here the threat of an 'ageing society' and the associated 'crisis' of current state-based provision – so-called 'unfunded' or 'pay-as-you-go' systems where pensions are paid through the taxation of current workers – is effectively transformed into an opportunity which can be grasped once the retirement savings of workers can be built up and invested in the financial markets (Minns 2001). Not dissimilarly, the relative competitiveness and apparent triumph of the Anglo-American 'model of capitalism' are traced to the presence of a vast pool of social security capital that supports the restructuring of the productive economy (e.g. Clowes 2000). It is the nature of these pension fund investment practices that is the principal focus for pension fund capitalism's detractors.

Critiques of pension fund investment, for the most part, turn on two related claims. First, fund investment concentrates on achieving short-term returns from secondary trading at the expense of a long-term concern with facilitating growth in the productive economy. While this claim is informed by a wider reading that casts contemporary financial markets as mechanisms for the speculative transfer of ownership claims across a whole host of assets (e.g. Henwood 1998), there are indications that specific features of pension fund investment prompt short-termism. The competitive process through which asset management contracts are awarded by funds' trustees, combined with the manner in which the success or otherwise of asset managers is benchmarked against their peers and market indexes, serves to institutionalise a focus on short-term performance (Langley 2004a). Funds typically undertake diversified investment strategies that are 'contrived to be both conservative – in the sense of concentrating on well-known brands and blue chip companies – and speculative – in the sense that they . . . slavishly follow market fads' (Blackburn 2002: 177). The overtly speculative side of investment ensures that, on a daily basis, attention focuses on the rapid and on-going opening and closing of opportunities for speculation in one type of asset or another. For example, pension funds became involved in the 1980s in so-called 'momentum investment' and index-tracker funds, whereby stocks are automatically purchased as their price rises and sold as prices fall. Moreover, pension funds became embroiled in a succession of largely discrete speculative waves as investment concentrated upon particular classes of assets: corporate restructuring and downsizing during the 1980s (Toporowski 2000); and the so-called 'emerging markets' and 'new economy' bubbles of the 1990s (Feng *et al.* 2001; Harmes 2001; Minns 2001).

Second, critics of fund investment claim that speculative short-termism not only starves the productive economy of desperately needed long-term capital, but also harms the prospects, wages, welfare and security of workers in particular. That 'labor's capital' (Ghilarducci 1992) invested through pension funds undermines the interests of workers is, then, a particularly frustrating paradox for many commentators and activists. Central to the paradox is the role that funds and their asset managers have played in extracting so-called 'shareholder value' from corporations. Shareholder value shapes, formats and performs an economy in which financial calculations such as ROCE (return on capital employed) dominate how the corporation is assessed, prompting destructive practices such as downsizing, sub-contracting, off-shoring, and mergers and acquisitions. Indeed, for some, shareholder value lies at the heart of a pervasive 'financialisation' of Anglo-America capitalism. Cutler and Waine (2001: 100), for example, describe financialisation as 'the marginalization of non-financial criteria for evaluating corporate performance' and 'the promotion of a regulatory framework conducive to the pursuit of shareholder value'. This 'regulatory framework' which is typically known as 'corporate governance' is primarily constituted through agency theory. As Lazonick and O'Sullivan (2000: 16) note, agency theorists 'believe that the market is always superior to organisations in the efficient allocation of resources' such that they are 'predisposed against corporate –

that is, managerial – control over the allocation of resources and returns in the economy'. For 'the market', read investors of all kinds, including pension funds.

Pension fund socialism

> In terms of socialist theory, the employees of America are the only true 'owners' of the means of production. Through their pension funds they are the only true 'capitalists' around, owning, controlling, and directing the country's 'capital fund'. The 'means of production', that is, the American economy ... is being run for the benefit of the country's employees.
>
> (Drucker [1976] 1995: 2–3)

As perhaps the key early proponent of the benefits of pension fund capitalism, highly influential management guru Peter F. Drucker also gave it an interesting spin. As he put it, the US had witnessed an 'unseen revolution' that had produced 'pension fund socialism'. 'Only in the United States are the employees through their pension funds also becoming the legal owners, the suppliers of capital, and the controlling force in the capitalist market' (ibid., p. 4). Drucker's tongue-in-cheek take on pension funds and 'socialist theory' nevertheless remains extremely illuminating thirty years on. As I have already highlighted, critics of fund investment stress not its 'benefit' for 'the country's employees', but the damage done to labour by labour's capital. Moreover, it is the democratic and egalitarian 'control' of fund investment that has become pivotal for critics and activists who wish to further workers' interests and establish a genuine pension fund socialism. As Hebb (2001: 2) summarises, 'The fundamental shift in the ownership of capital has not resulted in a corresponding shift in the control of capital.'

Writing at around the same time as Drucker, community activists Jeremy Rifkin and Randy Barber (1978) encouraged the US labour movement to re-orientate the focus of their campaigns from the reform of labour law to the control of multi-employer and public pension fund investment. Although the control of pension fund investment had been a subject within 'financial democracy' debates addressed by US liberal think tanks in the late 1950s (Ghilarducci 1992: 111–112), Rifkin and Barber are widely regarded to have kick-started thinking on what has been more recently described as 'a capital strategy for labor' (Hebb 2001: 2). Indeed, they provoked a rebuke from some of the early supporters of pension fund capitalism (e.g. Borjas 1979). Rifkin and Barber's ultimate goal was the rebirth of America's 'Graybelt' manufacturing heartland in the 'North' which, for them, had been subject to '"redlining"' by 'the banking community' and starved of investment (Rifkin and Barber 1978: 6). Given the concentration of 'the largest single pool of private capital in the world' in the multi-employer and public pension funds of the North, 'With control of these moneys, unions and public authorities can begin to take over more and more of the economic-planning and capital-allocation decisions that have, for so long, been the exclusive prerogative of the private capital sector' (ibid.: 10–11). Ultimately, control over 'pension-fund capital' is, for Rifkin and Barber, 'an opening wedge in the development of basic economic alternatives within the United States' (ibid.: 12).

US multi-employer funds – also known as 'Taft–Hartley funds' after the 1947 legislation that first regulated their organisation – are jointly established by employers and unions. Fund members are unionised, and are typically construction workers and teamsters who are likely to be employed by different firms during their working lives. Built up through the post-war era, multi-employer funds currently hold assets in excess of $430 billion (Marens 2004: 110). Although legally bound by a fiduciary duty to act in the interest of fund members, the boards of trustees that administer multi-employer funds are divided equally between union officials and representatives of the corresponding employers' association. As such, it is perhaps no surprise that multi-employer funds appeared to Rifkin and Barber as providing a realistic opportunity for labour's investment activism. However, given their massive holdings of labour's capital, achieving control over the investment practices of public pension funds was also an important objective for Rifkin and Barber. Though there is no guarantee that union officials will serve as trustees of public pension funds, the extensive unionisation of the state and local government employees that are the members of these funds does make representation on their boards a strong possibility (Rifkin and Barber 1978: 224–228). Currently only five of America's twenty largest pension funds by assets are single-employer schemes (General Motors, IBM, General Electric, Boeing, and Ford), with the remaining fifteen all public pension funds. The top five largest funds are all public funds, in a list that is topped by the California Public Employee Retirement System (CalPERS). CalPERS covers 1.4 million public employees and retirees and, at September 2005, had assets worth a massive $196 billion.[1]

The distinctive nature of many public pension funds in the UK, whereby member's contributions are not invested but instead flow into the state's coffers, rules them out of investment activism. There are, of course, a few notable exceptions which include the Universities Superannuation Scheme, the Trades Union Congress (TUC) pension fund, and a handful of local authority plans. Activists' attempts to install some sense of workers' control over investment in the last three decades have remained largely confined, then, to the US multi-employer and public pension funds. Strong advocacy networks have developed which extend into the academic community and include, for example, the Pensions and Capital Stewardship Project which is part of the Labor and Worklife Program at the Harvard Law School. Action and advocacy have concentrated on three main forms of activism. First, the channelling of labour's capital into so-called 'economically-targeted investments' (ETIs) that explicitly support unionised employment. Second, the use of 'screening' devices that bring 'ethical' considerations to bear in fund's investment strategies. And, third, 'shareholder activism' in support of corporate governance reforms that not only oppose the restructuring plans of recalcitrant managements, but also tend to create new legal rights for shareholders in the process.

Despite tripling in value since 1994 (Calabrese 2001: 93), the cumulative value of ETIs remains extremely small in the context of the overall holdings of US pension funds. Consider, for example, perhaps the most high profile ETIs that have received increased financial support over the last decade or so. The Union Labor Life Insurance Company and the American Federation of Labor-Congress of Industrial Organizations' (AFL-CIO) Housing Investment Trust (HIT) currently only holds in excess of $5 billion in real estate loans made to developers who employ unionised labour. HIT was joined by the Building Investment Trust (BIT) in 1988, a $1.5 billion conduit through which investors channel workers' capital into real estate (hotels, office buildings, etc.) that is managed by those who do not oppose the unionisation of labour (Marens 2004: 116). Despite a 1994 endorsement by the Department of Labor (DoL), suggesting that targeted investments did not necessarily stand in tension with the fiduciary duty of trustees to maximise returns on behalf of fund members, suspicions persist about union involvement in investment practices that arise largely out of the loans and kickbacks that came to bind the Teamsters' Central States fund and a string of Las Vegas casinos during the 1960s and 1970s. More recent campaigns, such as the Heartland Labor Capital Project co-sponsored by AFL-CIO and United Steelworkers of America, have nevertheless sought once again to raise awareness among trustees as to the possibilities of ETIs (Calabrese 2001).

Alongside ETIs, pension fund activism also includes the development and implementation of 'screening' techniques associated with so-called 'ethical' or 'socially responsible investing' (SRI). SRI draws on the legacy of many civic associations, most notably churches and universities, that have sought for centuries to avoid investment in, for example, the production of alcohol or military hardware. CalPERS, for instance, incorporates SRI criteria in the 'Permissible Country Index' (PCI) that it deploys in relation to its investment in emerging markets (see Chapter 8 in this volume). The PCI provides a set of weighted quantitative measures against which the appropriateness of investments are judged. Adherence to international labour standards does feature in the PCI, and poor scores in this regard provided the justification for CalPERS' decision to divest from Thailand, Malaysia, Indonesia and the Philippines in 2002. That said, the weighting given to labour standards remains low relative to financial market factors such as liquidity, volatility, settlement systems and transaction costs, and CalPERS continues to regard emerging markets as a short-term investment option.

The most significant form of pension fund activism, then, is arguably shareholder activism. O'Connor (2001) even goes as far to argue that corporate governance has displaced labour law to become the key site for contestation between capital and labour. A key initial milestone here was the coming together of three craft unions and seventeen public pension funds to found the Council of Institutional Investors in 1985. As Marens (2004: 113) notes, the formation of the Council was particularly significant as it focused activists' attention on the use of shareholder resolutions in order to cajole corporate governance reforms. The Council now represents more than 130 pension funds who, collectively, hold in excess of $3 trillion in assets. While Securities and Exchange Commission (SEC) rules prevent labour disputes from being raised through shareholders resolutions, all other decisions by corporate managers can be targeted by shareholder activists. As this form of investment activism took hold, it dovetailed with wider political moves on both the 'left' and 'right' to further shareholders rights and to encourage both institutional and individual investors to 'vote their shares'. Indeed, by the mid-1990s, DoL regulations required that all pension funds trustees vote on shareholder resolutions and even encouraged them to negotiate with managers and submit their own resolutions.

The shareholder activism of pension fund socialism has thus become increasingly bound up with the technicalities of proxy voting and shareholder resolutions. Resolutions are typically advisory in nature, such that even when they receive majority support they are not binding on management (Marens 2004). Once a company is targeted by a resolution, it is common for funds and other institutional investors to voice their concerns in private meetings with executives. These meetings take place in the shadow of the likely shareholder vote on the resolution and, if shareholders concerns are addressed, lead to the withdrawal of the resolution. Resolutions often address the independence of executive boards, the removal of financial disincentives that discourage takeovers (so-called 'poison pills'), and the structure of compensation boards that award excessive 'fat cat' executive salary packages including stock options, 'golden hellos' and 'golden parachutes'.

Leadership in the shareholder activism of pension funds has come from major public funds such as CalPERS, CalSTRS (California State Teachers Retirement System), and the New York City Employees Retirement System. The majority of individuals that serve as trustees on the boards of these funds have links to, or are widely regarded as sympathetic to, organised labour. CalPERS and the other funds are, according to William Greider (2005), 'pursuing far-ranging possibilities for reforming the economic system', and are nothing short of 'the vanguard of a new kind of reform politics'. CalPERS have been the standard bearers for US shareholder activism since the mid-1980s. They were the first of the massive public pension funds to heighten their proxy voting activity during this period, and late California State Treasurer Jesse Unruh was a key figure in the formation of the Council of Institutional Investors (Ghilarducci 1992: 126). More recently, the $300 billion of losses incurred by public pension funds as a result of the collapse of Enron have further galvanised CalPERS and CalSTRS, often in conjunction with trustees from New York, Connecticut, North Carolina, Iowa and elsewhere, to more aggressively pursue those who they see as damaging the interests of their future retirees (Greider 2005). Taking advantage of the Private Securities Litigation Reform Act of 1995 which clamped down on profiteering by the legal profession and gave institutional investors the lead role in investor class-action suits, the New York State Common Retirement Fund wrested a $6 billion payout from investment bankers in the wake of the WorldCom fraud (Donovan 2005).

Dissent from investment

In this final section of the chapter I want to argue that the politics of dissent over pension fund investment is far more ambivalent than tends to be assumed by advocates of pension fund socialism. To be specific, I wish to question the 'subject' of the politics of dissent from investment. Pension fund socialism constructs a singular and unified working-class interest in pensions by forging an ontological juxtaposition against finance capital as an already dominant other. However, the drawing of such a binary opposition is misleading and cannot be maintained, and the assumed coherence of a working-class interest also overlooks the diverse experiences of workers with regard to pensions. Let us examine these two sets of ambiguities in more detail in turn.

Pension fund socialism calls for a politics of resistance that opposes a clearly defined enemy – that is, what those writing in the Marxist tradition would typically call 'finance capital' or the 'financial fraction of capital' (e.g. Gill 2003; Harvey 1999). A sense of unity and purpose among workers is created through the securing of a singular foe – you are either with us or you are with them. The key to transformation appears to lie in wresting control over pension fund investment from finance capital. As I have argued elsewhere, however, pension fund capitalism is not simply a project co-ordinated by and operating in the powerful interest of finance capital, its exploitative and exclusionary form deliberately obscured through the manufacture of workers' 'false consciousness'. Rather, occupational pensions networks are constituted through hierarchical but nonetheless decentralised power relations in which techniques of calculation (such as asset management and actuarialism) and the assembly of financial subjects are central (Langley 2004b; 2006). Viewed in these terms, pension fund activism is of particular significance as it re-politicises finance and poses a potential challenge to the legitimacy of existing investment practices. As Greider (2005) puts it, 'remote skirmishes over esoteric financial rules' have become 'a very visible political fight'. As the standard bearer for pension fund activism, CalPERs has, in particular, been in the eye of the political storm. For example, considerable intrigue surrounded the de-selection of Sean Harrigan, the regional director of the United Food and Commercial Workers, as CalPERS board president in December 2004 (Williams Walsh 2004).

While emphasising the importance of the re-politicisation of investment through pension fund activism, a decentralised and constitutive reading of financial power also suggests working-class subjectivity is not as unambiguous as advocates of pension fund socialism would have it. Put differently and in the terms of Gibson-Graham (1996), 'capitalocentric' accounts that emphasise the all-pervasive power of capital and which, therefore, demand unequivocal opposition to capital in the name of the working class are especially problematic in pension fund capitalism. Capitalocentrism leads us to overlook the partial, fragmented, contingent and contested nature of financial power within pension fund capitalism. Individuals perform multiple economic and non-economic subject positions that cannot simply be reduced to their place in the capitalist relations of production. Workers who are members of pension funds are, at once, consumers, investors and shareholders, and are also likely to be men, baby-boomers, credit card holders, and fathers. In the words of Foucault (1976: 96), it follows that there can indeed be 'no great refusal' which steps outside of the power relations of pension fund capitalism to establish a pension fund socialism, but rather 'a plurality of resistances' which may be 'possible, necessary, improbable', 'spontaneous, savage, solitary, concerted', and 'quick to compromise, interested, or sacrificial' (cf. Amoore 2006). So, while pension fund activism may succeed in enlivening a radicalised working-class subjectivity, that subjectivity will be a partial, momentary and contradictory solidarity.

Shareholder activist campaigns for corporate governance reform are particularly illustrative of the problems of drawing a binary opposition between the interests of finance capital and those of the working-class. Consider the description of union shareholder activism offered by influential proponent Marleen O'Connor:

> Of course, labor shareholders have a general interest in promoting the long-term goals of adequate and secure workers' retirement income, and so seek corporate governance arrangements that prevent managerial self-dealing. Yet good corporate governance practices can benefit workers as well as shareholders; specifically, such practices serve as a floor that will lead to management turnover when firms perform badly. (2001: 70)

What is clear is that for those involved in shareholder activism, it is often prefaced not on an explicit challenge to finance capital and the drive for shareholder value, but on the assumption that 'good corporate governance' and financial performance simultaneously benefit pension fund members, workers, and wider shareholders. The phrase 'CalPERS effect', for example, is widely used by US asset managers and institutional investors. In the light of the clear-cut advocacy of CalPERS shareholder activism in readings provided by the likes of Greider (2005), what is particularly striking is that the 'CalPERS effect' does not refer to the consequences of the fund's activism on behalf of workers, far from it. Rather, the 'CalPERS effect' refers to the consequences for the stock prices of those corporations who are included on CalPERS annual hit list for poor financial performance and corporate governance practices. As the financial results and governance of these firms typically improve in response to pressure from CalPERS, so their stock price tends to outperform the relevant benchmark indices (CalPERS 1995).

More broadly, analyses that seek to question whether shareholder activism lives up to the promise of pension fund socialism tend to highlight important paradoxes. Marens (2004) concludes, for example, by noting that shareholder activism that operates in the name of 'good corporate governance' and extracts shareholder value may further erode the capacities of corporate managers to undertake strategies that deviate from production patterns that are flexible, lean, out-sourced etc. For Ghilarducci (1992: 131–2), meanwhile, pension fund activists have embraced discourses of property rights in corporate governance campaigns and, therefore, become defenders of one of the central pillars of financial power at the same time as seeking to further the interests of workers. In the words of CalPERS (1995: 1, original emphasis), shareholder activism is 'the prudent exercise of *ownership* rights, toward the goal of increased share value' (see also Chapter 8 in this volume).

To reiterate, it would be possible, following David Harvey (1999), to interpret these paradoxes as a function of a wider contradiction and thus retain a sharp distinction between the interests of finance capital and the working class. For Harvey, 'workers have a strong stake in the preservation of the very system that exploits them because of the destruction of that system entails the destruction of their savings' (ibid.: 263). In Harvey's Marxist terms, as Soederberg (2008) notes, workers' savings only arise from their exploitation in commodity production and, to ensure returns on their pension funds for their retirement, workers are forced to expose themselves further to that exploitation. What marks out the interests of workers from those of finance capital, from this perspective, is that workers by definition cannot rely solely on returns from investment. However, to take Harvey's position would require us to hold class identity as ontologically prior in processes of identification. It would also require us to understand class interests as fully constituted and overriding, rather than recognising that subjects' perceived and multiple self-interests (as workers, pension fund members, investors, etc.) are discursively framed and manifest in their reflective practices. We would, therefore, miss the ambiguities that mark dissent from investment. Significantly, we would also retain the assumption of a clear and unified working-class interest in investment.

Pension fund socialism seeks to operate in the name of the working class as a singular and coherent set of interests. Labour's capital is to be used to secure a very different economy to that which prevails at present, one in which the interests of the working class are to be privileged. Two dynamics ensure, however, that calling up a universal working-class interest in dissent from investment is highly problematic. First, as Ghilarducci (1992) reveals, pension fund activism reproduces and further entrenches a cleavage between unionised members of occupational pension schemes and other workers. As she puts it, 'Unions must satisfy a group of voluntary members, most of whom want a service union. Therefore, a union pension strategy … must advance traditional union goals: surviving, organizing, and bargaining' (ibid.: 130). It is this 'defensive' pension activism that for the most part prevails, rather than attempts 'to transform the relationship between workers and financial institutions' (ibid.: 121). Consider, for example, the relatively limited take-up of ETIs in contrast with much more widespread shareholder activism and screening. For pension fund activists, the retirement security of unionised workers who are members of occupational pension funds is prioritised, even though maximising rates of return on investment is, at the same time, also recognised as likely to be counter to the interests of workers in general.

Second, an enduring feature of Anglo-American occupational pensions is that they are not mediated or experienced primarily in terms of class. It is not simply that the distribution of occupational pensions is regressive, as higher-income earners are more likely to receive greater tax relief and larger benefits. Long-standing dynamics of inequality have also created large numbers of working-class households who are stubbornly excluded from occupational pensions and unionised employment, a situation that is particular acute for unemployed, part-time or temporary workers and working-class women. The flexibilisation of work and the creation of greater numbers of unprotected workers in the last quarter of a century have served to amplify these dynamics although, noticeably, women workers are now much more likely to be members of a pension scheme than in the past. For example, in the UK, 40 percent of employed women contributed to an occupational pension by the late 1990s, up from 25 per cent in 1967. Coverage of male employees fell from 66 per cent to 55 per cent over the same period (ABI 2000: 17). Radical politics and dissent from investment that recognise these cleavages and antagonisms cannot be reduced to the language of class.

As 'defined benefit' (DB) or 'final salary' single-employer occupational pension schemes are increasingly being replaced by 'defined contribution' (DC) or 'money purchase' plans (Langley 2004a; Mitchell and Schieber 1998), the highly differentiated experiences of workers in occupational pensions are, at once, further reinforced and rearticulated. To a greater degree than at any time since the early 1960s, workers who are members of DB schemes that offer collective insurance for old age guaranteed by employers are now the exception rather that the rule. Both DB and DC schemes translate tax-favoured contributions by employees and sponsoring employers into collective holdings of equities, bonds and other financial instruments. While the scale and ratio of employer and employee contributions vary across both DB and DC, it is difference in terms of benefits/returns and responsibility that primarily distinguishes the two types of fund. Members of DC plan, which are also known as '401(k)s' in the US as they commonly use the 401(k) tax code, are responsible for their own investment decisions, and typically choose from a range of mutual funds. The contribution of the plan to their retirement income is not guaranteed as under the 'final salary' promise, but is determined solely by the returns from their investments.

The upshot of the move from DB to DC, then, especially alongside ongoing attempts to minimise state-based pension provision, is an individualisation of responsibility and risk in saving for retirement that turns on the making of responsible investor subjects (Langley 2006). Retirement is presently represented as a technical problem to be solved by the individual who calculates, embraces and bears financial market risk through their investment practices during their working life. Put differently, our confrontations with the uncertainty of future retirement are immediately depoliticised and no longer elusive or contested once they become anchored in the realm of risk and individual investment. As others have suggested more broadly, the process of individualisation necessarily entails the disintegration of previously existing collective social forms such as class, family and welfare (Bauman 2001; Beck and Beck-Gernsheim 2001). Although the potential for class politics clearly does not evaporate with the move to DC, further ambiguities are certainly introduced into dissent from investment in general, and the specific assumption of a unified working-class interest looks increasingly outmoded and anachronistic.

Conclusion

Confronted by financial power and pension fund capitalism, advocates of pension fund socialism ground dissent from investment in a series of identity claims that create a unified collective working-class opposition to finance capital. In this chapter I have shown, however, that dissent from investment is far more ambiguous than tends to be assumed by advocates of pension fund socialism. These ambiguities arise from the web of relations that bind pension fund members and finance capital, and the absence of a singular working-class interest in pension fund investment. Such a reading will not sit well with pension fund activists and many scholars of finance who, like advocates of pension fund socialism, offer calls for financial resistance that suggest that omnipresent financial power requires united hostility to realise a consistent and coherent alternative (cf. de Goede 2005b). Often implicit within this activism and scholarship is the assumption that to deny a singular working-class interest and the possibility of 'a great refusal' is to somehow collapse pessimistically in the face of financial power.

In highlighting the ambiguities of pension fund socialism, however, I want to conclude, not pessimistically, but with a positive message and a call for further research into dissent from investment. Re-reading the work of Laclau and Mouffe (1985), Butler *et al.* (2000: 1) open by noting that 'new social movements often rely on identity-claims, but "identity" itself is never fully constituted; in fact, ... identification is not reducible to identity'.

There is an antagonism or incommensurability between identification and identity. But, as they stress, 'It does not follow that the failure of identity to achieve complete determination undermines the social movements at issue' (ibid.: 1–2). We should not fear the 'failure' of a single and coherent working-class interest in dissent from investment, but instead need to 'value this "failure" as a condition of democratic contestation itself' (ibid.: 2). Put differently, at the very moment that pension fund socialism opens up and re-politicises pension fund investment, the ontological primacy given to class simultaneously closes down and de-values the multiplicity of actual and potential forms taken by dissent from investment. For instance, pension fund socialists would, no doubt, see little of value in the parodies of the rational and scientific character of investment offered by comedy and art (de Goede 2005b; Raley 2005). Although it is the case that this carnivalesque dissent from investment may not expressly profess a wish to overthrow investment or hold out a blueprint for the future, it nevertheless provokes a disturbance in the meaning and purpose of 'investment'.

While further research is required into the place of 'the carnival of money' (de Goede 2005b) in dissent from investment, the pervasive processes of individualisation underway in Anglo-American pensions also suggest additional possibilities. There is a temptation to view individualisation as necessarily the enemy of (working-class) collectivism in dissent from investment. For Greider (2005), for example, California Governor Arnold Schwarzenegger's recent proposals to break up CalPERS by offering public employees DC accounts would disperse 'its financial power' and dilute 'its ability to exercise reform leverage'. Yet, while the individualisation of responsibility and risk de-politicises pensions, it also presents the prospect of alternative forms of everyday dissent that interfere with this rationalisation, challenge what it means to be 'an investor', and thereby contribute to the re-politicisation of investment. As I have argued elsewhere (Langley 2007), the investor subjects assembled through the individualisation of pension provision are necessarily 'uncertain subjects'. Contradictions such as the inability of investment – as a technology that (self-)governs through the calculative prism of 'risk' – to overcome future uncertainty ensure that the making of 'the investor' is highly contingent and can never be completed. Negotiations and contestation of the making of investor subjects are not, of course, unproblematic. Dissent from financial market investment on both sides of the Atlantic includes, for example, 'investment' in residential property, as individuals perceive their retirement and financial interests to be best served by 'trading up' and/or by participating in the 'buy-to-let' market. Nevertheless, the intensified subjectivisation of power carried through processes of individualisation also creates opportunities for immanent dissent that may be connected in unpredictable but potentially progressive ways. Just as practices are called for to invest more effectively in order to provide for retirement by, for example, diversifying a portfolio into high-risk 'emerging market' equities, so the door is left open to similarly individualised practices that may generate a collective force for compassion and solidarity.

One notable area for further research in this regard is the so-called 'ethical investment' practices that, in many ways, parallel the 'screening' pursued by some multi-employer and public pension funds. An ethical investor will typically choose from a menu of mutual funds that have been 'screened' and branded according to various 'positive' or 'negative' criteria, the former enabling investment in companies that, for example, are involved in recycling and conservation, and the latter leading to the avoidance of companies linked, for example, to the arms trade. Stock market indices such as FTSE4Good provide, meanwhile, a touchstone and benchmark for the performance of ethical investments. Dedicated websites, for example, socialfunds.com, and publications have also developed in support of ethical investment. $1 in every $8 invested in the US in 1998 made use of socially and environmentally responsible investment vehicles (Hebb 2001: 5). Ethical investment practices certainly transform everyday experiences of investment in important ways, and may indeed contest the assumption that principles are necessarily sacrificed in order to make a profit. Becker and McVeigh (2001), for example, are keen to stress that there is little evidence that ethical investments under-perform relative to the market in general. That the first concern of proponents is almost always to put to rest the assumption that investing in an ethical manner necessarily reduces returns is, however, potentially insightful. Further research is needed, then, that asks how tactics of ethical investment can question the dominant representation of individual investment as rational and integral to a secure and autonomous life, and at the same time merely appear to add moral bells and whistles to investment as self-care and collective gain. Either way, what is certainly clear is that recognising the absence of a unified working-class interest should not be taken as an indication of the impossibility of dissent from investment, far from it.

Note

1 www.pionline.com/page.cms?pageId=624. Accessed 14 February 2006.

References

Amoore, L. (2006) 'There is No Great Refusal': The Ambivalent Politics of Resistance', in M. de Goede (ed.) *International Political Economy and Postructuralism*, Basingstoke: Palgrave, pp. 255–274.

Bauman, Z. (2001) *The Individualized Society*, Cambridge: Polity Press.

Beck, U. and Beck-Gernsheim, E. (2001) *Individualization*, London: Sage.

Becker, E. and McVeigh, P. (2001) 'Social Funds in the United States: Their History, Financial Performance, and Social Impacts', in A. Fung, T. Hebb and J. Rogers (eds) *Working Capital: The Power of Labor's Pensions*, Ithaca, NY: Cornell University, pp. 44–66.

Blackburn, R. (2002) *Banking on Death or, Investing in Life: The History and Future of Pensions*, London: Verso.

Borjas, G.J (1979) *Union Control of Pension Funds: Will the North Rise Again?* San Francisco, CA: Institute for Contemporary Studies.

Butler, J., Laclau, E. and Žižek, S. (2000) *Contingency, Hegemony, Universality: Contemporary Dialogues on the Left*, London: Verso.

Calabrese, M. (2001) 'Building on Success: Labor-Friendly Investment Vehicles and the Power of Private Equity', in A. Fung, T. Hebb and J. Rogers (eds) *Working Capital: The Power of Labor's Pensions*, Ithaca, NY: Cornell University Press, pp. 93–127.

California Public Employee Retirement System (1995) 'Why Corporate Governance Today? A Policy Statement', 14 August. Available at: www.calpers-governance.org/viewpoint/default.asp

Clark, G.L (2000) *Pension Fund Capitalism*, Oxford: Oxford University Press.

Clowes, M.J (2000) *The Money Flood: How Pension Funds Revolutionized Investing*, New York: John Wiley and Sons, Ltd.

Cutler, T. and Waine, B. (2001) 'Social Insecurity and the Retreat from Social Democracy: Occupational Welfare in the Long Boom and Financialisation', *Review of International Political Economy* 8(1): 96–117.

De Goede, M. (2005a) *Virtue, Fortune, and Faith: A Genealogy of Finance*, Minneapolis, MN: University of Minnesota Press.

—— (2005b) 'Carnival of Money: Politics of Dissent in an Era of Globalizing Finance', in L. Amoore (ed.) *The Global Resistance Reader*, London: Routledge, pp. 379–391.

Donovan, K. (2005) 'Legal Reform Turns a Steward Into an Activist', *The New York Times*, online edition, 16 April.

Drucker, P.F (1976/1995) *The Unseen Revolution/The Pension Fund Revolution*, New Brunswick, NJ: Transaction Publishers.

Feng, H., Froud, J., Sukukdev, J., Haslam, C. and Williams, K. (2001) 'A New Business Model? The Capital Market and the New Economy', *Economy and Society* 30(4): 467–503.

Foucault, M. (1976) *The Will to Knowledge: The History of Sexuality*, vol. 1, London: Penguin.

Gerard, L.W (2001) 'Foreword', in A. Fung, T. Hebb and J. Rogers (eds) *Working Capital: The Power of Labor's Pensions*, Ithaca, NY: Cornell University Press, pp. vii–viii.

Ghilarducci, T. (1992) *Labor's Capital: The Economics and Politics of Private Pensions*, Cambridge, MA: MIT Press.

—— (2001) 'Small Benefits, Big Pension Funds, and How Governance Reforms Can Close the Gap', in A. Fung, T. Hebb and J. Rogers (eds) *Working Capital: The Power of Labor's Pensions*, Ithaca, NY: Cornell University Press, pp. 158–180.

Gibson-Graham, J.K (1996) *The End of Capitalism (As We Knew It): A Feminist Critique of Political Economy*, Oxford: Blackwell.

Gill, S. (2003) *Power and Resistance in the New World Order*, Basingstoke: Palgrave Macmillan.

Greider, W. (2005) 'The New Colossus', *The Nation*, February 28, online edition. Available at: www.thenation.com/doc/20050228/greider.

Harmes, A. (2001) *Unseen Power: How Mutual Funds Threaten the Political and Economic Wealth of Nations*, Toronto: Stoddart Publishing Co.

Harvey, D. (1999) *The Limits to Capital*, London: Verso.

Hebb, T. (2001) 'Introduction: The Challenge of Labor's Capital Strategy', in A. Fung, T. Hebb and J. Rogers (eds) *Working Capital: The Power of Labor's Pensions*, Ithaca, NY: Cornell University Press.

Henwood, D. (1998) *Wall Street: How it Works and for Whom*, New York: Verso.

Laclau, E. and Mouffe, C. (1985) *Hegemony and Socialist Strategy: Towards a Radical Democratic Politics*, London: Verso.

Langley, P. (2004a) 'In the Eye of the "Perfect Storm": The Final Salary Pensions Crisis and Financialisation of Anglo-American Capitalism', *New Political Economy* 9(4): 539–558.

—— (2004b) 'Investing For Retirement: The Structural Power of Finance and Anglo-American Occupational Pensions', paper presented to the International Studies Association Annual Convention, Montreal, March.

—— (2006) 'The Making of Investor Subjects in Anglo-American Pensions', *Environment and Planning D: Society and Space* 24(6): 919–934.

—— (2007) 'The Uncertain Subjects of Anglo-American Financialisation', *Cultural Critique*, Special Issue: Cultures of Finance, 65: 67–91.

Lazonick, W. and O'Sullivan, M. (2000) 'Maximising Shareholder Value: A New Ideology for Corporate Governance', *Economy and Society* 29(1): 13–35.

Leyshon, A. and Thrift, N. (1997) *Money/Space: Geographies of Monetary Transformation*, London: Routledge.

Marens, R. (2004) 'Waiting for the North to Rise: Revisiting Barber and Rifkin after a Generation of Union Financial Activism in the U.S.', *Journal of Business Ethics* 52(1): 109–123.

McKenzie, D. (2006) *An Engine, Not a Camera: How Financial Models Shape Markets* Cambridge, MA: MIT Press.

Minns, R. (2001) *The Cold War in Welfare: Stock Markets versus Pensions* London: Verso.

Mitchell, O.S. and Schieber, S.J. (1998) 'Defined Contribution Pensions: New Opportunities, New Risks', in O.S. Mitchell and S.J. Schieber (eds) *Living with Defined Contribution Pensions: Remaking Responsibility for Retirement*, Philadelphia, PA: University of Pennsylvania Press, pp. 1–14.

O'Connor, M. (2001) 'Labor's Role in the Shareholder Revolution', in A. Fung, T. Hebb and J. Rogers (eds) *Working Capital: The Power of Labor's Pensions*, Ithaca, NY: Cornell University Press, pp. 67–92.

OECD (1998) *Maintaining Prosperity in an Ageing Society*, Paris: OECD.

Raley, R. (2005) 'Virtual Money: Data Visualisation and Financial Capitalism', paper presented to the Cultures of Money workshop, University of Amsterdam, October.

Rifkin, J. and Barber, R. (1978) *The North Will Rise Again: Pensions, Politics and Power in the 1980s*, Boston: Beacon Press.

Soederberg, S. (2008) 'Deconstructing the Official Treatment for "Enronitis": The Sarbanes–Oxley Act and the Neoliberal Governance of Corporate America', *Critical Sociology* 34(2/3), in press.

Toporowski, J. (2000) *The End of Finance: Capital Market Inflation, Financial Derivatives and Pension Fund Capitalism*, London: Routledge.

Williams Walsh, M. (2004) 'California Pension Activist Expects to Be Ousted', *The New York Times*, online edition, 1 December.

8 Imposing social responsibility?

Pension funds and the politics of development finance

Susanne Soederberg

Since the early-1990s, private capital flows have become an important source of development finance for 'emerging markets' and are currently equal to four times the amount of international aid (International Finance Corporation 2005). Although foreign direct investment still constitutes the bulk of private capital flows, equity financing – by which publicly traded companies in the global South raise long-term capital through the sale of shares (equity) to investors – has become a significant source of credit for emerging markets. Since the 1990s, one of the main suppliers of equity financing has been Western-based institutional investors, such as pension and mutual funds. These new trends in development financing have underscored the creation of a growing number of assessment instruments for evaluating the ability of non-US public stock markets to support investment. Given the nature of equity finance, a central concern of these assessment exercises has been the compliance of the developing world with 'good' corporate governance practices, which are seen to reduce investor risk. Recently, however, various investors have sought to complement their understanding of good corporate governance practices with what may be broadly understood as 'socially responsible investment' (SRI) criteria.[1] Positive interpretations of SRI suggest that workers in the West may be able to harness the power of their investments – most often their accumulated pension funds – to promote beneficial social practices, such as good labour and environmental standards, in the rest of the world.

The investment assessment instrument of the union-based public pension fund California Public Employees' Retirement System (CalPERS) is a case in point. With an investment portfolio of $201 billion, CalPERS is the leading public pension fund in the US, and third largest in the world (CalPERS 2006). While the majority of CalPERS' funds are tied up in American corporations, an increasing amount is directed toward 27 emerging market economies. CalPERS draws on the information gathered by its investment assessment instrument, the Permissible Country Index (hereafter PCI or Index), in order to identify suitable investment climates. The Index, which forms the focal point of this chapter, provides an interesting study, as the 'activism' it is purported to reflect embodies the growing trend in corporate governance discourse to assume a greater concern for social issues under the banner of SRI. Through the application of its PCI, for example, CalPERS has sought to promote an understanding of corporate governance that is based on what it terms 'enduring value' in the developing world. The PCI aids CalPERS' investment committee in determining, on a quantitative basis, the levels of enduring value in an emerging market by measuring not only economic indicators (market factors), but also social indicators (non-market factors) involving equitable treatment of workers, the environment, and other commonly shared public assets.

Until now, the topic of equity financing has largely been treated in mainstream literature as an economic and technical instrument devoid of any considerations of politics and social power (cf. Hebb and Wójcik 2005). The argument developed here takes issue with this account and suggests that the PCI is neither a natural occurrence, nor has it emerged from an ahistorical and apolitical vacuum. Rather, CalPERS' assessment instrument is a contradictory and conflict-ridden strategy. The basic premises and objectives of the Index, including its appeal to SRI, are firmly rooted in the most recent version of neoliberal-led development policy, which international institutions refer to as 'entrepreneurial development' and which rests heavily on the promotion of the Anglo-American variant of corporate governance. This overarching capitalist strategy aims not only to encourage greater involvement of the private sector in development, but also legitimates deepening forms of dependency on, and discipline by, foreign capital in emerging markets as an attempt to ensure high rates of return on capital invested.

The PCI and the shifting geography of development finance

Before turning to a discussion of the content of the PCI, it is useful to highlight the nature of CalPERS' activism vis-à-vis emerging markets. CalPERS, along with other public pension funds, have acted as the main drivers of shareholder activism in the US, especially with regard to promoting the so-called good corporate governance agenda. There are important differences, however, between the type of activism pursued by CalPERS in the US and in the Third World. First, CalPERS, which is composed of 1.4 million union-based members of local public agencies in California, engages actively with its American corporate holdings. According to CalPERS, 'Shareowners collectively have the power to direct the course of corporations. The potential impact of this power is staggering. Shareholder activism is defined by a strategy of action that relies primarily on 'voice' as opposed to 'exit'' (Brancato 1997). In contrast, when engaging with publicly listed corporations in the global South, CalPERS appears to inverse its approach, preferring exit strategies as opposed to exercising voice. The reason for this difference in activism lies in the high levels of family and/or state ownership in publicly traded corporations in the developing world, which limits the ability of CalPERS to exercise voice in the same way it can within the American context.

Another related difference between the nature of CalPERS' activism in the US and in the developing world is the level at which good corporate governance practices are observed. Corporate governance can be addressed at a variety of levels from the national context (involving, for instance, rules and regulations making up the regulatory and legal framework of a country) to the company level (including appointments of non-executive directors, executive pay, board accountability, and so forth) (Gul and Tsui 2004). While CalPERS targets both levels in the context of the US, the public pension fund focuses exclusively on country factors with regard to emerging markets. Although the Index's national-level focus has come under significant criticism by its detractors for neglecting company-level reforms in emerging markets, the rationale behind this strategy is twofold. First, as a minority shareholder, CalPERS can effect very little change in Third World corporations. Second, if change is to take place at the company level, it must be accompanied by 'big picture' reforms at the level of legal and political systems.[2]

A third difference with regard to the nature of CalPERS' shareowner activism in the developing world is its temporal focus. While CalPERS generally tends to be a long-term investor (holding stock for seven to eight years) in the US, it engages in short-term behaviour when operating in emerging market economies. Indeed, given its penchant for exiting emerging markets when broad national indicators of the PCI point to unfavourable investment conditions, the nature of equity financing falls more into the camp of 'hot money', or short-term investments, rather than more stable and long-term investments, such as FDI. This observation stands in contrast to the above definition of equity finance offered by the International Finance Corporation (IFC), which stresses the 'long-term' feature of capital flows. The relatively short temporal nature of these investments also has important consequences with regard to its disciplinary features, such as living with the constant surveillance and scrutiny of the PCI, and the threat of capital flight and/or investment strike (e.g., when CalPERS removes or 'blacklists' a country from its PCI).

CalPERS management and board of directors, which includes both labour representatives and state officials, strongly believe in their proactive stance to ensure that companies in which the fund invests adhere to good corporate governance principles (CalPERS 2005). The PCI was designed to gauge the degree to which best practices in corporate governance are adhered to by governments in the Third World. Broadly, corporate governance refers to the relationships between a company's owners, managers, board of directors, and other stakeholders. It is important to underline that although there are many country-specific forms of corporate governance, CalPERS draws on the so-called Anglo-American model, with its emphasis on ensuring maximisation of shareholder value (Soederberg 2004). The inclination toward the US variant is not exclusive to CalPERS, but reflects a general consensus among policy-makers and private sector actors that the

Anglo-American model is the most desirable in achieving long-term profitability and economic efficiency (Reed 2004).

The Anglo-American model reflects the key interests of the PCI, namely: expanding the capitalist strategies of US institutional investors, and safeguarding their investments in the Third World through, for example, the creation of minority shareholder rights, protection of private property, and financial liberalisation. It is one example of what the IFC, mirroring the general shift in power from public to private sector forms of development financing, calls 'entrepreneurial development'. In the IFC's words, 'More and more development and aid organizations – multilateral banks, foundations, nonprofits – are looking at an entrepreneurial approach to development. They are asking how they can harness the power of private capital, free enterprise, and social entrepreneurship to bring about needed change' (International Financial Corporation 2005). The objective of this approach, according to the executive vice-president of the IFC, Lars Thunell, is 'to bolster the stability of existing capital markets and flows in the developing world by strengthening domestic financial institutions and deepening local currency markets' (ibid.). This is part of a broader shift within neoliberalism of strengthening the social and political institutions through which markets operate, and gives private capital a leading role in disciplining states to adopt market-reinforcing reforms (see Soederberg 2006). Thunell goes on to suggest that in order to achieve this goal, 'We need to improve corporate governance, so that more of the up-and-coming companies that are creating jobs can tap into the capital in the global economy' (International Financial Corporation 2005: 11). The preference for the Anglo-American model, however, is not simply an external imposition. It is warmly embraced by some indigenous capitalists in various parts of the developing world, such as India. The latter favour the American variant as it, unlike the German model, for example, does not provide a role for stakeholder involvement, such as employees and their unions (ibid.). As I suggest below, the general openness (or hostility, in the case of many East and Southeast Asian countries) to the Anglo-American model must be understood in historical terms; that is, as resulting from nation-specific relations of power between capital, labour, and the state.

The changing nature of neoliberal investment assessment Exercises

> American businesspeople are going to put capital where they feel they are welcome, where capital is honored and where they can get good returns.
>
> (John Snow, US Treasury Secretary, *Financial Times*, 14 June 2005)

Against the backdrop of the growth of shareholder activism in the US and the modest but growing interest by institutional investors in emerging markets, the CalPERS investment committee turned to Wilshire to devise a permissible markets analysis, also known as the PCI in 1987 (Wilshire Consulting 2005). As noted above, one of the main objectives of the Index was to gauge good corporate governance practices in emerging markets. With the onslaught of a deep recessionary environment in OECD countries in the early-1990s, coupled with relatively higher growth rates in various areas of the developing world, net equity flows to key areas of the global South began to pick up early in the decade, taking off in the mid-1990s. Given its heavy exposure in emerging markets, CalPERS, along with many institutional investors, was directly and adversely affected by the rash of financial crises in the global South, most notably the Peso Meltdown in 1994–1995, the East Asian Crisis in 1997, and crises in Russia and Brazil in 1998. In 1999, the CalPERS investment committee sought to redesign the manner in which the PCI assessed the stability and profitability of investment opportunities in developing countries. The amendment was significant as it included non-financial criteria in determining suitable investment sites in the developing world. The methodology of the PCI, for example, was revised to take into account two broad sources from which risks (defined as 'the standard deviation of returns') were believed to emanate, namely: (1) country factors, which concentrated on a narrowly defined concept of political risk; and (2) market factors, which related to issues such as market liquidity and volatility, market regulation, such as investor protection inscribed in a country's legal system, capital market openness, settlement proficiency, and/or transaction costs (Wilshire Consulting 2006).

In response to the Enron-style debacles in the US in the early 2000s, and the heavy losses incurred by institutional investors, including CalPERS, Wilshire was asked, once again, by CalPERS' Investment Committee to revise the instruments of the PCI. The major change to the permissible country criteria was a broader understanding regarding the definition of 'country factors' or political risk, which encompasses the following: (1) transparency; (2) productive labour practices; and (3) an expanded understanding of political stability (see Table 8.1). It should be emphasised that Wilshire does not determine which factors and sub-factors comprise the PCI. These factors are selected by the CalPERS board of directors, although the revised PCI was initiated by both the Treasury Department of California and the former CEO of CalPERS, Sean Harrigan.[3] According to a senior associate at Wilshire, it is the consultancy firm's job 'to find appropriate, credible independent third-party sources that evaluate the factors and sub-factors'.[4]

The first country factor is political stability. Like the rest of the PCI indicators, political stability is composed of two parts: a macro-factor and several sub-factors. Political stability (the macro-factor) refers to progress in the creation of basic democratic institutions and principles, such as guaranteed elimination of human rights violations (e.g., torture), and a strong and impartial legal system. Political stability is seen as a vital component in guaranteeing the development of a free market in the Third World, which in turn will attract and retain long-term capital. There are several sub-factors that further define political stability: (1) civil liberties; (2) independent judiciary and legal protection; and (3) political risk, which covers the extent of internal

Table 8.1 *Permissible Country Index (PCI) / CalPERS: country and market macro-factors*

Country macro-factors (or political risk factors	*Weight (%)*	*Market macro-factors*	*Weight (%)*
Political stability	16.7	Market liquidity and volatility	12.5
Transparency	16.7	Market regulation / legal system / investor protection	12.5
Productive labour practices	16.7	Capital market openness	12.5
		Settlement proficiency / transaction costs	12.5
Total assigned weight	50.1		50

Source: Wilshire Consulting, 'Permissible Equity Markets Investment Analysis'. Prepared for The California Public Employees' Retirement System. Santa Monica, CA: Wilshire Consulting, 2005, pp. 4, 11.

and external conflict, corruption, the military and religious influence in politics, law and order, ethnic tensions, democratic accountability, and bureaucratic quality. Together, these are intended to map the extent to which there exists government stability, a high quality of socio-economic conditions, and a positive investment profile (Wilshire Consulting 2005: 6).

The second country factor is transparency. Wilshire sees this factor as primarily comprising financial transparency, which involves four sub-factors: (1) freedom of the press, including the existence of 'elements of a free press necessary for investors to have truthful, accurate and relevant information on the conditions in the countries and companies in which they are investing' (Wilshire Consulting 2005: 6); (2) monetary and fiscal transparency; (3) stock exchange listing requirements; and (4) accounting standards.

The third and final country factor is productive labour practices. To assist in the evaluation of this macro-factor, Wilshire sought the assistance of Verité. A US-based, non-profit research organization, Verité has served CalPERS in a consultative role since 2000, providing information and analysis of labour protections (or, lack thereof) in 27 emerging markets. Verité's matrix, which considers 42 indicators of labour standards compliance, is the first of its kind to be used for investment purposes (Verité 2005). In response to the divestment from four Southeast Asian countries in 2002, Verité reported the following regarding its methodology:

> We looked at the laws, the institutional capacity to implement the laws and then we looked at what was really going on the ground – child labour, forced labour, freedom of association and discrimination. . . . We had in-country researchers in those Southeast Asian countries using

> questionnaires to interview governments, labour unions, NGOs and business groups. Then we used more traditional research data to make an overall assessment.
>
> ('US pension fund quits Asian countries', *BBC World News*, 21 February 2002)

Under this schema, markets are evaluated based on their ratification of and adherence to the principles laid out by the International Labour Organization (ILO), which 'cover labour rights and prohibitions on abusive labour practices, and the degree of effectiveness of implementation through relevant laws, enabling regulations and their degree of enforcement through the judiciary process' (Wilshire Consulting 2005: 7). The productive labour practices macro-factor is accompanied by the following four sub-factors: (1) ILO ratification of the eight core conventions;[5] (2) quality of enabling legislation; (3) institutional capacity to enforce; and (4) effectiveness of implementation. These sub-factors are heavily weighted toward the quality of enabling legislation and the effectiveness of implementation (ibid.).

The PCI and 'enduring value': the social factor

Despite the fact that neither CalPERS nor Wilshire explicitly uses the term SRI to describe the PCI, and instead insists that the Index assesses good corporate governance practices abroad, CalPERS board member and Treasurer of the State of California Phil Angelides drew on the notion of 'enduring value' in 2002, not only to promote the fact that the revised Index allocates equal weight to both financial and social criteria, but also to justify the decision to exit several South-east Asian countries. According to Angelides, 'enduring value' should act as a guiding principle for investments as opposed to short-term economic thinking.

> These reformers understand that the current *laissez-faire*, let-'er-rip system damages important social values – equitable treatment of workers, the environment and other commonly shared public assets – and that both workers and retirees (and the state taxpayers who put up the money for public pension funds) have a strong self-interest, personal as well as financial, in husbanding the distant future: a healthy society and strong economy for themselves and their families.
>
> (Greider 2005: URL)

To demonstrate that its expanded understanding of corporate governance had teeth, CalPERS announced in 2002 that it was going to pull out of all of its investments in Thailand, Malaysia, Indonesia, and the Philippines, not only because of financial criteria regarding issues of corporate governance – assessing the openness of a capital market, the sorts of protection offered to investors, and how effectively a market is regulated – but also due to non-financial issues, such as concerns about social conditions in these countries, particularly with regard to labour conditions.

CalPERS' exit strategy had immediate and devastating ramifications for these countries.[6] For example, although the $65 million invested in the Philippines in 2002 represented only 0.04 per cent of CalPERS' global fund, it was five times the average daily trading volume on the Filipino stock exchange in 2001. The day the exit of funds was announced, the Philippine Stock Exchange Composite Index tumbled 3.3 per cent. There were, therefore, important and immediate economic implications stemming from the pull-out. The decision to divest triggered a run on foreign investments in the Philippines, which caused the economy to suffer and led to countless job losses. According to the Philippine Ambassador to the US, Albert del Rosario, given the size of CalPERS, it is important to remain on the fund's permissible country listing because it represents the coveted 'seal of good housekeeping', which signals to the global investment community that the Philippines is 'an attractive and viable investment location' ('CalPERS Flips and Flops in Philippines – Again,' Bloomberg News, 22 April 2004).

Although sensitive to the socioeconomic consequences of CalPERS' decision to divest from several Southeast Asian countries in 2002, Robin Blackburn sees the move as

> a striking victory for the movement for social responsibility in investment ... The countries targeted [by CalPERS] in the move to maintain special export zones where social protection of the workforce is particularly weak. Altogether there are believed to be some 27 million workers in 800–1,000 special export zones worldwide. The ban on labour organisation in these zones has been an intense concern of the anti-sweatshop movement, and CalPERS' decision is certainly a success for this campaign.
> (Blackburn 2002: 517)

As we will see below, Blackburn was not alone in interpreting the revised PCI as an attempt at SRI. Some observers have gone so far as to state that CalPERS has become the first public pension fund to look beyond traditional economic factors ('US pension fund quits Asian countries', BBC World News, 21 February 2002).

Drawing on the findings of its investment assessment instrument, CalPERS decided to stay away from the Thai, Malaysian, Indian, and Sri Lankan equity markets in 2003, despite the fact that 2002 stock market returns, in dollar terms, averaged 136 per cent in Thailand, 82 per cent in India, 30 per cent in Sri Lanka, and 23 percent in Malaysia (Blackburn 2002). On the face of it, this decision might suggest that the public pension fund is more interested in establishing what it considers to be a better investment climate for its money than entering into short-term gains, which are tied to relatively higher risks. This position is supported by CalPERS' claim that its divestures have had a positive effect on the overall governance structures in the global South. According to Wilshire's research, the PCI seems to have an effect on the country and market performance of the selected 27 developing countries: 'In the 2002 [PCI] report, the final scoring ranged from a high of 2.63 out of a possible 3.00 to a low of 1.15. The 2003 scores ranged from a high of 2.75 to a low of 1.25. The 2004 scores ranged from a high of 2.83 to a low of 1.50, while the 2005 scores ranged from a high of 2.88 to a low of 1.46' (Wilshire Consulting 2005: 15).

The PCI is not without its critics, however. CalPERS board members – 10 out of 13 of whom are union members, union officers, or current and former politicians, and most of whom depend or depended on union support and endorsement – have been accused of using the PCI to further their careers. According to some observers, CalPERS' attempt to grandstand its ethical investment (as opposed to market activism) was driven by votes, not a social conscience (Edwards 2002).[7] The PCI country factors, which on the surface show a concern for social issues, appealed to the California taxpayer and union members. This tactic, some suggest, was aimed at riding 'the SRI-wave', which took off after the 1999 anti-globalisation protest at the WTO meeting in Seattle, and has since been harnessed by a highly lucrative ethical investing business, whose total assets under management comprised $2.16 trillion in 2003 and $2.29 trillion in 2005.[8]

Detractors of the PCI also argue that by choosing to divest from four Southeast Asian countries in 2002 on the basis of poor labour standards and human rights records, CalPERS was turning its back on its fiduciary duties to its shareowners given that the four countries in question were registering high returns. According to one observer, 'The use of (public employee retirement system funds) to subsidise economic development efforts is inappropriate … [T]he greatest good a (state pension fund) can do for its state is to maximise return on investments and reduce the contributions necessary from taxpayers' (Monks and Minow 2001: 128).[9] Of course, at the heart of this criticism lies the question of whether the latest revision of the PCI represents spin, or an attempt to increase investment returns through SRI.

Another major criticism was the fund's inconsistent usage and incorrect rating process of the PCI. After intense lobbying by the Philippine government and the Filipino community residing in the US, CalPERS reversed its decision to blacklist the country in May 2002. The financial reverberations were immediate: stocks in the Philippines immediately rose 1.3 percent and the Philippine peso soared to a 12-month high. However, in February 2003, Wilshire once again advised CalPERS to divest from its Philippine holdings. Instead of heeding this advice, CalPERS devised a 'cure period' ('CalPERS Flips and Flops,' 2004). Reinforcing the deep-seated idea of the 'backwardness' of Third World countries, a cure period allows for one year of grace before the fund would liquidate its investments in any emerging market that slips from the public pension funds' permissible list. In March 2004, Wilshire announced that the Philippines was to receive an overall score of 1.86, well below the passing score of 2.0. This announcement caused the Philippine stock index to plunge to its lowest point in six weeks. Despite Wilshire's advice, and after intense lobbying by the Philippine government and wider Filipino community, CalPERS issued a statement in April 2004 that it would remain in the Philippines. On 19 April 2004, Wilshire changed its overall score of the Philippines from 1.86 to 2.12. This clearly reveals the internal inconsistencies of the PCI initiative, as well as its fickle politicisation of social concerns in the Third World.

While the above criticisms are useful in highlighting the political features of the PCI, they neither shed critical light on the capitalist nature of the Index, nor explain how and why this strategy has been reproduced. The primary reason for this neglect lies in the fact that the Index is assumed to be merely an economic and technical instrument. Mainstream debates fail to capture the connection of the PCI to the wider discourse and policy of entrepreneurial development, as well as the underlying dynamics of capital accumulation from which both strategies emerged. Those involved in mainstream debates fail to grasp that the 'progressive sheen' of the PCI cannot be divorced from the wider relations of domination and exploitation involved in delivering the ultimate investment goal: a relatively higher return on CalPERS' original outlay than the fund can earn by investing either in the US or in other industrialised countries.

In what follows, I argue that the deeper (capitalist) nature of the PCI may be revealed through the identification of three overlapping factors. First, the content of the Index perpetuates the commonsense assumption that development is a neutral and universal concept that aims to promote material prosperity through growth. Second, the PCI relies on an economistic frame for assessing the investment potential of countries. This perspective is assumed to be scientific and, therefore, unproblematic. And third, the content of the Index assumes that the Third World is culturally homogeneous and its governance structures (legal, economic, and corporate) are backward. Through this objectification process, which is also reinforced in the first and second assumptions, the PCI represents highly complex national social formations in ahistorical and apolitical terms. Together these factors not only prime a developing country to be objectified and thus understood in terms of categories that can be measured with regard to its ability to provide a good investment site, it also renders the disciplinary action to withhold funds or subject the country to a 'cure period' as an unproblematic and indeed necessary strategy to ensure market stabilisation. We now look at each of the three points more fully.

The neutrality and universality of 'development'

The Index and entrepreneurial development remain above critical reproach largely because they resonate well with a deep-seated, Western, commonsense understanding that economic growth leads to progress. As Gilbert Rist observes, this understanding of 'development', which has dominated official discourse and policy since the end of World War II, 'offers the promise of general abundance, conceived in biological imagery as something "natural", positive, necessary and indisputable' (Rist 2002: 214). Consequently, the debates have remained silent on the question of how and why the knowledge contained in the PCI is readily accepted by policy-makers, the media, shareowners, and scholars as a natural fact.

To transcend the technical and economistic treatment of the Index, it is important to question the assumption of progress, as this highly political concept beats at the heart of the official understanding of development. Progress is defined in terms of material prosperity, which is, in turn, generated by economic growth. According to the PCI and entrepreneurial development, the ability of countries to attract equity finance assists in growth. The IFC, for instance, insists that harnessing the power of private capital and free enterprise – represented as 'positive' power – is necessary to bring about *needed change* in the developing world (International Finance Corporation 2005, my emphasis). It is believed that this change will reduce economic risks and protect shareholder value by ensuring that the 'underdeveloped' countries strive toward establishing 'good' (read: Anglo-American) corporate governance practices through, for example, implementing 'well-functioning' (universal) legal and political systems, modernising stock exchanges, stabilising capital market flows, decreasing commission rates and other transaction charges, and so forth. The questions that emerge here, but which are rarely posed in the dominant discourse, are: On whose terms is change in the 'developing' world 'needed'? Who benefits from this change? And, what social, political, and cultural dislocations are associated with this change, and why?

To address these questions it is useful to combine the capitalist nature of the PCI with an interrogation of its cultural dimensions of knowledge and production of social space. This strategy allows us to grasp that the key sources of power of the PCI lie not only in the coercive features of the Index (exit strategies, blacklisting 'bad' investment sites, cure periods), but in its ability to normalise, and, therefore, reproduce, the knowledge rooted in official development discourse and policy. What is at stake here is concealed by the neutrality of the term 'development', namely the production of knowledge and exercise of power over the Third World (Escobar 1995: 9):

> Most forms of understanding and representing the Third World are still dictated by the same basic tenets. The forms of power that have appeared act not so much by repression but by normalisation; not by ignorance but by controlled knowledge; not by humanitarian concern but by the bureaucratisation of social action. As the conditions that gave rise to development became more pressing, it could only increase its hold, refine its methods, and extend its reach even further. The materiality of these conditions is not conjured up by an 'objective' body of knowledge but is chartered out by the rational discourses of economists, politicians, and development experts of all types.
>
> (Escobar 1995: 53)

To grasp the inner nature of the PCI and its ability to replicate the conditions of capitalism by normalising and universalising the meaning of good investment sites, I highlight two ways in which the spatial dimension of the production of knowledge is rooted in capital relations of exploitation and domination (Lefebvre 1991). First, entrepreneurial development and the PCI are social constructs that are forged by particular individuals, groups, and institutions within social space (Lefebvre 1991; Harvey 2001). Entrepreneurial development represents an intensified phase of neoliberal-led development policies and practices over the past several decades. Two novel attributes of this neoliberal variant are: (1) the more explicit and direct control of financial actors vis-à-vis policy formation, such as the 'new conditionality'; and (2) the increasing presence of foreign investors in the global South, and an emphasis on the 'social' aspects of good governance, or SRI.

The space within which the knowledge underpinning entrepreneurial development and the PCI are both produced and reproduced reflects dominant capitalist interests in the US. In an attempt to deal with the effects of the tendency toward capital accumulation, American institutional investors, such as CalPERS, expand geographically into new regions by exporting capital, extending toward the creation of what Marx referred to as the world market (Marx 1981). David Harvey describes this as a process of the spatial displacement of capital (Harvey 2001), referring to a strategy in which capitalists seek to find outlets for their surplus capital by 'opening up new markets, new production capacities and new resource, social and labour possibilities elsewhere' (Harvey 2003: 64). As Marx suggested, 'If capital is sent abroad, this is not done because it absolutely could not be applied at home, but because it can be employed at a higher rate of profit in a foreign country' (Harvey 1999: 434). Marx's observation resonates with Wilshire's emphasis on the importance of economic growth as the primary motivation for investing in developing countries. According to Wilshire, growth 'is the reason for investing in the emerging markets, including superior relative expected returns and expanding opportunity set for investment. Last year [2005] the emerging markets collectively out-performed their developed markets counterparts globally' (Wilshire Consulting 2006: 2). One of the largest sites of foreign investment has been corporate borrowing, which grew from $21 billion in 2002 to $111 billion in 2006 ('How the developing world is striving to free itself of debt,' *Financial Times*, 8 February 2007).

Economics as 'scientific' knowledge: naturalising the hegemony of market episteme

Despite its emphasis on country factors, the PCI grants primacy to the economy. Both the means and end of the Index is to promote a well-functioning market by granting it as much freedom from government intervention as possible. This position is firmly rooted in the hegemonic understanding of economic growth and the material prosperity it generates (i.e., market episteme), which tends to reduce all aspects of life to the needs and proper functioning of the market and serves to remove and, therefore, sanitise the political, material, and cultural aspects of societies and recast them ahistorically in terms of the neutral realm of science. On this view, economics is represented as somehow embodying a scientific and therefore accurate representation and truth about the world (Escobar 1995). As Arturo Escobar notes, there is a close, albeit distorted, connection drawn between the scientific knowledge of economics, and its implicit claims to neutrality, and what he refers to as the 'cultural code', or cultural discourse of economics.

The assumption that markets are inherently rational, as long as they are left to their own devices, is an important feature of the cultural code of economics and serves as the cornerstone of the Index's ability to recreate the status quo by neutralising and thus normalising disciplinary relations of exploitation and domination. It does so in the following two ways. On one hand, the understanding that markets are inherently rational depoliticises and, therefore, naturalises the knowledge upon which the PCI attempts to exercise its disciplinary power, as it removes any problematic issues, such as social conflicts, contestation over material power, and so forth, from the political and cultural realms and recasts them in terms of the sanitised and neutral realm of 'science'. While CalPERS claims that its revised Index gives equal weight to market and country factors, for instance, it should be underlined that the country factors have been selected to encourage governments of emerging markets to pursue the neoliberal utopia of unregulated freedom of the market. Country factors are scored on the basis of how well national governments provide the proper conditions (e.g., legal entitlements, sound economic policy based on fiscal austerity, financial deregulation, trade liberalisation, and so on) for market actors to flourish under the conditions of competition in order to promote economic growth.

On the other hand, the assumption of the rationality of the market allows CalPERS to continue to place the blame for economic crises or slowdown at the door of the developing world, thereby justifying ever more intrusive forms of surveillance and control through neoliberal knowledge. Given the assumption of rational and efficient behaviour of financial actors such as CalPERS, the occurrence of crises is largely blamed on internal factors of state failure, or in neoliberal parlance, poor governance structures and lack of sound macroeconomic fundamentals of developing countries. As we saw above, the PCI was subject to revision each time a major crisis occurred, whether it originated in the Third World (e.g., East Asia) or in the US (e.g., Enron). The underlying assumption in each revision of the Index was not an acknowledgement of market failure, but rather of state failure to provide a free-market environment. Crony capitalism, rent-seeking behaviour, and weak legal systems, for example, were believed to have led to the distortion of the competitive tendencies of rational economic actors. By locating blame with the Third World countries, CalPERS' revised Index mirrored, and therefore legitimised, the knowledge produced by the IMF, the World

Bank, and G–7 countries in reaction to the major financial crises that occurred during the 1990s, which culminated in the creation of the New International Financial Architecture (Soederberg 2004).

An important consequence of this neoliberal knowledge, which is rooted in the 'economics as a science' assumption, has served to naturalise further the efficiency and desirability of Anglo-American forms of corporate governance. One criticism of the high concentration of family ownership of indigenous, publicly listed corporations, for instance, is that the management and board of directors are effectively insulated from market discipline, due to their lack of exposure to outside voices, such as minority shareholders. The assumption here is that in the presence of good governance structures, such as the democratic and legal systems found in the US, there will be less chance of market failure; that is, financial actors like CalPERS will act rationally. Yet, as the recent Enron-style debacles in the US revealed, the same short-term, speculative and irrational 'herd-behaviour' is at play in the highly deregulated financial markets of the First World as it is in the Third World (Patomäki 2001; Harmes 1998).

There is an important feature of the cultural code of economics that Escobar overlooks, however. While the assumption of rationality appears to legitimise the reductionism that occurs in the portrayal of economics as a science, it also helps to cloak the social power inherent in capital by treating the latter as some sort of neutral object or thing. There are at least two immediate and interrelated outcomes in treating capital as a thing as opposed to a social relation. First, the dominant treatment of capital as an object devoid of social power fails to acknowledge the exploitative relationship that occurs between capitalists and labour in the creation of surplus value. Investors such as CalPERS hold titles of ownership and receive interest (dividends). The latter are not generated in thin air but, in order to share in future surplus value production, must at some point confront labour (Harvey 1999: 276). Second, by treating capital as a thing, the cultural code of economics conceals the role and class nature of the bourgeois state, and thereby depoliticises and declasses the gloss of 'good governance' in which the country factors of the Index are encased.

Equity finance is not an object, but has its base in money, which is viewed here as an integral moment of the social relations of capital. Seen from this perspective, money and, by extension, equity finance wield social power. Those who exercise this social power seek to cultivate command over spatial organisation. Authority over the use of space becomes a crucial means for the reorganisation and reproduction of social power relations (Harvey 1989). This command over space, and subsequent power struggles to resist this command, are concealed in the discourse and policy of entrepreneurial development; and the PCI, as money which takes the form of equity financing, is reduced to a neutral object. One such expression of this power is the ability of American capitalists and their state to construct particular forms of knowledge that assist in protecting US capital abroad. The manner in which a specific variant of corporate governance is championed over others is a case in point. It is not purely objective forms of 'scientific knowledge' that drive the general consensus among mainstream scholars, policy-makers, and the media that East Asian forms of corporate governance are 'weak' and 'underdeveloped' compared to their American counterparts, the latter having bred the largest and most socially devastating forms of business fraud in US history during the early 2000s.

The technical and economic aspects of the Index also downplay how the historical configuration of relations of power within a particular national formation can delimit the degree to which Anglo-American forms of good governance can be effectively and swiftly implemented (the one year of 'cure period') without deeper social conflicts and/or possible threats of economic and political destabilisation. A basic prerequisite for the implementation of Anglo-American reforms in the PCI is the fundamental reorganisation of the social relations of production and exchange in a given social formation. For instance, given the high concentration of family-owned, publicly run corporations in East and Southeast Asia, minority shareholder rights cannot be guaranteed by mere technical changes without ensuring major social and political struggle and dislocation through the implementation of neoliberal forms of social engineering (Zhuang *et al.* 2000).

Cultural homogenisation and objectification

The act of denying a country its individual history, culture, and political characteristics objectifies national social formations, so that 'scientific' assessments of its investment potential can be undertaken. This process of 'othering' also permits capitalists to control social space within these countries by naturalising the importance of reducing all economic, political, and social activities to the goal of convincing investors that the country is a good investment site. The country categorisation of the Index is rooted in cultural imperialism that feeds off of, and is reinforced by, what Edward Said refers to as 'orientalism', occurring through the spatial (re-)organisation of capital. An example of this process may be found in the manner in which the PCI establishes two main investment categories involving 24 'developed' countries and 27 'emerging markets' (Said 1979; Escobar 1995: 9). This representation demarcates and recreates a geopolitical space, or imaginative geography, which showcases the evolutionary phases of 'progress' across the globe. For instance, a large majority of the world's countries, including approximately 140 that fall outside the two categories of the PCI, are viewed not only as high risk and, therefore, unworthy of investment, but also as failures of development, due to their unwillingness and/or inability to embrace Western expert knowledge, technology, and management skills (market episteme).

The PCI does not allow for any criteria differentiation between countries. Take, for example, the term 'emerging market economies', which was constructed by the IFC in 1981 to encourage foreign investment in select countries in the global South. It has reduced the historically distinct cultural, social, and political characteristics of entire countries to potential investment sites, or 'financial markets'. Yet, as Escobar suggests, this 'discursive homogenization' (which entails the erasure of the complexity and diversity of Third World peoples, so that a squatter in Mexico City, a Nepalese peasant, and a Tuareg nomad become equivalent to each other as poor and underdeveloped) is necessary to exercise power over the Third World (Escobar 1995: 53).

The benefits of creating a better investment climate are portrayed by the Index and, more broadly, those championing entrepreneurial development, not only as a win-win situation for developing countries and foreign investors, but also as universal. According to the World Bank, 'investment climate improvements are the driving force for growth and poverty reduction. A good investment climate is one that is better for everyone in two dimensions. It benefits society as a whole, not just firms. And it expands opportunities for all firms, not just large or influential firms' (2004: 35). The knowledge entailed in the prescription of desirable investment sites is further normalised by portraying the interests and goals (material gains) of foreign investors and (apolitical and asocial) markets of (homogenised) Third World countries as fundamentally the same, and thereby side-stepping issues of power, struggle, class, contestation, gender, and race.

The neutral, scientific discourse of economics removes the complexity and diversity tied to issues of poverty and inequality in the Third World and therefore effectively homogenises and dehumanises the social and political landscape upon which good investment sites are to be constructed and assessed. Moreover, it acts to smooth over the highly uneven and exploitative nature of global capitalism. This stance is evident in two features of the factor pertaining to productive labour practices that falls under the country or political risk category of the PCI. While labour codes speak directly to SRI concerns, upon closer inspection of this category, it becomes clear that the Index does not strive to empower workers. Rather, it appeases their demands while remaining within the neoliberal-led development framework so as not to distort the existing levels of exploitation of labour necessary to ensure high returns on CalPERS' investment, or at least higher returns than could be gained in the US. On one hand, while Verité provides insight into the treatment of workers in the formal sector, it ignores the informal sector. While the neglect of the latter may relate to its elusive character, it is problematic that the PCI does not begin to question the connection between the highly uneven and exploitative nature of global capitalism under neoliberal rule. This unevenness may be seen by the rapid expansion of the informal sector, which has come to represent a significant and increasing portion of the labour market in the Third World. According to the ILO, 'more than 80 per cent of new jobs created in Latin America and Africa in recent years have been in the informal economy' (Altvater 2002: 79). In the Philippine case, for example, 82 per cent of the non-agricultural workforce and 90 per cent of the manufacturing sector are outside the formal sector. The growth of the informal sector implies that workers are, among other things, in a precarious position to exert pressures for socioeconomic reform, such as legislation regarding fair labour practices. Indeed, the connection between higher profit rates in emerging markets and parallel levels of rates of exploitation are conveniently neglected by the PCI.

On the other hand, the ILO standards upon which Verité bases its assessments strive to encourage union competition and discourage centralised collective bargaining. As Teri L. Caraway argues, the ILO's understanding of freedom of association is distinctly liberal and promotes the formation of 'free' as opposed to 'powerful' trade unions (Caraway 2006). Depending on the historical configuration of state-labour-capitalist relations, the ILO position can lead to the weakening as opposed to empowering of trade unions. This position is not surprising, however, given the dominant neoliberal position that trade unions lead to rent-seeking activities and therefore threaten good governance practices in both the government and the publicly listed corporation.

Conclusion: moving beyond 'enduring value'?

I have argued that the PCI is not a neutral assessment exercise to ensure good returns on foreign investment in the global South, but rather a political strategy that assists in the recreation of conditions for continued spatial expansion of capital accumulation. This is largely accomplished through coercive measures, such as exit strategies, as well as the construction of specific forms of knowledge that normalise the disciplinary and exploitative relations inherent in the 'new conditionality' imbued in entrepreneurial development. The result is the naturalisation of the premise that Third World countries should strive to attract equity financing in their bid to achieve development. The latter is understood in capitalist terms of economic growth and material prosperity.

The limitations for social change with regard to politicising the management of social security capital identified in this chapter should be complemented by the insights provided in our discussion regarding the lack of control unions wield in public pension funds and publicly listed corporations in which they are alleged 'owners' (see Munck Chapter 11 in this volume). Indeed, the latest reforms of the PCI were initiated in a top-down manner, with the Treasury Department of California and the former CEO of CalPERS leading the way. In terms of the union-led reforms, although workers' deferred wages comprise the material strength of CalPERS, in practice, 'these beneficiaries have little autonomy and no direct influence on the corporations they nominally own' (O'Barr and Conley 1992: 3). The PCI was, therefore, not instigated from the bottom up by the individual unions (so-called 'shareowners') that comprise CalPERS. Legal control over the public pension fund resides with the State of California, which established it. This does not mean that unions linked to CalPERS have not played an important role in instigating corporate governance reforms in the US, especially high executive pay packages, as well as seeking to convince the investment committee at CalPERS to boycott corporations that engage in anti-union campaigns. However, union-led activism tied to CalPERS has remained largely passive with regard to corporate governance and its newly extended definition that embraces SRI in emerging markets.[10]

While this discussion has sought to draw attention to the manner in which SRI, seen here as an extension of the neoliberal project of corporate governance, has been constructed to conceal intrusive and disciplinary strategies on the part of institutional investors, we should not lose sight of the spaces of hope that lie within this capitalist project. If we recall, the paradox underlying the PCI and entrepreneurial development entailed not only intensified forms of exploitation and domination, so as to secure the expansion of social security capital, but also the growing political and social unrest associated with the legitimacy crisis of neoliberal-led capitalism. Possibilities for social change lie here. Significant forms of resistance to growing levels of exploitation have taken shape at both the local and global levels. These protest movements are aimed at curbing the power of corporations, regardless of their nationality, and making them more socially and environmentally accountable. There are, for example, numerous anti-sweatshop networks (e.g., Clean Clothes Campaign, UNITE HERE, Students Against Sweatshops, No Sweat, etc.) and faith-based institutional investors (e.g., the Inter-Faith Centre on Corporate Social Responsibility) that work closely with workers in both the informal and formal sectors across the globe, as well as fight for basic human rights and access to health (cheaper drugs for HIV/AIDS patients), education, and welfare services for all citizens. The unionised membership base of CalPERS would do well to learn from and engage with these organisations more carefully, and work toward radicalising the 'social factors' that comprise the PCI. In other words, CalPERS should work toward using 'voice', by forming alliances with local unions and progressive NGOs in emerging markets, as opposed to 'exit' as a disciplinary strategy.

Notes

1 A standard definition of socially responsible investing (SRI) refers to 'an investment approach which, in addition to conventional financial criteria, evaluates and selects companies based on social and ethical criteria such as legal compliance, employment practices, human rights, consumer issues, contribution to the community, and environmental issues, while seeking stable returns' (Kawamura 2002: 14).

2 Confidential interviews at CalPERS, 2 May 2005.

3 Confidential interview with representatives from the Treasury Department of California on 6 May 2005.

4 Confidential e-mail exchange with a Senior Associate at Wilshire on 21 June 2005.

5 For more information, see the ILO's website: www.ilo.org/public/english/standards/norm/wharare/fundam

6 Although the majority of CalPERS' assets are invested on a long-term basis in US publicly traded corporations, in 2005, the fund held $3.9 billion in assets in emerging markets. See 'CalPERS adds to emerging markets list', Benefits Canada, 20 April 2005·

7 See N. Edwards (2002).·

8 To put things in perspective, while assets under professional management (i.e., non-SRI assets) are substantially greater than their SRI counterparts ($24.4 trillion as of 2005), over the 1995–2005 period, SRI assets rose more than 258 per cent, whereas non-SRI assets increased by 249 per cent over the same time line. Social Investment Forum (2005) on Socially Responsible Investing Trends in the United States, Social Investment Forum Industry Research Programme: www.socialinvest.orgareas/research/trends/sri(_)trends(_)report(_)2005.pdf

9 According to the *Wall Street Journal*:

> In the boom years of the 1990s, CalPERS outperformed most other public employee pension funds; but in the down years of 2000 and 2001, it performed at an average of one percentage point below its peers – a difference of millions of dollars. The fund's value has dropped from a high of $177 billion in October 2000, to about $149 billion in July 2002. In that same year CalPERS pulled out of Southeast Asia on the basis of poor labour standards and human rights records.
>
> ('CalPERS: Enron Deals a Mistake,' *Wall Street Journal*, 18 July 2002)

10 Interview with administrative member of the California State Council (SEIU). Sacramento, California, 5 May 2005.

References

Altvater, E. (2002) 'The Growth Obsession', in L. Panitch and C. Leys (eds) *Socialist Register: A World of Contradictions*, London: Merlin Press, pp. 45–62.

Blackburn, R. (2002) *Banking on Death or Investing in Life: The History and Future of Pensions*, London: Verso.

Brancato, C.K. (1997) *Institutional Investors and Corporate Governance: Best Practices for Increasing Corporate Value*, New York: Irwin.

California Public Employees' Retirement System (2005) 'Corporate Governance and Core Principles and Guidelines: The United States', CalPERS. Available at: www.calpers-governance.org/principles/domestic/us/page01.asp.

—— (2006) 'Facts at a Glance, CalPERS'. Available at: www.calpers.ca.gov/eip-docs/about/facts/investme.pdf.

Caraway, T.L. (2006) 'Freedom of Association: Battering Ram or Trojan Horse?' *Review of International Political Economy* 13(2): 210–232.

Edwards, N. (2002) 'Pragmatism Rules in Asia's Ethical Investing Debate', Association for Sustainable and Responsible Investment in Asia. Available at: www.asria.org/pro/news&events/ethical_investing_debate.htm.

Escobar, A. (1995) *Encountering Development: The Making and Unmaking of the Third World*, Princeton, NJ: Princeton University Press.

Greider, W. (2005) 'The New Colossus', *The Nation*, 28 February 2005. Available at www.thenation.com/doc/20050228/greider

Gul, F. A. and Tsui, J.S.L. (2004) 'Introduction and Overview', in F.A. Gul and J. S.L. Tsui (eds) *The Governance of East Asian Corporations*, London: Palgrave, pp. 1–15.

Harmes, A. (1998) 'Institutional Investors and the Reproduction of Neoliberalism', *Review of International Political Economy* 5(1): 92–121.

Harvey, D. (1989) *The Urban Experience*, Baltimore, MD: Johns Hopkins University Press.

—— (1999) *The Limits to Capital*, London: Verso.

—— (2001) *Spaces of Capital: Towards a Critical Geography*, London: Routledge.

—— (2003) 'The "New" Imperialism', in L. Panitch and C. Leys (eds), *Socialist Register 2004: The New Imperial Challenge*, London: Merlin Press, pp. 67–83.

Hebb, T. and Wójcik D. (2005) 'Global Standards and Emerging Markets: The Institutional-investment Value Chain and the CalPERS Investment Strategy', *Environment and Planning A* 37: 1955–1974.

International Finance Corporation (2005) 'Emerging Markets Heading for Banner Year in 2006: IFC Notes Progress, Development Challenges Ahead', International Finance Corporation. Available at: www.ifc.org/ifcext/home.nsf/Content/Emerging_Mkts_2006.

Kawamura, M. (2002) 'How Socially Responsible Investment (SRI) Could Redefine Corporate Excellence in the 21st Century', NLI Research Institute, No. 160, p. 14.

Lefebvre, H. (1991) *The Production of Space*, Cambridge, MA: Blackwell.

Marx, K. (1981) *Capital* , vol. 3, London: Penguin.

Monks, R.A.G. and Minow, N. (2001) *Corporate Governance,* 2nd edn, Oxford: Blackwell).

O Barr, W.M. and Conley, J.M. (1992) *Fortune and Folly: The Wealth and Power of Institutional Investing*. Homewood, IL.

Patomäki, H. (2001) *Democratising Globalisation: The Leverage of the Tobin Tax*, London: Zed Books.

Reed, D. (2004) 'Corporate Governance Reforms in Developing Countries', in D. Reed and S. Mukherjee (eds) *Corporate Governance, Economic Reforms and Development: The Indian Experience,* Oxford: Oxford University Press, pp. 19–41.

Rist, G. (2002) *The History of Development: From Western Origins to Global Faith*, London: Zed Books.

Said, E. (1979) *Orientalism*, New York: Vintage Books.

Soederberg, S. (2004) *The Politics of the New International Financial Architecture: Reimposing Neoliberal Domination in the Global South*, London: Zed.

—— (2006) *Global Governance in Question: Empire, Class, and the New Common Sense in Managing North–South Relations*, London: Pluto Press.

Verité (2005) 'Emerging Markets Research Project: Year-End Report. Prepared for California Employees' Retirement System' Available at: www.calpers.ca.gov/eip-docs/investments/assets/equities/international/permissible/calpers-verite-final-report-2004.pdf.

Wilshire Consulting (2005) 'Permissible Equity Markets Investment Analysis', prepared for the California Public Employees' Retirement System, Santa Monica, C. A.: Wilshire & Associates.

—— (2006) 'Exposure Draft – Permissible Equity Markets Investment Analysis', prepared for The California Public Employees' Retirement System, Santa Monica, C.A.: Wilshire & Associates.

World Bank (2001) *World Development Report 2002: Building Institutions for Markets*, Oxford University Press.

—— (2004) *World Development Report 2005: A Better Investment Climate for Everyone*, New York: Oxford University Press.

—— (2005) *World Development Report 2006: Equity and Development*, Oxford University Press.

Zhuang, J., Edwards, D., Webb, D. and Capulong, V.A. (2000) *Corporate Governance and Finance in East Asia: A Study of Indonesia, Republic of Korea, Malaysia, Philippines, and Thailand*, Manila: Asian Development Bank.

Part IV

New directions in labour organising?

9 Challenging labour market flexibilisation

Union and community-based struggles in post-apartheid South Africa

Marlea Clarke

The 1994 election of the African National Congress (ANC) in South Africa's first democratic election was celebrated as a victory for the country's working class. There was good cause to believe an ANC victory would result in the socio-economic transformation of the country. On the one hand, the ANC was a militant mass movement at the centre of the national liberation struggle with a programme for radical socio-economic change. This programme included the redistribution of resources and delivery of social provisions, and the restructuring of the labour market to improve working conditions and workers' rights. On the other, the ANC was in a formal alliance with the Congress of South African Trade Unions (COSATU), the country's largest and most militant trade union federation. From both the ANC's and COSATU's perspective, the introduction of new labour laws and labour market institutions was central to reforming and re-regulating the labour market in order to improve socio-economic conditions of the majority of the population. Further, COSATU viewed reforms as an important step towards consolidation their role in policy-making in order to ensure economic developments addressed poverty and inequality.

Staying the course, however, did not prove to be easy for the new government. The ANC formed the new government at a time when pressures to liberalise the economy and increase the flexibility of labour markets were strong. Further, the new government inherited a country marked by economic instability, pervasive poverty, rising unemployment, and massive social inequalities. As discussed below, the government began to introduce policies of privatisation, trade liberalisation and deregulation. Similar to restructuring initiatives begun in the 1980s under the previous National Party (NP) government, these policies were aimed at integrating South Africa into the global economy and improving the country's international competitiveness. These policies undermined the regulatory scope and aim of new labour laws and, as a result, unemployment has steadily risen alongside the expansion of casual, informal and other forms of precarious employment arrangements. Expectations among black people, especially the black working class, of significantly improved standards of living, wages and working conditions have remained largely unfulfilled as macroeconomic policies have failed to create or sustain 'decent' jobs or address deeply entrenched poverty and inequality structures. Restructuring has foisted flexibilisation on workers, while privatisation and liberalisation have reduced or deprived communities of basic social services and have extended market forces to all areas of workers' lives. On a political level, reforms have also contributed to the demobilisation of the labour movement and its declining capacity to organise, mobilise and represent marginalised workers and others most impacted by restructuring.

The adoption of neoliberal policies and the marginalisation of the union movement in South Africa raise important questions concerning the strategies of labour movements and the potential for effective forms of collective resistance. As the chapter details, in contrast to the active role unions played in the apartheid era community struggles through 'social movement unionism' – a fusion between labour organising and broader social movements – the last decade has seen a shift in union strategies towards a more traditional 'business' model of unionism. Union leaders have used alliance structures, tripartite forums and the new labour relations system to try to secure the best deal possible for their members in the context of the ANC's adoption of market-based reforms. In this context, the chapter explores 'old' and 'new' forms of contestation by unions and new social movements and argues that COSATU's retreat from social movement unionism to a more traditional 'business' model of unionism in the post-apartheid period has shaped and limited the federation's ability and capacity to organise and mobilise those most affected by neoliberal restructuring and rising precariousness.

With the scope of unionism increasingly restricted to 'workplace' rather than broader social issues, a range of new social movements have emerged to challenge government policies and the negative impacts of neoliberal restructuring. As the chapter details, only recently has the union movement begun to address divisions between unions and other groups in civil society, and the artificial separation between workplace and social issues by committing itself to re-build social movement unionism and to build stronger coalitions with social movements. Nonetheless, the emergence of new social movements, and COSATU's recent commitment to re-building social movement unionism and increasing union memberships among casual and other precarious workers are positive signs that workers may begin to challenge the politics and policies of the ANC government. Still, for this to happen, the union movement needs to rethink its relationship with the ANC and the union movement's broader strategy and vision for transforming post-apartheid South Africa in ways that are likely to build a more democratic and equal society.

Labour and the South African transition

As is now well known, the dismantling of apartheid and creation of a democratic system of representation were a negotiated process in South Africa.

The ANC scored a landslide victory in the country's first democratic election in 1994, winning nearly 63 per cent of the nearly 20 million votes cast, just shy of the two-thirds majority it needed to write the new constitution with few concessions to other parties (Murray 1994: 210). Central to the ANC's election platform was the Reconstruction and Development Programme (RDP) – a programme that had been developed through extensive consultations with unions, social organisations and the civic movement throughout the early 1990s – that closely linked reconstruction with development, and prioritised meeting basic needs and democratising the state and society. Although the ANC's economic proposals did have some ambiguities and contradictory aspirations, the RDP remained the most detailed and widely publicised set of commitments to economic justice for the black majority. Further, the ANC had committed itself to a programme of labour market transformation aimed at improving workers' rights, creating jobs and fighting poverty.

COSATU was a major political actor in the transition and played a pivotal role in drafting the RDP. The federation's role in the transition was shaped by its history in the anti-apartheid struggle. COSATU was formed in 1985 at the height of community and township struggles against apartheid. Many of the key trade unions that were part of COSATU's formation have their roots in the Durban strikes of 1973 and the related emergence of an independent black union movement in the years following the strikes. Of course, the origins of the black trade union movement date back much further, to the late 1920s and early 1930s, and to the establishment of the South African Congress of Trade Unions (SACTU) in 1955. SACTU established a strong alliance with the ANC, and established a tradition of 'political unionism'. This form of unionism was based on the view that the political conditions in the country meant that union and political struggles could not be separated (Webster 1988). However, state repression and the exclusion of black unions from the industrial relations system under apartheid made unionisation extremely difficult, and many unions all but disappeared in the 1960s. The period following the 1973 strikes saw the formation of a new group of unions organising black workers. Many of these unions continued with the tradition of 'political unionism' begun with the formation of SACTU.

Rapid unionisation in unorganised sectors and the crossing over of other unions and federations meant that COSATU's membership grew rapidly in the months following its launch. Although some unions were wary of a close alliance with the national liberation movement and argued that building shop-floor structures should be the basis for trade unionism in South Africa, most affiliates supported the tradition of political unionism. From its inception COSATU aligned itself with the ANC and played a leading role in mobilising workers and communities in the struggle against apartheid. In contrast to the narrow focus on union members and on collective bargaining issues common in business unionism, COSATU adopted social movement unionism. This type of unionism concerns itself with issues that extend beyond the shopfloor and beyond a particular group of workers, and therefore often involves alliances with community groups (Robinson 1993; Ross 2004). The adoption of social movement unionism meant that the federation focused on workplace and bargaining issues facing union members, while also taking up a range of broader social and economic issues facing the working class more broadly. Unions placed great importance on active membership participation and education, and sought to build the democratic capacities of workers. Strong shop floor structures were built, with rank-and-file workers playing a strong and critical role in policy processes, organising campaigns, community struggles and day-to-day functions of the union.

COSATU's approach and focus shifted in the late 1980s as political and economic reforms began to take place. The federation began participating in various newly established tripartite structures that promoted negotiated settlements between government business and the state and began focusing increased attention on reforms to labour laws and to the industrial relations system. Unions also sought to reform existing institutions such as the government-sponsored National Manpower Commission (NMC) and to 'proactively engage' with government and business over a range of macro-economic policy and workplace issues, including new labour legislation, constitutional rights, industrial restructuring, industrial training and workplace restructuring. Unionists and other analysts characterised this 'proactive engagement' and participation in macro-economic policy formulation and workplace restructuring initiatives as a shift away from 'social movement unionism' to 'strategic unionism' (see, for example, Von Holdt 1993). Advocates of this approach argued that this approach was not a retreat into mere reformism or corporatism, rather involved a strategic vision of a labour-driven process of social change that was of crucial importance to transformation and democratisation in South Africa (ibid.).

The trend towards tripartism and 'strategic unionism' continued. A successful COSATU-led campaign against a new value added tax (VAT) led to the creation of a new tripartite forum, the National Economic Forum (NEF) in 1992. For labour, this forum was an important step in stopping unilateral action and decision-making on economic issues by government as the Forum was established as a decision-making body on socio-economic issues facing the country. The unbanning of the ANC and the South African Communist Party (SACP) in 1990 led to the formalisation of the alliance, referred to as the tripartite alliance, the following year. COSATU then participated in the ANC's Economic Policy Conference in 1992 and helped draft the RDP, which later became the ANC's election platform in 1994. Although officially excluded from the Convention for a Democratic South Africa (CODESA), the formal political negotiations process aimed at ending apartheid, four COSATU representatives joined the SACP's delegation to CODESA.

COSATU's alliance with the ANC, its central role in drafting the RDP, its formal role in newly established tripartite bodies, and its strong and rapidly growing membership led the federation to believe that it would play a central role in shaping post-apartheid policies and politics. The federation also believed that policies developed within the alliance in the years prior to the elections would be introduced as official government policy after the elections. Indeed, as Buhlungu (2005) notes, COSATU expected that the ANC would actively champion the interests of workers. Some of these hopes were initially realised. As promised, labour market reform during the ANC's first term in government focused on introducing new labour legislation that would create a more co-operative industrial relations system with an increased role for organised labour. A series of labour laws, influenced by international employment standards and South Africa's Bill of Rights contained in the country's new constitution, were promulgated to implement the Ministry of Labour's five-year programme. Four key statutes were introduced: the Labour Relations Act 66 of 1995 (LRA), the Employment Equity Act 55 of 1998 (EEA), the Skills Development Act 97 of 1998 (SDA), and the Basic Conditions of Employment Act 75 of 1997[1] (BCEA).

The LRA and BCEA were central with regard to employment standards and trade union rights. The new LRA established the rules of collective bargaining, granted workers a meaningful right to strike (without fear of dismissal), and formalised and codified organisational rights. The Act also introduced a new dispute resolution system and laid a basis for worker participation in the workplace. The BCEA was the most important piece of legislation in terms of regulating working conditions, and by 2004 covered approximately 7.15 million employees (Statistics South Africa 2004a). The Act established minimum conditions of employment and extended them to most formally employed workers. The new employment law dispensation aimed to improve workers' rights and extend protection to vulnerable workers, especially those who had previously been excluded from legislative protection.

New labour market institutions and tripartite structures were also established, such as the Employment Conditions Commission (ECC), and the National Economic Development and Labour Council (Nedlac). The ECC was established by the BCEA with its main task being to advise the Minister of Labour on Sectoral Determinations (determinations setting wages and working conditions for 'unorganised' workers, or workers in sectors without bargaining councils). Nedlac replaced the National Economic Forum (NEF), which had operated as a tripartite forum to discuss and reach agreement on economic and social policy issues between 1992 and 1994. The new institution was a statutory body, with representation from organised labour, organised employers and community-based groups. Nedlac's mandate was broader than the NEF, and expanded areas of negotiation to include labour policy and key aspects of fiscal, industrial and development policy. COSATU played a critical role in shaping the new regulatory framework and was a strong force in newly established tripartite institutions.

According to some unionists and writers, the consolidation of labour's institutional role in policy-making and labour market structures was a significant gain for organised workers, even representing a form of 'left corporatism' (Adler and Webster 1996, 2000; Patel 1993).

However, as will be discussed below, the ANC has not continued to actively champion the interests of workers. In fact, new labour laws and the new industrial relations system have not brought about the type of reforms workers and their union expected. Moreover, tripartite institutions have not cemented a central role for labour in policy formulation and employment standards setting. Instead, as we shall see three factors including: (1) the ANC's adoption of free-market economic policies; (2) COSATU's marginalisation within tripartite structures; and (3) weaknesses in new laws have led to a growth in unemployment and various forms of precarious, low-waged employment and rising inequalities. Indeed, alongside the decline in full-time, permanent employment in sectors protected by collective bargaining and labour laws has been the proliferation of casual, informal and other types of precarious, or 'flexible' employment, unprotected by labour laws and union organising. Policies of privatisation and liberalisation have resulted in a steady deterioration of working and living conditions for many South Africans, thus contributing to rising poverty and inequality. Overall, political developments and labour market reforms have contributed to a steady decline in union membership and undermined COSATU's capacity to organise, mobilise and represent those workers most impacted by neoliberal restructuring.

Neoliberalism and labour market flexibility in post-apartheid South Africa

Despite their victory at the polls, the new ANC government faced a range of constraints and pressures in developing economic policies. Poor economic performance during the ANC's first few years in office, criticism from the domestic business sector, and sustained international pressure from the World Bank, the IMF and Western governments regarding policy development contributed to the ANC re-thinking its economic strategy (Marais 2001). Consequently, soon after the election the government began to retreat from the more 'people-driven' development strategy outlined in the RDP and started adopting policies aimed at securing foreign investment and increasing the country's international competitiveness. For example, in December 1995, the government unilaterally announced its commitment to the privatisation of state assets and soon after introduced policies aimed at privatising water and other municipal services.

High hopes generated by the RDP-inspired economic restructuring strategy were further dashed when the government abolished the RDP office and announced its neoliberal macroeconomic programme, Growth, Employment and Redistribution (GEAR), in June 1996 without consulting its alliance partners. One of GEAR's primary aims was to attract foreign investment to South Africa, which the government saw as key to reviving economic growth. Therefore, the emphasis on state-led development and redistribution in the RDP was replaced with a focus on trade and market liberalisation, debt reduction and stringent fiscal deficit reduction targets, and the privatisation of state assets and public utilities – including water, electricity and waste management at the municipal level. The ANC's adoption of GEAR revealed the government's growing preoccupation with macroeconomic policy ahead of other policy priorities. In contrast to goals such as job creation, reduction in poverty and equitable economic growth present in the RDP, GEAR emphasised trade liberalisation and reduced social expenditure. A point we shall return to below, GEAR also called for increased flexibility in the labour market, largely through the introduction of 'regulated flexibility'.

In line with GEAR, the country's trade and industrial policies were largely marked by a market-led approach, with an emphasis on traditional supply-side measures to induce competitiveness and export-oriented growth. Despite speculation that the new government would reverse policies of trade liberalisation initiated by the previous regime and adopt a more cautious approach to tariff reform, the opposite took place. The new government adopted both multilateral and unilateral trade liberalisation. In 1994, South Africa signed the Marrakech Agreement of the General Agreement on Tariffs and Trade (GATT), and in 1995 applied formally to the World Trade Organisation and began implementing a new tariff reduction programme. This new programme resulted in a significant reorganisation of South Africa's tariff structure. By 2002 the country's trade regime had been substantially liberalised; virtually all quantitative restrictions had been eliminated and the tariff regime had been rationalised, with the number of lines and tariff bands significantly reduced (Draper 2003).

Increased global competition, combined with the implementation of GEAR and related policies of privatisation and trade liberalisation, put pressure on the labour market and made regulation difficult. Policy shifts resulted in the push for increased labour market flexibility, and have shaped the government's capacity and political will to monitor and enforce new legislation (Clarke 2006). Labour flexibility – including flexibility in wages, working conditions and employers' ability to adjust the size and nature of their workforce through, for example, outsourcing and the increased use of causal or temporary workers – was achieved through the introduction of a framework of 'regulated flexibility'. It was most overtly introduced and promoted in the 1997 Basic Conditions of Employment Act 75 (BCEA), which provided extended and expanded protection for workers but with extensive provisions for variation. Apart from certain key protections (or 'core' rights), standards could be varied through collective bargaining, through exemption procedures, and by individual contracts of employment. Standards could also be varied through Sectoral Determinations, introduced by the Minister on the advice of the new Employment Conditions Commission (ECC). Each of these methods has provided significant scope for amending wage rates, hours of work and other employment conditions. Additional variation (outlined in the *Ministerial Determination: Small Business*) was granted to small businesses employing less than 10 workers. This Determination provided for downward variation in overtime hours, pay for overtime work, averaging of hours, family responsibility leave and annual leave for small businesses (GG 20587). In short, this Ministerial Determination meant that employers in small business were granted increased flexibility, while the floor of rights for employees was reduced significantly.

Overall, the new regulatory framework provided for quite extensive forms of flexibility – directly through downward variation provisions in the legislation, and indirectly through weak monitoring and enforcement (Clarke 2006). Research conducted on the use of exemption provisions suggests that businesses have quickly taken advantage of this provision. According to Harsch (2001: 17), by the end of 2000 it was reported that about 400 businesses, employing approximately 400,000 workers, had already applied for exemptions from BCEA provisions. Based on available data, variation provisions have also been widely utilised, with the vast majority of applications for variation granted. For example, only six (2 per cent) of applications for variation were refused in 2002. The result was that 5,303,302 workers were affected by variation (Department of Labour 2002: 38). In the 2004/2005 reporting period, 848 applications were received for exemption or variation from certain provisions of the BCEA. Excluding those that had not been finalized when the Department reported on figures, the success rate was 63 per cent, with applications for exemptions from overtime provisions the most common (34 per cent), followed by weekly and daily rest periods (14 per cent) (Godfrey *et al.* 2006). Further, despite opposition from the small, medium and micro enterprises (SMMEs) sector over new legislation, particularly the BCEA, exemption provisions have provided exactly the kind of flexibility this sector had demanded. The Department of Labour reported that SMMEs accounted for 59 per cent of the 7,373 exemption applications received in 2004 (Altman 2005: 17). Similar to previous years, the vast majority (77 per cent) of all applications were approved in 2004 (ibid.).

Finally, despite the DoL's initial goal of extending protection to vulnerable workers, pressure for continued and expanded flexibility resulted in the more limited application of the BCEA to those workers in formal employment. While previous legislation excluded those employees who worked less than three days per week ('casuals'), most sections of the new BCEA were applicable to those who work more than 24 hours per month for one employer. This provision marked a significant gain for many workers who were previously unprotected. However, those who did not fit the definition of 'employee' (such as independent contractors, homeworkers, self-employed and informal workers) were still excluded from coverage. Further, many casual, temporary and fixed-term contract workers were effectively excluded from the Act since protection was based on a model of full-time, continuous employment (Clarke 2006). As Halton Cheadle, one of the drafters of the new statutes, recently acknowledged, laws are 'failing to protect the most vulnerable: the informal, the marginal and the casual' (2005: 5). And, contrary to expectations by many unionists and scholars that supported labour's move towards 'strategic unionism' and tripartism, labour's role in tripartite institutions has not resulted in improved wages and working conditions for most 'vulnerable workers', and workers and unions have not been able to use tripartite structures or bargaining councils to gain more influence over restructuring and the use of casual labour.

Precarious employment and inequality

Increased global competition, neoliberal restructuring and the ANC's capitulation to domestic and international pressure for increased flexibility in the labour market have had a negative impact on levels of employment, wages, and the quality of employment. Flexibility and exemption provisions in new labour laws and the limited coverage of social security and employment standards legislation have meant that a growing numbers of workers remain unprotected and have only limited access to social security programmes, and sometimes none at all. Largely as a result of priorities outlined in GEAR, social grants expenditure as a percentage of GDP fell between 1997 and 2002 (Pauw and Mncube 2007). Although the government has recently increased social spending and has increased the number of people eligible for grants and the real value of social grants, the system still fails to provide an adequate safety net for the millions who are unable to find work. Drawing on national statistics, Robinson (2006) argued that in September 2005, 7.8 million people of working age were unemployed and none of them were eligible for a state grant.

Macro-economic policies, poor monitoring and enforcement of new labour laws combined with flexibility provisions and the limited reach of employment standards legislation have also facilitated workplace restructuring. Employers have outsourced and subcontracted work to smaller companies, many of whom have lower wages and benefits than larger companies and who take advantage of flexibility and exemption provisions to reduce employment standards for their employees. Thus, restructuring has facilitated the creation of poorly protected and remunerated jobs, justified by employers as necessary to reduce labour costs and regain competitiveness. As a consequence, the following trends have been noted: rising unemployment, a steady reduction in protected workers with permanent, full-time jobs in core sectors of the economy, and a proliferation of precarious employment. According to official data, if discouraged jobseekers are included, the unemployment rate was 29.2% in 1995 and by early 2004 it had increased to 41.2% (Statistics South Africa 1998, 2004a: xii). Youth unemployment was particularly severe; by 2004 it was estimated that 70% of the unemployed were under the age of 35 (IMF 2005: 53). Although unemployment appeared to drop slightly at the end of 2005, to 38.8% (about 4.3 million), this decline was, at least in part, the result of new definitions of 'employed' used by Statistics South Africa. Beginning in September 2004 a one-hour minimum was added to the definition of 'employed', thereby increasing the number of workers counted as 'employed'. According to Statistics South Africa, 'the *employed* are those who performed work for pay, profit or family gain in the seven days prior to the survey interview *for at least one hour*, or who were absent from work during these seven days, but did have some form of work to which to return' (2004b: xxv, emphasis added). However, unless an individual meets a far narrow definition of 'employed', they are not eligible for employment standards coverage and social security protection.

Alongside high and rising levels of unemployment has been an expansion in informal work. Restrictions on black business and informal traders during the apartheid period had kept the informal sector quite small. However, in the mid-1980s the apartheid regime began to relax laws and restrictions on black business ownership and small business development in the townships, resulting in the steady growth of small businesses and informal trading. The ANC's support for the small business sector has contributed to the rapid growth of small and micro-enterprises, many of them not registered for tax or other purposes and therefore part of 'the informal sector'. For example, those employed in informal work increased from 15.9 per cent to 20 per cent between 2002 and 2005. Informal work made up a larger percentage of those people employed in some sectors, such as the retail sector and the clothing industry. According to the Labour Force Surveys, informal retail work rose steadily in the post-apartheid period, and by March 2005 made up close to 36 per cent of employment in the sector (Statistics South Africa 2004b). A similar pattern of informalisation has been apparent in other sectors, such as the clothing industry. Clothing firms have responded to the new, more competitive environment brought about by trade liberalisation by outsourcing and sub-contracting more of their production to unregistered operations (informal factories), or to small home-based operations. At the same time, South African retailers have taken advantage of the new tariff structure to increase volumes of clothing from overseas producers and have begun sourcing clothing directly from small, informal clothing producers. Overall, there has been a decline in formal sector employment and rise in informal, home-based work in the sector. According to Statistics South Africa data, an estimated 64,000 formal sector jobs were lost in the clothing, textile and footwear industries between January 2003 and June 2006 (Kriel 2006).

Informalisation has been accompanied by a proliferation of temporary and casual forms of employment. According to government labour force statistics, the number of workers employed in casual jobs (seasonal, temporary, casual or fixed-term contract work) has steadily increased, from 22 per cent to 28 per cent between September 2001 and March 2006 (Statistics South Africa 2002b: 46; Statistics South Africa 2006: 36). Qualitative and quantitative research in specific sectors suggests that casual work and other forms of precarious employment with uncertain hours, scheduling and pay have grown more rapidly than what is documented by national statistics. For example, casual employment in the retail sector is more widespread than national statistics suggest as 'permanent' employment in the retail sector includes both permanent full-time workers as well as those employed as 'permanent casuals'. For instance, store-based research on the retail sector reveals that casual employment is the norm in most large retail stores, often making up close to 60% of those employed (see Kenny 2004 and Clarke 2006).

Given the intersection of race and skill levels in South Africa, it is no surprise that employment shifts have contributed to changes in the racial composition of the labour force and to rising inequalities. The number of black workers employed in full-time, permanent jobs has shrunk, while greater numbers of the working class have moved into casual, non-unionised, unprotected jobs and occupations. In particular, African workers have borne the brunt of job losses in the formal sector. This is consistent with the decline in the primary sectors, which have historically been the most important employers of African workers relative to other racialised groups. According to Barchiesi, 'by the end of the 1990s, full time waged employment was a reality for only less than one third of the African economically active population and approximately 40% of the overall national EAP' [Economically Active Population] (2007: 4). Similarly, restructuring in South Africa has been profoundly gendered. Restructuring has intensified poverty, especially among rural women and black women, while employment changes have reinforced gender and racial inequality in the country. Racial and gender inequality has persisted in unemployment rates, employment form and protection, employment income, and in the incidence of low and uncertain wages. Overall, employment changes have created new divisions between workers and widened existing differentials among them; thus amplifying racial and gender segmentation in the labour market. Hence, just as legislative reforms formally eradicated all forms of discrimination carried over from apartheid legislation, other socio-economic changes have re-shaped and reinforced divisions and inequality in the labour market.

In addition, the privatisation of public sector companies (specifically municipal services) and cost recovery in service delivery have contributed to continued, even rising, socio-economic inequalities. The logic of tight fiscal management and market-orientation has meant users pay the full cost of the provision of basic services. This has, in effect, 'clawed back' many of the services newly extended to poor communities. Water and electricity infrastructure has been extended to new areas, but even the poorest households are expected to pay full market prices or they will be cut off. Statistics released by the government's delivery monitoring service revealed the extent of the problem: there were 154,601 more electricity disconnections than connections in the first three months of 2002 (Clarke and Greenberg 2003). Using a conservative estimate of five people per household, this meant more than 770 000 people had their electricity cut off. Those who could not pay their bills also risked having their homes re-possessed and household items sold to recover arrears. In addition, labour market restructuring, privatisation and cutbacks to social services (alongside the rapid increase of AIDS[2] and other diseases) are forcing many women back into traditional family forms to provide unpaid care for family (often extended family) members.

In sum, despite some progress in employment standards and social policies over the last decade, the government has failed to address the social and economic inequalities of the country. There is a general consensus that incomes have declined and poverty and overall inequality have increased (see, for example, Pauw and Mncube 2007). In a range of policy areas, especially trade and industrial and labour market policies, the government failed to represent the interests poor and working-class communities. Attracting foreign investment and improving the country's international competitiveness took precedence over meeting the needs of poor and working South Africans. It is no surprise that social tensions have increased in recent years as the country continues to move away from a racially-divided society, to an increasingly class-divided society (Southall 2007). As we shall see in the section below, unions have struggled to respond to employment restructuring and shifting forms of inequality. Partly as a result of the slow pace at which unions have responded to socio-economic restructuring and the impact of these policies on marginalised workers and communities, new social movements have emerged and begun to play an important role in challenging the ANC's policy direction.

Responding and resisting: union strategies to restructuring

Collective bargaining and traditional forms of organising and representing workers are beset by various challenges emerging from the shifting political and economic context and from labour market restructuring. Although some unions have responded proactively to workplace restructuring initiatives and processes of casualisation, most – especially unions in industries that continue to be dominated by full-time, permanent employment – have been slow to respond. For the most part, COSATU continued to embrace a model of 'strategic unionism', despite the failure of this strategy and their waning influence on both government and business. As such, the union movement has remained narrowly focused on workers in formal employment, especially those in full-time, continuous employment in core sectors of the economy, and on tripartite structures and agreements aimed at protecting their members and strengthening labour legislation and expanding its coverage. Although the federation has argued that agreements have been successful in finding ways to retain and create quality jobs, there is little evidence to suggest that they have done anything to produce new jobs for the unemployed millions or protect existing jobs for those in sectors where employers continue to casualise the workforce and introduce other ways of increasing flexibility.

In the years following the introduction of the new regulatory framework, unions focused on using new laws to strengthen collective bargaining and improve minimum standards for workers in poorly organised sectors. Unions believed they could take advantage of their organisational and political strength to negotiate strong sectoral wage agreements for workers in poorly organised sectors – including retail, cleaning, security and agriculture – and push to have wage agreements extended to non-parties, thereby improving the wages and working conditions of unorganised workers. COSATU also believed, and for good reason given its history in the anti-apartheid struggle and its alliance with the ANC, that it would be able to use tripartite institutions and structures (such as Nedlac and the ECC) to improve wages and working conditions, to defend and advance workers' rights, and to challenge the neoliberal economic and development strategy the government seemed to be following with increased zeal.

For the most part, this strategy has met with very little success. Although some unions and scholars have continued to defend tripartism and seem to believe that for these structures to function properly, COSATU simply needs to increase its capacity to 'make effective use of the institutions it helped create' (Adler and Webster 2003), there is little evidence to suggest that COSATU has, or could have in the near future, anything more than waning influence within tripartite structures. Instead, the power of capital vis-à-vis labour suggests that national and international business demands are more likely to be met in government policy. There is certainly much evidence of this, such as the fact that none of COSATU's major socio-economic demands have been implemented as government policy and few of the federation's basic demands, in areas such as job creation and inflation-related wage increases, have been accepted since 1994 (McKinley 2004). And, despite the federation's expectations that Nedlac and other tripartite structures would result in an increased role for unions in policy-making and in the ongoing transformation of the economy, COSATU has been increasingly marginalised within Nedlac structures, and major economic policies, such as GEAR, were implemented without ever having been discussed within Nedlac structures (Bassett 2000). Indeed, even the government has acknowledged that Nedlac has not functioned properly, and that key stakeholders are often unable to attend crucial meetings. According to one of the representatives of business to Nedlac, 'There are few directors generally attending meetings at Nedlac. Within the government, Nedlace is no longer taken seriously' (Letsoalo 2005).

Tripartism and alliance politics have certainly not proven successful. As noted above, at independence COSATU entered into a strategic alliance with the ANC and SACP in order to advance working-class interests in the new government. Even COSATU, if reluctantly, has recently acknowledged alliance politics and alliance structures have failed. To quote at length:

> COSATU thought it would meet in the Alliance or with the government to plan how to discipline capital and get it to play a constructive role in the ongoing transformation of the economy and our country. This type of Alliance does not exist and, if we are to be honest, will not emerge in the foreseeable future. ... Fundamentally, the balance of forces in the Alliance today ... prefer that the Alliance appears united in ceremonious occasions but largely acts only as cannon fodder for mobilisation during the elections. In the run-up to the elections, relations improve and a new sense of unity and respect for one another emerges. Once the elections are over, we go back into the painful reality of being sidelined for another five years. (COSATU 2003: 9)

In addition to the failure of tripartism and alliance politics, organised labour's hope that they could use their organisational strength and the new industrial relations system to advance workers' interests has also failed to materialise. For the most part, unions have not been able to use new labour regulations to strengthen the bargaining council system or to use bargaining council agreements to restrict or regulate the use of casual and temporary labour. After several years of stabilisation, the latter part of the 1990s saw the number of bargaining councils in decline, as did the ability of existing councils to effectively implement and monitor their agreements. Declining union membership and strength, linked in part to the rise of casual and temporary employment, have contributed to weakening the bargaining council system and the steady decline in the number of functioning bargaining councils. According to Godfrey, Maree and Theron (2006: 96), there were 104 councils in 1983, 87 in 1992, 80 in 1995 and only 57 by 2004. By 2005 bargaining councils covered just less than a third of employees that could potentially be covered by collective bargaining, and less than 5 per cent of all such employees were covered by extended agreements (ibid.: 94).

The decline in the number and effectiveness of bargaining councils has resulted in a general trend towards decentralised bargaining at the enterprise level. Since South Africa does not have national minimum wage legislation, this trend means that workers in weakly organised workplaces and informal employment are more likely to have wages set by individual employment contracts with employers, thus being most vulnerable to downward pressure on wages and working conditions through flexibility provisions in the BCEA. And, similar to Nedlac's marginalisation in national economic policy-making and COSATU's declining political strength within the tripartite structure, COSATU has tended to play a minor role in setting new sectoral wage determinations. In contrast, employers have strategically used negotiating structures tasked with setting sectoral wage agreements to set new industry-wide employment conditions which provide extensive flexibility for businesses. Indeed, union negotiators have often been forced to adopt defensive positions in response to employer demands for greater flexibility, rather than using negotiations to extend protection to casual and other vulnerable workers. For example, retail employers' demands for increased flexibility were largely accommodated in the new sectoral determination for the retail sector, introduced on 1 February 2003. Employers' proposals for extensive flexibility in wage rates and working hours (through the averaging of hours of work and the compressed working week) were realised in the new determination (Clarke 2006).

Surprisingly, COSATU remains committed to the alliance, to tripartite structures and to continuing its strategy of 'strategic unionism'. Still, the federation has begun to acknowledge the weaknesses and limitations of these strategies and corporatist-type structures. The federation and individual affiliates have begun to recognise that rather than 'strategic unionism', a more traditional, bureaucratic 'business' model of unionism has largely replaced social movement unionism in the country. Similar to 'business' unionism elsewhere (Banks and Metzgar, 1989; Ross, 2004), a more hierarchical relationship between the union leadership and the membership has emerged in South Africa, with leaders focusing their attention on technical and legalistic processes and narrowly-defined material interests of the membership. In general, unions have tried to address membership losses and the impact of economic restructuring on workers by negotiating agreements with business and government, and have tended to retreat from organising and servicing their members. Thus, tripartism and the adoption of 'strategic' unionism have inadvertently contributed to a demobilisation of the union movement and a marked decline in the role and influence of COSATU in South African society and politics.

In order to address these problems, COSATU has begun to re-examine union structures and strategies, and has initiated a union renewal process aimed at increasing union membership in poorly organised sectors and among casual workers, and has committed itself to (re)build social unionism (COSATU 1999). At this point, it is unclear whether any of the traditions of social movement unionism embedded in COSATU in the 1980s have survived, and if they will be able to be revived over the next several years. One of the factors that might be decisive in this process is whether the unions are successful in organising and represent those workers and communities affected by neoliberal economic restructuring and labour market changes, and whether unions begin building real alliances with the newly emerged community-based organisations.

The emergence of new social movements

Beginning in the late 1990s, precisely when COSATU was hamstrung by Alliance politics, new community-based groups began emerging and organising around a range of socio-economic issues (Ballard *et al.* 2006; Bassett and

Clarke 2008). While some of these groups have their roots in the mass democratic movement under apartheid, and central members and leaders of some organisations have a history of political activism within the trade union movement, political parties – such as the SACP and ANC – and other political movements, contemporary social movements in South Africa have been characterised as 'new' since most of them have emerged and grown in the post-apartheid period, many since the late 1990s (Ballard *et al.* 2006).

These groups are not homogeneous and their strategies, goals and tactics have been quite diverse. However, what they share is a critique of the government's adoption of neoliberal economic policies, and they commonly emerged in response to the impact of these policies on poor and working-class communities, specifically on social reproduction and poverty. Notable examples of these social movements are the Anti-Privatisation Forum (APF), the Anti-Eviction Campaign (AEC), and the Soweto Electricity Crisis Committee (SECC). These groups have gained prominence in recent years and have played an increasingly important role in challenging government policies and mobilising communities most affected by the impact housing evictions and water and electricity cuts-offs as a result of government policy shifts. For instance, the APF was formed in 2000 as a loosely structured forum (involving such affiliates as the SECC) to challenge market liberalisation and its impact on communities, specifically the impact of the privatisation of municipal service delivery on social reproduction and poverty in the townships (interview, Dale McKinley, July 2006).

The social characteristics of membership of new social movements are revealing: many groups, particularly members of APF affiliates, such as the SECC, generally come from the marginalised and vulnerable sections of society. While the general membership tends to be women, often pensioners, the leadership – like the union movement – is dominated by men and those involved direct action, such as electricity reconnections that are carried out by young men (Egan and Wafer 2006). This gender and age profile of social movements is no surprise; women, women pensioners in particular, are the recipients of the government's old age pension and, given high and rising levels of unemployment, they are often the sole breadwinners in their households and bear the brunt of rising unemployment and cost-recovery policies linked to the privatisation of municipal services (Hassim, 2006; Ballard *et al.* 2006). Indeed, as Hassim (2006: 359) and others have argued (Budlender 2004; Clarke 2006), women have been the shock absorbers of high levels of unemployment, informalisation, casualisation, and 'of the failure of the state to provide a comprehensive and efficient system of social security and healthcare'. As community activist, Ashwin Desai has said, the APF's constituencies are women and 'the poors'.

Groups that have been involved in direct action – such as reconnecting electricity supplies to households that have had their electricity cut-off as a result of households' inability to pay for privatised service delivery – have also engaged in lobbying efforts and media work and have worked to organise poor and marginalised communities in situations where union organising has been absent or in decline. There are some success stories: thousands of households have had their electricity reconnected, even if illegally and possibly only temporarily; and the APF built a constitutional rights legal case against water privatisation and the installation of pre-paid water-meters that will soon be heard by the Johannesburg High Court, and may make its way to the Constitutional Court.

Still, while the potential of these new groups should not be underestimated, there are some clear limitations to their activities since they generally are organised around single issues, are based in small geographic communities, and continue to be quite divided by political goals and tactics. And, the continued separation of 'workplace issues' and 'social/community issues' by both the union movement and new social movements reveals some serious limitations to the organising and political strategies of both groupings. Surprising, neither the unions nor these new social movements appears interested or able to organise or represent precarious workers. As Buhlungu (2006: 84–85) correctly notes, these groups, such as the APF, have failed to attract unionised workers into its affiliates nor they been able to organise workers in informal, casual and other forms of precarious employment. With neither new social movements nor the traditional trade union movement have made any real inroads in organising precarious workers, some new organisations have begun to emerge. In the late 1990s a new group, *Sikhula Sonke* (meaning 'we grow together'), formed to organise casual women farmworkers, and, in 2003, a community-based group, *Men on the Side of the Road Project*, emerged to organise and represent the large and growing number of male day-labourers in the country.

While it is too early to assess their impact, the emergence of these groups suggests that diverse political struggles and new ways of mobilising workers are beginning to emerge. However, these groups are still new, are small and remain concentrated in only a few sectors, and are not integrated into either the union movement (COSATU) or affiliated with new social movements. COSATU's commitment to re-building social movement unionism and building stronger links with community groups suggests that stronger links between COSATU and new movements are being sought and may soon emerge.

Conclusion

For more than a decade, COSATU has been grappling with how to shape South Africa's transition while also confronting the impact of national and global processes of socio-economic restructuring. As was outlined in this chapter, COSATU's expectation that its close ties with the ANC during the anti-apartheid struggle would culminate in a socio-economic reform programme that would meet the needs of poor and working-class South Africans has not materialised. Instead, the government has generally used its close ties with COSATU to restrain the latter's push for extensive socio-economic restructuring and redistribution while proceeding with a programme to liberalise the economy (Bassett and Clarke 2008). The impact of liberalisation and flexibilisation has been devastating on many workers and communities, with rising inequalities, pervasive poverty, and the deepening 'jobs crisis' clear consequences of these policies. Job insecurity is rife and the gains initially won by labour are now being eroded, with union membership and power declining vis-à-vis growing employer offensives.

COSATU's preoccupation with institutional structures and formal negotiation processes has created new dynamics and tensions between workers, often intensifying and facilitating processes of socio-economic restructuring. As a result, despite the union movement's long history of collective action both within the workplace and community, COSATU has played a weak role in the rejuvenation of community groups that have played a critical role in challenging government policies and resultant problems in service delivery in recent years. With political fights over the issue of who will succeed Thabo Mbeki as President of the ANC in 2007 heating up once again, and as the country moves towards its next national election (scheduled for 2009), there are some signs that new, and different forms of contestation are beginning to emerge. First, the federation has begun focusing on union renewal strategies, and has highlighted the importance of organising casuals and other precarious workers. Second, COSATU has begun focusing attention on strengthening and rebuilding the union moment along the lines of previous forms of social movement unionism. As part of this strategy, the union movement has begun forging links with social movements.

These moves suggest that COSATU is, perhaps finally and decisively, moving away from the framework of 'strategic' or business unionism – shaped by a strategy of trying to transform economic processes and policies from 'within' – and instead shifting back towards social unionism. As argued elsewhere, under a best-case scenario, the next few years will see COSATU move out of its political stasis and use the political space open to unions and social movements to press for a redesign of post-apartheid democracy (Bassett and Clarke 2008). Though previously, there have been proposals that a coalition of community activists and trade unionists might come together to back a stronger challenge to the state, to reorient its policies towards the poor and working class, COSATU always seemed to pull back from opportunities to cement this relationship and help coordinate a new, broadly-based, national working-class movement. Instead, previously, the trade union federation retained its focus on their political Alliance and on tripartite forums and structures to challenge socio-economic processes and policies. The federation's recent and renewed commitment to re-building social movement unionism, and to organising casual workers suggests that this time might be different. Certainly COSATU needs to widen its constituency to incorporate the growing number of precarious workers in the labour market, but these workers need to be recruited as part of a broader political project, not just as a goal to increase union membership.

Notes

1 Both the LRA and BCEA were amended with effect from 1 August 2002.

2 Until at least 1998 South Africa had one of the fastest expanding epidemics in the world. According to the Department of Health Study of 2002, HIV prevalence is between 25.5 and 27.6 per cent among antenatal clinic attendees, and between 20 and 24 per cent among all people aged 15–49 years old (*South Africa HIV/AIDS Statistics* 2005).

References

Adler, G. and Webster, E. (1996) 'Challenging Transition Theory: The Labor Movement, Radical Reform and Transition to Democracy in South Africa', *Politics and Society* 23(1): 75–106.

—— (2000) *Consolidating Democracy in a Liberalizing World: Trade Unions and Democracy in South Africa*, Johannesburg: Witwatersrand University Press.

Ballard, R., Habib, A. and Valodia, I. (eds) (2006) *Voices of Protest: Social Movements in Post-Apartheid South Africa*. Pietermaritzburg: University of KwaZulu-Natal.

Banks, A. and Metzgar, J. (1989) 'Participating in Management: Union Organizing on a New Terrain', *Labor Research Review*, 14(Fall): 1–55.

Barchiesi, F. (2007) 'Schooling Bodies to Hard Work': The South African State's Policy Discourse and Its Moral Constructions of Welfare', paper presented at the North Eastern Workshop on Southern Africa (NEWSA), Vermont.

Bassett, C. and Clarke, M. (2008) 'The Zuma Affair: Labour and the Future of Democracy in South Africa', *Third World Quarterly* 29(4).

Budlender, D. (2004) 'Some Are Still More Equal Than Others', *Amalungelo, 15* (March{-]April), pp. 52–53.

Buhlungu, S. (2005) 'Union-Party Alliances in the Era of Market Regulation: The Case of South Africa', *Journal of Southern African Studies* 31(4): 701–717.

—— (2006) 'Upstarts or Bearers of Tradition? The Anti Privatisation Forum of Gauteng', In R. Ballard, A. Habib and I. Valodia (eds) *Voices of Protest: Social Movements in Post-Apartheid South Africa*, Pietermaritzburg: University of KwaZulu-Natal Press, pp. 67–87.

Cheadle, H. (2005) 'Labour Market Flexibility: Will a Social Pact Help?' Paper presented at the Harold Wolpe Memorial Seminar, 5 October, Johannesburg.

Clarke, M. (2006) *'All the Workers?' Labour Market Reform and Precarious Work in Post-Apartheid South Africa, 1994–2004*, unpublished dissertation.

Clarke, M. and Greenberg, S. (2003) *Global Influences on Macro-economic Policy and Practice in Post-apartheid South Africa*, Cape Town: Women on Farms Project.

COSATU (1999) *Repositioning COSATU to Meet the Challenges of the New Millennium*, Book #1, Johannesburg: COSATU, Special National Congress, 18–20 August.

—— (2003) *COSATU Central Committee Report: 2nd Central Committee, Organisational Renewal to Deepen Service to Our Members*, Johannesburg: COSATU.

Department of Labour (2002) *Department of Labour Annual Report, 2001 / 2002*. Pretoria.

Draper, P. (2003) *To Liberalise of Not to Liberalise? A Review of the South African Government's Trade Policy*, Working Paper, Braamfontein: South African Institute of International Affairs.

Egan, A. and Wafer, A. (2006) 'Dynamics of a "Mini-Mass Movement": Origins, Identity and Ideological Pluralism in the Soweto Electricity Committee', in R. Ballard, A. Habib and I. Valodia (eds) *Voices of Protest: Social Movements in Post-Apartheid South Africa*, Pietermaritzburg: University of KwaZulu-Natal Press, pp. 45–65.

Godfrey, S., Maree, J. and Theron, J. (2006) *Conditions of Employment and Small Business: Coverage, Compliance and Exemptions*, DPRU Working Paper No. 06/106. Cape Town: Development Policy Research Unit.

Harsch, E. (2001) 'South Africa Tackles Social Inequities', *Africa Recovery* 14(4): 12–19.

Hassim, S. (2006) 'The Challenges of Inclusion and Transformation: The Women's Movement in Democratic South Africa', in R. Ballard, A. Habib and I. Valodia (eds) *Voices of Protest: Social Movements in Post-Apartheid South Africa*, Pietermaritzburg: University of KwaZulu-Natal Press, pp. 349–370.

Kenny, B. (2004) *Divisions of Labor, Experiences of Class: Changing Collective Identities of East Rand Food Retail Sector Workers through South Africa's Democratic Transition*, unpublished dissertation.

Kriel, A. (2006) 'Morris' Job Data Not Authoritative', retrieved February 15, 2007, from www.busrep.co.za/index.php?fSectionId=553&fArticleId=3480005

Letsoalo, M. (2005) 'State "no longer takes Nedlac seriously"', retrieved February 10, 2007, www.mg.co.za/articlePage.aspx?articleid=251455&area=/insight/insight–national

Marais, H. (2001) *South Africa: Limits to Change: The Political Economy of Transition*, 2nd edn, London: Zed Books.

McKinley, D. (2004) 'Democracy, Power and Patronage: Debate and Opposition within the ANC and the Tripartite Alliance since 1994', paper presented at the Conference on Opposition in South Africa's New Democracy, June.

Murray, M. J. (1994) *The Revolution Deferred: The Painful Birth of Post-Apartheid South Africa*, London: Verso.

Patel, E. (1993) 'New Institutions of Decision-Making: The Case of the National Economic Forum', in E. Patel (ed.), *Engine of Development?* Cape Town: Juta.

Pauw, K. and Mncube, L. (2007) *The Impact of Growth and Redistribution on Poverty and Inequality in South Africa, Country Study*, Brasilia: International Poverty Centre, United Nations Development Programme.

Robinson, I. (1993) 'Economistic Unionism in Crisis: The Origins, Consequences and Prospects of Divergence in Labour-Movement Characteristics', in J. Jenson and R. Mahon (eds) *The Challenge of Restructuring: North America Labour Movements Respond*, Philadelphia, PA: Temple University Press, pp. 19–47.

Robinson, V. (2006) 'From GEAR to ASGI', retrieved January 15, 2007, from www.mg.co.za/articlePage.aspx?articleid=263813&area=/budget_2006/bud_insight/

Ross, S. (2004) 'Social Unionism and Membership Participation: What Role for Union Democracy?' Paper presented at the Annual Conference of the Canadian Political Science Association, Political Economy Section, Winnipeg, Manitoba.

Southall, R. (2007) 'Introduction: The ANC State, More Dysfunctional than Developmental?' In J. Daniel, A. Habib and R. Southall (eds) *State of the Nation 2006–2007*, Pretoria: HSRC, pp. xvii–xlv.

Statistics South Africa (1998) *Labour Statistics, Survey of Total Employment and Earnings, Statistical Release P0271*, Pretoria: Government of South Africa.

—— (2004a) *Labour Force Survey March 2004: Statistical Release P0210*. Pretoria: Statistics South Africa.

—— (2004b) *Labour Force Survey September 2004. Statistical Release P0210*, Pretoria: Statistics South Africa.

—— (2005) *Labour Force Survey March 2005. Statistical Release P0210*, Pretoria: Statistics South Africa.

—— (2006) *Labour Force Survey March 2006: Statistical Release P0210*. Pretoria: Statistics South Africa.

Von Holdt, K. (1993) 'Strategic Unionism: The Debate', *Southern Africa Report* 8(3–4): 36–40.

Webster, E. (1988) 'The Rise of Social-Movement Unionism: The Two Faces of the Black Trade Union Movement in South Africa', in P. Frankel, N. Pines and M. Swilling (eds) *State, Resistance, and Change in South Africa*, Johannesburg: Southern Book Publishers, pp. 174–196.

10 After the collapse

Workers and social conflict in Argentina

Viviana Patroni

The December 2001 social uprising in Argentina awakened a new confidence within the imaginary of resistance movements, both inside the country and abroad. Excitement grew as broad sectors of the population became more convinced about the viability of popular struggles against neoliberalism. However, the sweeping transformations that were being forecast at the time have not to date materialised, at least not in the sense of producing a major political reordering. While the expected direction has not been followed, the process initiated after the crisis has nevertheless given way to a number of fundamental changes. In particular, the economic recovery experienced in Argentina since 2003 has altered the parameters within which key social actors, labour especially, have configured their opposition and struggles. Under the new conditions of economic growth, increasing employment, and strong political support for the current administration of President Néstor Kirchner, the movement of the unemployed – an alternative that generated a great many expectations as an exponent of novel ways of organising against neoliberalism – has suffered from deep divisions. The movement of the unemployed – better known as the *piquetero* movement – has also been subject to political isolation and a steady decline in its capacity to organise and mobilise those most affected by the negative transformation of Argentine labour markets. The traditional labour bureaucracy historically connected to Peronism, the CGT (*Confederación General del Trabajo*/General Confederation of Labour), after the major losses it suffered during the 1990s, has acquired a renewed prominence as an ally of a popular administration. In addition, initiatives within unionism that during the early 1990s with the formation of the CTA (*Central de Trabajadores Argentinos*/Central of Argentinian Workers) appeared well positioned to challenge the undemocratic and bureaucratic practices of the Peronist labour leadership have encountered mounting obstacles and have thus experienced difficulties in remaining significant as organisational alternatives. The experience of the CTA, the main focus of this chapter, demonstrates the complexity that has been involved in articulating alternatives inclusive of the various experiences of a fragmented working class.

Neoliberalism transformed Argentina in profound ways. From the time of the early neoliberal policies enforced by the military dictatorship between

1976 and 1983 up to the last wave of restructuring under the Convertibility Plan in the 1990s, more than 25 years of neoliberalism altered every single aspect of life in the country. These changes were especially evident in the new realities of work faced by most Argentines, in particular the deterioration of wages and labour conditions, the growth of unemployment and precarious forms of employment, and the deregulation of labour markets. In the 1990s, the working class responded in a number of ways to the drastic deterioration in living standards and decline in the quality of jobs that accompanied the neoliberal policies implemented in that decade. Labour's ability to challenge these burdens, though, was limited by the impact of the reforms themselves and by the connection of some sectors within labour to the Peronist party that was responsible in the 1990s for the reforms that so negatively affected labour markets. Notwithstanding these constraints, the collapse of the economic plan that became so central in the articulation of neoliberalism in Argentina during the 1990s was in large part determined by the growing social mobilisation of those sectors most affected by changes in labour markets. This was clearly the case with the *piqueteros* and also, as I will argue more emphatically, with the emergence of important challenges from within the union movement itself. Indeed, as the once very powerful CGT struggled to accommodate to the new neoliberal realities imposed on it, new challenges to its position emerged from within the labour movement. The CTA was one such challenge.

In examining the responses to neoliberalism in Argentina that emerged from the working class during the 1990s and the capacity of those responses to influence the configuration of alternatives to neoliberalism in the post-crisis period, my discussion will focus on the CTA, its relation to the traditional labour movement, and to other organisations of the unemployed. The main goal of the chapter is to account both for the significance of the experience of the CTA and also the increasing difficulties it has faced since 2001 in maintaining its position of prominence as a social and political actor. Despite the strength it gained during the 1990s – not only as an alternative working class organisation but also as a political force striving to provide a voice for the large segment of demands emerging from those marginalised through the process of restructuring – since the early 2000s the CTA has been in a situation of impasse. My argument is that, regardless of the strength the CTA gained during the appearance of more active mobilisation since the end of the 1990s until the election of Kirchner in 2003, the political capital it accumulated has not been enough to secure a significant role for the organisation in either the determination of public policy or the continual shaping of a more forceful and democratic form of unionism. In particular, the significant demobilisation of the organisation of the unemployed, the reaffirmation of the privileged position of the CGT within the government, and the CTA's increasing internal tensions form a cluster of challenges that have not been easily addressed. In many respects, the challenges the CTA has encountered in this new post-crisis political juncture are somewhat paradoxical since current conditions seem considerably more conducive to reasserting both key demands in the area of salaries and labour rights and an agenda for labour union democratisation.

In the next section of the chapter, I will concentrate on the main changes that occurred both in the position of labour as a political actor in Argentina and in the structure of labour markets resulting from the policies followed during the 1990s. In the third section, I will trace the emergence of the CTA and some of the characteristics that have made it such a worthwhile experiment in the search for union alternatives. The purpose of this discussion will be to provide the necessary background to examine, in the fourth section of the chapter, the conditions that account for the positioning of the CTA in the most recent phase of economic growth. In the conclusion, I will identify some of the main challenges faced by the CTA today.

Labour markets and the neoliberal debacle

Since at least the 1940s conceptions about development in Argentina gave privileged expression to ideas that connected industrialisation, a robust domestic market, high rates of employment, and the crucial role of the state in the economy with economic growth and improved standards of living. The demise of these principles was the direct consequence of the overwhelming victory of neoliberal ideas introduced with the military coup of 1976. This year saw the end of a period of at least three decades in which industrialisation – pursued under the tutelary role of the state – set the boundaries for the tenuous and increasingly unsustainable consensus that had delimited social conflict in Argentina. Labour, and more concretely its overwhelmingly hegemonic Peronist leadership, was a key political actor throughout the period and none of the governments that came to power during this era, not even those with an anti-labour stand, effectively threatened the structural and institutional bases of labour's enormous power (Cavarozzi 1986: 43).

In this context, those who continued to relate economic decline and political instability in Argentina to the over-regulation of the economy, the suffocation of private initiative, and the inordinate power of unions found themselves repeatedly overpowered by the weight of the arguments in support of industrialisation as a path to development. It is not surprising then that after 25 years of Argentine neoliberalism, those now involved in the construction of alternatives to it also attempt to recover some of the discourse that previously influenced the debate on development in the nation. At stake is the imperative to find an alternative to what has produced the steady deterioration of the country's economy, marked by its deindustrialisation, mounting foreign debt, the drastic deterioration of working conditions, rising unemployment and underemployment levels and, with them, the unprecedented growth of poverty and inequality.[1] Some of these tendencies have been in evidence since very early on in the process of neoliberal restructuring initiated by the military regime in 1976, but they reached their peak during the 1990s.

While neoliberalism was thus not new to Argentina in the 1990s, it was during this decade that it acquired its most dynamic and, moreover, its most destructive shape. In fact, it was in 1991 that the Convertibility Plan, establishing a fixed exchange rate between the domestic currency and the dollar, set the framework within which the last wave of structural reforms acquired new strength.[2] The process of economic restructuring produced a number of deep structural constraints and bottlenecks. Creating a situation that was ultimately unworkable, these barriers became the straitjacket within which successive administrations until 2001 tried to manage the deepening economic crisis neoliberalism had provoked (Basualdo 2001). While the troubling manifestations of the costs of imposed economic stability were evident via a number of early signs, probably no warning was more compelling than the transformation of labour markets and the rise of poverty that this particular transformation brought about.

Several factors contributed to the perverse performance of labour markets. The first and central aspect was, without doubt, the negative evolution of the industrial sector. In general terms, currency appreciation, particularly as the decade progressed, in combination with trade liberalisation, generated a number of difficult challenges for domestic industries by opening these industries to increasing competition from artificially low-priced imports. Under these conditions only firms capable of increasing efficiency at high enough levels to compete with imports survived the process.

Second, one of the most important instruments in the survival kit of manufacturing enterprises was the adoption of new technology. Nonetheless, an overvalued currency favoured the adoption of imported technology that tended to be capital intensive (Gastaldi *et al. 1997*: 87). Both trends, the elimination of less competitive firms and growing investment in labour-saving technology, resulted in productivity gains. In terms of employment levels, however, the disadvantage of this process was that displaced labour was not easily incorporated into other economic sectors. The problem was compounded by the fact that, as I will discuss below, one of the main characteristics of structural adjustment under the convertibility plan was the cyclical nature of economic growth. Moreover, growing labour productivity was also the outcome of the re-organisation of labour processes aimed at increasing the intensity of work. Without hesitation, it can be said that the weakening structural position of labour unions, and therefore their diminishing capacity to protect working conditions and even the most elemental labour rights, go a long way towards explaining rising labour productivity (Monza 1995: 146). Increasing productivity was not sufficient to affect the tendency for salaries to decline. Thus, by the end of the decade real salaries were 23 per cent below their 1986 level and 30 per cent below the level of 1980 (Mancebo 1998: 187).

Third, the privatisation of state companies became another source of labour displacement. In fact, privatisation was in many cases concomitant with sharp reductions in company staff and, therefore, resulted in considerable increments in state companies' levels of productivity (Beccaria and López 1996: 40). Fourth, a determining variable cutting across all these tendencies and certainly worsening their impact was the various recessionary processes that punctuated the decade (1995 and 1998–2001). Notably, though, some of the negative transformations of labour markets were evident even in periods of economic growth (1991–1994 and 1996–1998). Finally, one of the few sectors that performed well during the 1990s was exports.[3] However, the main characteristic of this sector was its growing 'primarisation', that is, the increasing participation of resource-intensive products (Nochteff 1998). The production of these exports was intensive in the use of capital and thus could not provide a dynamic alternative for the absorption of the workers who had been displaced from other economic activities undergoing major restructuring during the 1990s.

The interplay of all the above-identified variables resulted in an exponential growth of unemployment during the decade, from 6 per cent in 1991 to 18.3 per cent in 2001. Underemployment also rose dramatically in the 1990s as did the incidence of precarious forms of employment, in particular those jobs that did not offer any form of social security or formal contracts (Beccaria and López 1996: 60). In other words, most workers who lost their formal jobs were increasingly re-absorbed into the labour market through precarious forms of employment. In the metropolitan area of Buenos Aires, for example, the number of precarious jobs grew from 26.7 per cent in 1990 to 40 per cent in 2000.

The escalating incidence of precariousness evidences one of the most critical transformations during the 1990s. Precariousness, informality, unemployment, and underemployment were the outcome of a complex set of economic variables that tilted the balance of power further in favour of capital. A number of other variables weakened even further the capacity of labour to prevent a further deterioration in working conditions. One especially important factor was the lack of a comprehensive programme of unemployment insurance. In fact, the lack of decisive initiatives on the part of the government to transform the conditions faced by most workers was an important variable determining – during the 1990s, and beyond – the negative conditions under which workers re-entered the world of work. It is in this respect that one must consider the impact of employment programmes in sustaining the current trends in labour markets.

During the 1990s, as conditions in the labour market deteriorated and as poverty increased, the government implemented several social and employment programmes. Among the latter were *Reinserción Laboral* (Labour Reintegration), *Empleo Joven* (Youth Employment), and *Plan Trabajar* (Programme to Work). Following the prescription of the World Bank and the IMF, these programmes targeted a very specific and small portion of the population. Thus, for example, the most important employment programme during this period, *Plan Trabajar*, only reached 150,000 beneficiaries although unemployment affected at the time approximately 5 million people (Ogando 2004).

In general, employment plans under this category offered temporary three- to six-month contracts for community public works projects with very low remunerations (between $100 and $200 per month). According to one study, in 1997 these programmes were responsible for 80 per cent of the new employment in the public sector (Hidalgo 1999: 134). In every respect, these programmes came to contribute to the general tendency toward growing precariousness and instability in labour conditions, and, it may be added, toward accepting relief from complete exclusion from labour markets on a similar basis.

The serious political crisis unleashed with the December 2001 uprising and the pressing need to find some containment to social protest are factors that explain in large part the urgency with which governments, after 2002, attempted to put into motion some relief programmes with a much larger reach in terms of the intended beneficiary population. By mid-2002 the administration of then President Saa had put in effect a programme that, while replicating to a large extent the objectives of *Plan Trabajar*, was much broader in its scope. The new programme, entitled *Programa Jefes y Jefas de Hogares* (Programme for Unemployed Heads of Family), reached 2,000,000 beneficiaries in the whole country by the end of the year. The targeted population was ostensibly all unemployed Argentines with children under the age of 18. Beneficiaries receive $150 pesos (the equivalent of US$50) and are considered 'employed' for the purpose of official statistics, a fact that has allowed the government to reduce the official measure of unemployment by about 4 per cent. Further, not only are programme benefits extremely low in terms of meeting a family's basic needs, but access to the programme does not imply health care or social security coverage. Additionally, because beneficiaries are expected to participate in some type of employment programme, many of them have become, in practice, an alternative source of labour for jobs that were previously formal. For example, the Minister of Labour signed an agreement with the Ministry of Tourism in 2003 through which 500 beneficiaries of the programme were assigned positions in the tourist information services (CELS 2004: 33).

As the economic crisis worsened after December 2001, all indicators in labour markets continued to deteriorate. Thus by mid-2002, unemployment had reached 22 per cent of the working population. The strong economic reactivation Argentina has experienced since 2003 (the economy grew 8.9 per cent that year and 9 per cent in 2004, 8.7 per cent in 2005, and approximately 8.5 per cent during 2006) has resulted in some relief in unemployment figures. According to official figures, by the last quarter of 2004, unemployment had been reduced to 12.1 per cent of the economically active population and to 10.4 per cent in 2006. However, the figures are calculated by including as employed those who participate in some form of employment programme, a rather contentious form of measuring unemployment, as I have suggested above. When beneficiaries of these programmes are excluded from the calculations, the unemployment rate increases to 12.8

per cent (Lozano *et al.* 2006: 2). Most of the jobs created during the first few year of economic recovery continue to be contractually precarious or informal. According to a study undertaken by the CTA, 52.9 per cent of jobs created during the third quarter of 2004 corresponded to jobs where workers did not enjoy any kind of social security protection (Lozano 2005: 6). The persistently high rates of unemployment and underemployment certainly strengthened the negative conditions under which workers re-enter the world of work. But the lack of decisive initiatives on the part of the government to transform the conditions faced by most workers is also an important variable. Nonetheless, during 2006 it appears that it was jobs in the formal economy that had experienced the highest growth. However, in sectors where low-skilled workers constitute the major labour input, informal employment has continued to be the rule. This latter situation is the case, for instance, in the growing service sector, including the small-scale enterprises connected to the industrial and agricultural sector (*Página 12*, 9 May 2007). It is important to remember, though, that insofar as the reduction of unemployment has been based fundamentally in the growth of economic activity, there are no guarantees that the situation can be sustained in the long run.

The evolution of salaries is another fundamental aspect to consider. According to recent figures, salaries have experienced some real gains for the first time in the new century. From 2002 until the end of 2005, inflation reached almost 75 per cent, becoming a major area of concern in a country used to very high rates of inflation and hyperinflation (*Clarín*, 9 January 2006). While there were improvements in salaries, inflation eroded the gains made on the salary front. Preventing a full indexation of salaries to inflation was in fact a primary component of the official strategy to contain inflation. The evolution of salaries, though, has registered important changes during 2006. According to the official figures, real salaries grew on average 18.9 per cent during this year while inflation would have reached only half that figure (*Página 12*, 8 Feb. 2007). Interestingly, it was salaries among those working without legal protection that increased slightly above those in the formal private sector (20.6 per cent for the former against 19.4 per cent for the latter). The change in the performance of salaries for informal workers must be placed, though, in the context of the abysmal conditions informal workers face: while between October 2001 and December 2006 salaries for formal workers increased on average 125 per cent, the increment was only 57 per cent for informal workers. The cumulative effect of the performance of salaries for the two groups of workers is evidenced in the fact that the average salary for formal workers is almost double the level of that for informal workers (ibid.).

Resistance and contestation: the responses from labour

Although the rapid, drastic, and negative impact of structural reforms on labour during the 1990s implied the creation of conditions that were not conducive to the effective defence of labour rights, workers nevertheless presented major challenges to these policies. Importantly, though, it was the emergence of actors outside the traditional and powerful labour movement represented by the CGT that was pivotal in articulating some resistance to the devastating impact of neoliberalism in Argentina. This unusual situation arose because the political context within which structural adjustment proceeded in Argentina during the 1990s put the CGT in a position from which it was impossibly difficult to escape without incurring heavy costs. At the core of the dilemma was the fact that it was a government being led by the Peronist party – not just labour's historical ally but rather its natural party – that was carrying out so vehemently the reforms. In many respects the shifts in policy applied by the Menem administration (1989–1999) to the crisis Argentina faced by the end of the 1980s were part and parcel of the Peronist party's internal changes, most notably, the displacement of labour from the central position it had occupied for decades (Gutierrez 2001).

The dwindling capacity of the CGT to influence government policy, particularly under a Peronist government, presented the organisation with a reality that it was not well equipped to confront. Armed with the institutional, financial, and organisational tools as a result of its corporatist relationship with the state, the CGT had been a pivotal political force in contemporary Argentina. In fact, with the exception of the military dictatorship between 1976 and 1983, the CGT had exercised the kind of power that had allowed it to determine, in many cases, the viability of both economic programmes as well as the governments that promoted them. In contrast to this earlier display of strength, the aggressive stance against labour rights and traditional unionism adopted by President Menem was met only with some tepid resistance on the part of the CGT. Even when some sectors in this labour confederation eventually became more resolute in their opposition to Menem, they never posed the kind of challenge which could have brought the president's drastic package of reforms to a halt. While many observers predicted that the new realities imposed by neoliberalism, especially under Menem, were going to deliver the final blow against corporatism and, therefore, against the CGT, in reality, the demise was only manifested in partial ways.

Quite certainly, growing unemployment, underemployment, and the increasing incidence of contingent and precarious work had dramatically limited the power of the CGT's member unions. Moreover, the organisation's reluctance to take a more clearly oppositional stance against the government cost it dearly in terms of legitimacy. However, there were sectors within the CGT that did oppose the Menem government and that became increasingly disassociated with its failing project as the decade went on. As I will discuss below, Hugo Moyano, the leader of a dissident faction within the CGT, in particular managed to remain a powerful figure, a fact that allowed him, after the election of Kirchner, to regain some of the space the CGT had lost during the 1990s.

Additionally, the political tensions generated by the CGT's overall weak stance toward Menem were serious enough to prompt some more progressive and independent unions to leave the confederation altogether in 1992. These dissident unions, most prominently the Association of Public Employees (ATE) and the Central of Education Workers (CTERA), reorganised themselves under the new Congress of Argentine Workers, the body that would later become the Central of Argentine Workers, the CTA. During the 1990s, the CTA grew to encompass other unions in different sectors of the economy, but its most important area of expansion was found in sectors outside the traditional arena of union affiliation. This growth came about particularly as a result of the capacity of the CTA to attract to its rank-and-file a large number of unemployed workers, most of them through their affiliation to the FTV (Federation of Land, Housing and Habitat (*Federación de Tierra/ Vivienda y Habitat*).

It was the institution of direct or individual forms of affiliation – as opposed to the traditional model based on the representation of constituted unions – that allowed the CTA to provide a channel of organisation for these sectors. In this way, the CTA was able to present a significant and novel alternative in response to the weakening structural position of the working class and its increasing fragmentation. The flexibility in the CTA's structure plus its very acute sense of what should constitute new alternatives in labour organising also allowed the organisation to become one of the main poles of attraction to important new social experiments in Argentina. In particular, for example, as several workers took over factories in an attempt to save their jobs, it was not difficult for them to find in the CTA a source for political support and alternative for affiliation (Palomino: 84).

It was its novel forms of representation that allowed the CTA to achieve prominence as a vehicle for the organisation of the unemployed and to gain a lead role in the struggles this sector waged with increasing determination since the mid-1990s. The FTV, the sector within the CTA representing the unemployed, sustained a rapid process of growth during the late 1990s.[4] This growth was expressed not only in its number of affiliates, but also in its increasing capacity to become a pivotal political influence within the *piquetero* movement of laid-off workers. The *piquetero* movement was and continues to be a highly heterogenous movement, marked by sharp political and organisational differences, and divided into factions.[5] However, despite these divisions there has also been the emergence of a common set of demands, primarily for work programmes. Another common characteristic among *piqueteros* has been the use of roadblocks as a form of protest. To an important extent, it was the reality of growing precariousness – a phenomenon that affected the unemployed as much as those with a job – that conditioned long-established forms of working-class struggle, in particular, strikes and general strikes.[6] Since strikes were obviously not within the repertoire of the jobless, forms of protest that before were only marginal, such as road blockades, became extremely important during the 1990s in the expression of discontent toward government policies.

While unemployed and poor communities were the main actors in the roadblocks – largely because this was one of the few forms of protest available to them – formal workers and students were also important participants. Organisations like the CTA were instrumental in drawing together the lines of communication among all these sectors and, therefore, in facilitating important levels of integration among different forms of protest. The CTA represented, in this respect, a major anti-neoliberal effort to bring together a range of demands from sectors affected in particular ways by the process of restructuring and to articulate them through various but coordinated forms of struggle and protest.

Although the organisations of *piqueteros* gained both momentum with their struggles and legitimacy as political actors during the 1990s, the number of very concrete problems related to their capacity to coordinate their struggles at the regional and national levels remained substantial. Fractures in the movement resulting from differences, particularly in strategies toward government administrations, were deepened under the new administration of President Kirchner. To be sure, the relative propensity and degree of willingness to maintain open communication with governments have been a traditional line dividing these organisations (Epstein 2003: 20–21). Differences regarding the role to be played by their organisations in the distribution of work programmes have also been a source of division among *piqueteros*. Some *piquetero* groups have seen this function as problematic since, in the eyes of some, it transforms them into intermediaries between the government and their grassroots.

The work programmes became in fact a critical issue not only dividing the *piquetero* movement but also facilitating its manipulation by the government. As I mentioned above, through these programmes the government attempted to provide some relief to the serious crisis of unemployment which developed during the 1990s. In practice, though, not only were the programmes not effective in providing an instrument to address the overwhelming problems of poverty and the deterioration of working conditions; they also became a convenient instrument for the extension and consolidation of patronage and, therein, the splintering of opposition movements.

There are two points that are particularly relevant with respect to the role of the *piquetero* organisations in the distribution of work plans. The first is that the number of plans under their control was very small. Indeed, the number of those plans secured through the agency of a *piquetero* organisation represents approximately only 5 per cent of existing plans (100,000 beneficiaries). Despite this small percentage, however, the role of the *piquetero* organisations as agents in the implementation of government social policy affected in important ways their own dynamics as political organisations and gave their leadership a new element of power over the rank-and-file. Second, and more importantly, the government was also able to use its power to allocate work plans through various organisations of the unemployed as an instrument to discriminate among them. In practice, this meant there was an added premium to an organisation's capacity to maintain a position of dialogue with the government. For instance, the FTV, the organisation of the unemployed connected to the CTA, and the CCC (*Corriente Clasista Combativa*), the two *piquetero* organisations more inclined toward negotiations with the government were selected by President Duhalde in 2002 to integrate the national body that advises the government on the implementation and performance of the programme (Epstein 2003: 26). Proximity to the government has also meant that the CTA and the CCC have been able to capture a proportionally large number of work plans.

Under the present Kirchner administration, there have been proposals once again (in early 2006) to transform work plans and to establish a Training and Employment Insurance programme aimed at facilitating the reinsertion of the unemployed into the labour market. The CTA has been very critical of the approach, pointing to the political need of the Kirchner government to transcend perceptions of a social 'emergency'. Seen from the CTA perspective, these particular government plans tend to reduce the solution to the negative structural transformation of labour markets to economic reactivation alone. Moreover, the CTA has argued, the emphasis on training and employment counselling carries with it the erroneous assumptions that employment opportunities exist for everyone and that the only thing the unemployed need is to have the right skills (CTA 2006: 2–3).

One step forward . . . two steps back?

With the election of Néstor Kirchner – a government capable of gaining strong levels of support – a very different political context for the CTA and the *piquetero* movement emerged. Some of the organisations within the movement of the unemployed tried to position themselves as the main interlocutors of the state – this was particularly the case with the FTV – which caused the stakes to rise even higher. As a wide range of *piquetero* organisations faced increasing isolation from other political and social forces, the conflict within the movement also took on a new, much more critical dimension.[7]

The growing political challenges faced since the 2001 crisis by organisations that had become so prominent until that time deserve careful consideration. The expectations generated by the reactivation of the economy as well as growing employment levels have reduced the impact of the demands and policy prescriptions that had provided direction for the strategy followed by the CTA during the 1990s and into the new century. This new reality contrasts considerably from the success the CTA enjoyed earlier in its attempt to inject broader political objectives into the wave of protests around the issues of unemployment and poverty. One example of the CTA's achievements in this area was the three weeks of protests organised during

July and August 2001. The actions involved roadblocks, massive demonstrations in downtown Buenos Aires, public sector employee and teacher strikes, and other forms of community-based protests such as blackouts and '*cacerolazos*' or pot banging. Key among the participants were the organisations of the unemployed, particularly the representatives of districts such as La Matanza, the area where the two renowned leaders of the movement, Luis D'Elía for the FTV and Carlos Alderete for the CCC were based.[8] Probably the most important outcome of these days of protest was the consolidation of the role of organisations of the unemployed as leaders in the opposition to the government's latest adjustment plan at the time.

The CTA was also the main force, as part of the National Front Against Poverty (FRENAPO), behind the organisation of a national referendum around the creation of a national employment and training insurance (*seguro de empleo y formación*) programme. This programme had been a central demand of the CTA for a few years, so the organisation's ability to mobilise a number of social forces behind it – in particular human rights organisations, student associations, some unions, and other social actors – was an important sign of its increasing influence across a large sector of social and political organisations. The preparation for the referendum involved the creation of a large number of local councils and their articulation at the national level, including a national congress held in Buenos Aires. Thus, the campaign was instrumental in fostering the organisation and coordination of a very broad spectrum of forces. The request for a public referendum did not gain official support, but an unofficial referendum was carried out nonetheless in December 2001, with results that encouraged the organisers: while FRENAPO had set its target at 2 million votes, approximately 3.1 million Argentineans voted in the referendum. In many respects, these results could also be read as an indicator of the very high levels of discontent and the obvious desire to express it that existed in Argentina. But, held as the referendum was from 14 to 17 December, just on the eve of the events that were to unleash mass mobilisations and the resignation of the national government, the potential political impact of the referendum results was undermined by the uprising of 19 and 20 December.

Still, these were momentous political events at the time, showing not only the capacity of the CTA to mobilise large sectors of the population, but also its effectiveness in beginning to sketch out the main components of an alternative to neoliberalism. However, the CTA's prominent position was reduced in the wake of the rapid political changes that followed. First, part of the challenge during the period immediately succeeding the crisis was the exponential growth in the number of new social actors outside of the CTA's sphere of influence, most noticeably Neighbourhood Assemblies. But probably more significant in affecting the potential of the CTA was – and this has continued to be the case – the twofold effect of growing political isolation of some sectors among the organisations of the unemployed and the demobilisation of others. In turn, increasing fragmentation among the newly organised sectors, and this is clearly the case with the unemployed, have proven to be unworkable given the lack of a more overarching political alternative. Moreover, the CTA's *piquetero* contingent, while still very large, has lost the capacity it once possessed to provide some form of leadership for the movement as a whole. The close connection of the FTV to the Kirchner government has certainly isolated it from other organisations of the unemployed. But the current weakness of the unemployed movement as a whole also lies in the serious divisions that exist among its various sectors, including those influenced by more radical political forces. Rising levels of employment, if sustained in the longer run, will further reduce the weight of this sector and with it some of their demands for more inclusive channels of political participation and economic growth (Dinerstein 2001). In this respect, the experience of the organisations of the unemployed speaks to the trajectory of many social movements and their rather limited horizon when their practices are connected only weakly to broader political demands or political actors. But that those links are not easily established or sustained can be shown by the example of the CTA itself. The situation in post-2001 Argentina, therefore, might also be taken as a sobering reminder of the sometimes thorny process through which union struggles and demands reverberate and dissipate among social actors outside of traditional spheres of labour influence and vice versa.

Second, the weakening of the CTA's capacity to represent marginalised sectors has been paralleled by its less than optimal level of growth as a union force. For example, since 2003 – that is with economic recovery since that time – organised workers have taken the lead in terms of pushing for change in the long process of wage deterioration in the country. Interestingly, many of these struggles have been undertaken at the very local level, in some cases challenging the directives of a given union itself. Thus, the CGT and even the CTA have been overwhelmed by the outbreak of various labour conflicts over which they have not been able to exercise any control. In some ways this inability to effectively represent emerging working-class demands might be a reflection of the reduced appeal of the CTA as a new force capable of presenting an option against the bureaucratic and anti-democratic practices of traditional unionism in Argentina.

Additionally, there are also some important structural obstacles that the CTA needs to overcome. A persistent stumbling block in its ability to consolidate its power as a union organisation has been the continual denial of all governments from the 1990s onward to alter existing Argentine labour legislation in a way that would make it possible for more than one union in a firm to be legally entitled to represent workers (Brienza 2007: 4). It is only those unions with legal entitlement (*personería gremial*) that enjoy all benefits of the law, including protection against firings and other penalties imposed by the employer. The labour law grants the right for other unions to exist, but they do not have the right to negotiate on behalf of the employees in a workplace and are not protected against employers' reprisals.

The existence of unions working under these limiting legal conditions has negatively affected the capacity of the CTA to challenge the supremacy of unions affiliated to the CGT.

There are very good explanations for the unchanging nature of labour legislation when it comes to the monopoly of representation still enjoyed by the CGT. Not only is the CGT a historical ally of the Peronist party – strained as the relationship might have become during the 1990s – but the old logic of corporatism continues to apply (Patroni 2001). Governments know that in a moment where conditions are propitious for a reactivation of labour struggles, the safest route to control them is to support a labour leadership committed to the protection of the government's political and economic plans. Thus, the CGT under the leadership of Moyano has repositioned itself effectively in the negotiation of salaries, a fact that has given it a new opportunity to strengthen its position as the hegemonic labour sector in the country. The CTA, in contrast, has lost its capacity to influence in a decisive way the debate on issues that are fundamental in terms of social justice and that still remain unresolved.

In fact, unemployment and precarious forms of employment continue to afflict a very large sector of the Argentine working class. According to the CTA, economic growth without some type of forceful intervention on the part of the state in employment creation cannot provide a solution to the structural conditions that have generated these problems in labour markets. Moreover, economic growth can only provide a means toward the resolution of some of the most pressing problems for workers in Argentina if it is connected to state policies that aim at assuring a fairer distribution of income. While redistribution is thus a key component in the CTA's proposal for change in Argentina, its positive effects on employment can only be cemented through legal guarantees for greater democracy within unions. Accordingly, the CTA has invested considerable energy in trying to procure the changes in labour legislation necessary to extend the democratic functioning of its unions. So far, though, the results have been negative and the democratisation of unions continues to be another important deficit in the transformation of the country.

Finally, the election of President Kirchner and his performance so far have been extremely effective in raising expectations of change without open confrontation. Indeed, the nationalist and more progressive stance of the Kirchner government has found a welcome reception among some factions within the CTA. It is thus no surprise that the changes outlined above have been reflected also in mounting internal divisions within the organisation with respect to their position vis-à-vis the government.

Notwithstanding the obvious impact of very complex circumstances, the CTA's responses have been tempered also by some internal changes. In particular, the decision in December 2002 to build a political movement on the basis of the forces accumulated within the CTA represented a new way of conceiving the role of a labour organisation at this particular juncture in

Argentina. This transformation certainly created new points of tension. More specifically, there are a number of issues still not resolved within the CTA in terms of its capacity to generate unity among the struggles of different sectors of the working class. In moving toward taking on a new role as a political movement, the CTA has, in fact, made this problem of unity a function of a broader dilemma of how to formulate alternatives that can respond to the multitude of new demands posed by mobilised sectors of the population (Patroni 2002). If as a new alternative for union organising the CTA has certainly presented various labour sectors with an option to organise and to respond to the drastic deterioration of living and working conditions over the past 30 years, this does not necessarily mean that it can have an equally innovative role as a political force. The complexity of the dilemma can be appreciated given the fact that, in practice, the re-shaping of the CTA as a political force has so far only given way to the participation of various of its leaders as candidates for different political parties (Svampa 2007: 7).

Conclusion

Judging from the course social conflict has taken in Argentina in the years since the 2001 crisis, it is evident that the expectations created at that time for a renewal of political contestation to neoliberalism have not become a reality. The new pressures generated in the unfolding of the post-2001 scenario in the country have also resulted in the weakening of the political influence the CTA had enjoyed up until then. Nonetheless, the CTA must still be recognised as continuing to present a potentially important new option, both for labour and for the broader sectors it has so far successfully included in its struggles. The challenge for the organisation, daunting as it may be, is to envisage alternatives to broaden the political debate around the potential of economic growth to reduce the burden of informality and poverty. Ultimately, finding a way out of the shattering experiences of marginality and poverty that so many Argentines face constitutes the pre-condition to convey deeper meaning and structure to the rather weak forms of democratic representation that the country, as the rest of the Latin American region, has to date produced.

The cost that labour continues to be called upon to bear in the recovery of Argentina from its economic collapse – a cost measured in particular in the lack of an assertive public policy to reduce the incidence of precariousness and informality in labour markets – is a reminder of the actual reach of the reform governments that are the heirs of neoliberalism in the region. In addressing the problem of employment, the CTA has correctly attempted not only to respond to the devastating effects of neoliberalism on labour markets but also to establish a direct link between the setback suffered by workers and the crisis of development that afflicts the country as a whole. Thus, redistribution is also the central economic policy in the proposal that the CTA has formulated as its vision of sustainable and equitable development in Argentina. The problem consists, of course, in how to gather the necessary political strength to advance such an agenda.

Ironically, the decision of the CTA to place its efforts in the construction of an alternative capable of affecting the Argentine political map may have created a fault line that now sits at the core of the organisation's capacity to deepen its role as a labour organisation. This is all the more so since the CTA still remains unclear in its analysis of the specific way in which concrete labour struggles and demands relate to the struggles of other sectors in the country. The problem is compounded by the urgent need to define a scope for alliances while at the same time attempting to hold on to the expression of more radical labour perspectives. Ultimately, the direction of change within the CTA will be determined by its capacity to realise its potential in terms of the continual construction of truly representative forms of labour organisation.

Notes

1 For example, see CTA (2002a, 2002b).

2 The Convertibility Plan was conceived as an anti-inflationary program and became law in April 1991. It established a fixed exchange rate of US$1 for $1 Argentine peso. At that rate, the Central Bank was required to sell all the dollars demanded by the market and to take out of circulation the domestic currency received in the transactions. The law also established that the monetary base of the country could not be larger than the amount of international reserves in the central bank. Additionally, the law banned price and debt indexation and the practice, then quite widespread, of including an indexing clause in contracts.

3 On average, exports increased 2.6 per cent annually between 1990 and 1994 and 14.7 per cent between 1994 and 1997. While their growth rate was reduced after that year, exports continued to increase throughout the period of convertibility.

4 This Federation, organised on territorial lines, is the most heterogeneous, and it also brings together sectors generally outside traditional unions: landless peasants, First Nations, shantytown dwellers, tenant associations, and neighbourhood associations organising around issues related to the cost and delivery of newly privatized public services and other problems in their communities.

5 For an excellent study of the movement, see Svampa and Pereyra (2003).

6 Nonetheless, it is important to remember that there were a large number of general strikes in Argentina during the 1980s and 1990s.

7 Thus, for instance, Luis D'Elía – the leader of the FTV and also a member of the Buenos Aires Provincial Legislative Assembly at the time – categorised as a serious mistake the use of 'insurrectional' forms of protest against a government that presents an alternative to neoliberal policies in Argentina (Fernández Moores 2003a).

8 La Matanza is a municipality close to downtown Buenos Aires. The former site of important industries, the area is now home to 1.5 million inhabitants, 300,000 of whom live in 180 shantytowns and '*asentamientos*', areas where the land was taken through popular mobilisations and where housing was built through the organisation of community cooperative organisations like the FTV who have substituted quite effectively for the lack of any public service.

References

Basualdo, E. (2001) *Sistema Político y Modelo de Acumulación*, Buenos Aires: Universidad Nacional de Quilmes.

Beccaria, L. and López, N. (1996) 'Notas sobre el comportamiento del mercado de trabajo urbano', in L. Beccaria and N. López (eds) *Sin Trabajo: Las características del desempleo y sus efectos en la sociedad argentina*, Buenos Aires: UNICEF/ Losada, pp. 17–45.

Brienza, H. (2007) 'Trabajadores pobres, dirigentes ricos', *Le Monde Diplomatique*, Southern Cone Edition 8(91): 4–5.

Cavarozzi, S. (1986) 'Political Cycles in Argentina Since 1955', in G. O'Donnell, P.C. Schmiter and L. Whitehead (eds) *Transitions from Authoritarian Rule: Latin America*, Baltimore, MD: Johns Hopkins University Press, pp. 19–48.

CELS (2004) *Derechos Humanos en Argentina. La lucha por la libertad y la democracia sindical*, Buenos Aires: CELS/CTA.

Clarín, 9 January 2006.

CTA (2002a) *Apuntes sobre nuestra estrategia*, Buenos Aires.

—— (2002b) *Shock distributivo, autonomía nacional y democratización. Aportes para superar la crisis de la sociedad argentina*, Buenos Aires: Editorial La Página.

—— (2006) 'Mesa de Políticas Sociales IEF-CTA Sin cambio de planes. Acerca de las medidas de reconversión del Programa Jefes y Jefas de Hogar', Buenos Aires.

Dinerstein, A.C. (2001) 'A Silent Revolution: The Unemployed Workers' Movement in Argentina and the New Internationalism', *LABOUR, Capital and Society* 34(2): 166–183.

Epstein, E. (2003) 'The Piquetero Movement of Greater Buenos Aires: Working Class Protest During the Current Argentine Crisis', *Canadian Journal of Latin American and Caribbean Studies* 28(55–56): 11–36.

Fernández Moores, L. (2003a) 'La polémica entre piqueteros crece y es cada vez más dura', *Clarín Internet*, 25 November. www.old.clarin.com/diario/2003/11/25/p-00301.htm.

Gastaldi, S. *et al.* (1997) *Empleo en la Argentina: Clave para una Mayor Prosperidad*, Buenos Aires: Fundación Bemberg.

Gutierrez, R. (2001) 'La desindicalización del Peronismo', *Política y Gestión* 2: 93–112.

Hidalgo, J. C. (1999) *Mercado de Trabajo: Teorías económicas, plan de convertibilidad y opción de desarrollo*, Santa Fe: Universidad Nacional del Litoral.

Lozano, C. (2005) *Los problemas de la distribución en la Argentina actual*, Buenos Aires: Instituto de Estudios y Formación de la CTA.

Lozano, C., Rameri, A. and Raffo, T. (2006) *Seguirá elinando la desocupación? Una mirada sobre la última información del mercado laboral*, Buenos Aires: Instituto de Estudios y Formación de la CTA.

Mancebo, M. (1998) 'El nuevo bloque de poder y el nuevo modelo de dominación (1976–1996)', in H. Nochteff (ed.), *La economía argentina a fin de siglo:fragmentación presente y desarrollo ausente*, Buenos Aires: Eudeba, pp. 169–202.

Monza, A. (1995) 'Situación actual y perspectivas del mercado de trabajo en la Argentina, in Ministerio de Trabajo y Seguridad Social', *Libro blanco sobre el empleo en la Argentina*, Buenos Aires.

Nochteff, H. (1998) 'Neoconservadorismo y subdesarrollo. Una mirada a la economía argentina', in H. Nochteff (ed.) *La economía argentina a fin de siglo: fragmentación presente y desarrollo ausente*, Buenos Aires: Eudeba, pp. 17–46.

Ogando, A. (2004) 'Desocupados y Planes Sociales en el Posmenemismo', *Rebelión*, available at: www.rebelion.org/argentina/040409ogando.htm

Página 12 (2001) 23 June.

—— (2001) 14 December, pp. 6–7.

—— (2007) 'Creciendo desde el infierno', 8 February.

—— (2007) 'Más precarios, pero mejor pagos', 9 May.

Palomino, H. (2003) 'The Workers' Movement in Occupied Enterprises: A Survey', *Canadian Journal of Latin American and Caribbean Studies* 28(55–56): 71–96.

Patroni, V. (2001) 'The Decline and Fall of Corporatism? Labour Legislation Reform in Mexico and Argentina during the 1990s', *Canadian Journal of Political Science* 34(2): 249–274.

—— (2002) 'Structural Reforms and the Labour Movement in Argentina', *LABOUR, Capital and Society* 35(2): 252–280.

Svampa, M. (2007) 'Profunda rupture de las lealtades', *Le Monde Diplomatique*, Southern Cone Edition 8(91): 6–7.

Svampa, M. and Pereyra, S. (2003) *Entre la ruta y el barrio: La experiencia de las organizaciones piqueteras*, Buenos Aires: Editorial Biblos.

11 Globalisation, contestation and labour internationalism

A transformationalist perspective

Ronaldo Munck

Globalisation has generated a multi-layered and multi-faceted process of social contestation. The first wave of capitalist globalisation (1875–1914) saw the labour movement as the incipient driver of that contestation. The current wave of globalisation (1989–present) coincides with what most observers see as the terminal decline of the labour movement, and other social actors are seen as the main agents of contestation. But what if the labour movement is entering a new cycle of activism and militancy, precisely through the contestation of neoliberal globalisation? Is it inconceivable that a global contest between labour and capital might now emerge as Marx predicted? Be that as it may, we should now move beyond the verdict of Manuel Castells, among others, that 'the labour movement seems to be historically superseded' (Castells 1997: 360).

This chapter unfolds in four distinct moments, seeking answers to these questions and advancing what I call a transformationalist labour perspective on globalisation. In the first section, I examine current debates and practical developments around the emergence of global unions. Does global capitalism lead inexorably to global unions, or should it? The second section is retrospective, examining the emergence of labour internationalism as a response to the first wave of economic internationalisation. Might we see a revival of this 'classic' Marxist confrontation between labour and capital on a global scale? The third section takes up the so-called new internationalism and examines how labour is joining the new social movements in contesting globalisation. Are we moving towards a global working class, or 'multitude', that is taking on global capitalism? Finally, I consider what a transformationalist or radical reform strategy for labour might mean in the current era of globalisation. There are no simple answers, but we have to at least start asking the right questions.

Global capital/global unions

The year 2007 began auspiciously, from a transformationalist labour perspective, with the announcement by a group of influential US, British, and German trade unions that they would join forces to confront the power of transnational corporations (Morgan 2006). The organisations involved were the UK's largest private sector union, Amicus, the influential German engineering union, I.G. Metal, and the American United Steel Workers and International Association of Machinists, representing between them nearly six and a half million workers. For traditional, or at least mainstream, trade union leaders to recognise that the days of the national trade union were numbered was a major step. While transnationals may pit countries and workforces against one another, trade unionists have started working to create a transnational union to challenge the power of global capital. Could it be that the 1970s vision of trade unions acting as a countervailing power to multinational corporations is coming to fruition?

It is now widely believed among labour specialists that the international trade union movement and, more specifically, the recently unified peak organisation, the International Trade Union Confederation (ITUC) – which brings together the International Confederation of Free Trade Unions (ICFTU), the Global Unions Federations (GUF) and the World Confederation of Labour (WCL) – are at a crossroads in terms of how they might meet the challenge of globalisation. For Marcel van der Linden (2003b: 20) 'it remains very likely that the coming of transnational internationalism will be a difficult process interspersed with failed experiments and moments of deep crisis'. We can probably agree with that statement, whether we hold an optimistic or pessimistic view on the likelihood of a new era of labour transnationalism. What is at stake in this context, however, is not our estimation of the capabilities of this or that organisation, but the question of what the main dilemmas facing the global labour movement are. Of course, we cannot resolve this issue in a few pages. But we can try to lay out, in a simple way, the main scales of activity that labour operates on in the current period, before going on to discuss actual labour strategies in the next section.

At an international level, the new International Trade Union Confederation (ICFTU/GUF/WCL) seeks to articulate labour interests at the level of international financial institutions and transnational corporations (TNCs). Compared to the period of the post-war boom, the era of neoliberal globalisation has seen very little space created for durable class compromises to be negotiated with either of these interlocutors. The main dilemma for international labour organisations is whether they should continue to operate as if that class compromise were possible, through the cultivation of social partnerships and generally 'responsible' modes of engagement and activity. The alternative, of course, is a more wholehearted engagement with the global justice movement, and activist practices more akin to those of civil society organisations. What is in question, then, is whether existing trade union structures and procedures can adapt to the demands of the new global order.

In terms of the overarching spatial and social divide between formal sector workers in the affluent North and those in the dominated South, a major dilemma has been the issue of international labour standards. Should the international labour movement argue, on the basis of fairness and legitimacy, that core labour standards should be incorporated into the remit of the World Trade Organisation (WTO)? Or are these labour standards a covert form of Northern protectionism at odds with the interests of workers in developing countries? As Rebecca Gumbrell-McCormick puts it: 'The ICFTU believes that there is a danger of a "global race to the bottom" and that it must be prevented by binding rules to establish minimum standards for workers in the global economy' (2004: 526). The problem for workers in the majority world is that the 'social dialogue' approach, and the social economy model it is premised on, remain unavailable to them. For a global labour movement this is a serious dilemma, and one not amenable to cosmetic resolution.

Increasingly, we find the regional moment of labour activity coming to the fore. Whether it is at the level of the European Union (EU), North American Free Trade Agreement (NAFTA), Mercosur or Asia-Pacific Economic Cooperation (APEC), trade unions need to respond to the new regional modalities of capitalist development. As Nigel Haworth and Steve Hughes have argued, 'There is a positive aspect to regional labour activity today. A combination of three factors – internationalisation of capital, the Social Clause/Labour Standards debate and regional integration – has provided labour with a need, a platform and a context for action' (2002: 163). Certainly the regional transnationalism of the South does not share the same dynamic of the EU, for example. But clearly this domain will gain in importance. The dilemma it poses to labour is whether it displaces the national terrain and whether, in some way, it lessens the importance of global labour solidarity.

With respect to the once dominant or even exclusive national level of labour activity, there is now a gradual realisation that the nation-state is far from irrelevant as a parameter for much of labour's activity. As Bill Dunn concludes in a recent study of globalisation, labour, and the state: 'There appear to be many respects in which it remains both possible and necessary for workers to fight at the national level' (2006: 47). Even if labour is mounting a transnational campaign, say on core labour standards, nation-states remain a key target insofar as they are the constituent members of international financial institutions. Upscaling labour struggles because the national terrain is hostile is not always possible or desirable. Further, it is not clear that the national trade union is an adequate vehicle to defend the national working class from the deleterious effects of neoliberal globalisation, let alone to secure substantial gains for the working class.

There is a growing tendency across social movements to accept that we might 'think globally' but that we need to 'act locally'. Andrew Herod has argued persuasively that 'workers may think that if they cannot organise globally, there is no point in attempting to organise at other scales' (2001: 118). This is not only politically paralysing, but also ignores the extent to which TNCs can be effectively challenged locally. This is not presented as a 'small is beautiful' or 'local trumps all' argument, but simply recognises that workers need not (indeed, often cannot) respond to capital's movement at the same scale. While it is clear that local pressure points may be effective in challenging a TNC, there is still the dilemma posed for workers worldwide who might accept that 'another world is possible' in principle, but who do not see a global vision that is achievable coming from traditional labour organisations.

Clearly these different scales of labour activity are not like rungs on a ladder; in practice they overlap, as one would expect given the uneven and combined development of capitalism itself. Taking one dispute that has received sustained scholarly attention as an example, namely, the Liverpool lock-out of 1995–1998, we can see the complexities of labour contestation. There were sustained arguments that the dockers had to '*go global*' more consistently, and that only international labour solidarity could overcome the negative national terrain (see Castree 2000, for a review of this case). One could also argue, however, that the dense social networks of the *local* labour and community movements in Liverpool were the only reliable basis for sustaining such a long struggle. Likewise, it could be argued that a decisive yet less confrontational approach through official *national* trade union channels in the transport sector might have produced more positive results. The point here is not to rake over these debates, but simply to reinforce that labour's contestation of capitalism and its effects will more often than not be multiscalar.

In a revealing comment, leading Latin American trade unionist and one-time ICFTU director Kjeld Jakobsen has admitted that, 'For all its millions of unionised workers, the world trade union movement cannot bring the neoliberal experiment to an end on its own' (2001: 78). We might go further and argue that organised labour on its own will not even be able to develop an adequate social and spatial strategy to defend its position in the era of neoliberal globalisation. Thus, our conclusion will inevitably be to argue for a new global social movement unionism (popularised by Moody 1997, albeit from a traditional Fordist workers' perspective). While recognising that a rapprochement between organised labour and the global justice movement will not be easy, it is clear that the new capitalism requires a new unionism. That movement will need to create new places and spaces and learn to play by new rules, distinct from those of the nation-statist era, if it is to empower working people worldwide.

At the end of the twentieth century, international trade unionism was confronted by a tragic paradox: as globalisation unleashed a new great proletarianisation, there were more wage-earners than ever before – around three billion (Freeman 2006); but the labour movement had been decimated by its neoliberal policies. There has been a dramatic increase in the effective global labour force over the last two decades, with a recent International Monetary Fund study (IMF 2007) suggesting it has risen fourfold. A

United Nations projection suggests that effective global labour supply could more than double again by 2050 (cited in IMF 2007: 180). While the overwhelming majority of this labour force will remain unskilled, it is the increase in the proportion of skilled workers which is most notable. The integration of workers from the 'emerging market' (i.e. former state socialist) and 'developing' (i.e. former Third World) countries has created the conditions for the emergence of a global working class, as the ongoing integration of workers into the global marketplace proceeds apace. However, the trade union and socialist movements are emerging from a period in which they were seriously weakened, if not decimated, by capitalism's 20-year-long neoliberal offensive.

The new ITUC claims to represent 166 million workers through its 309 affiliated trade union organisations in 156 countries and territories. The ICFTU had previously brought the GUF (formerly known as International Trade Secretariats) under its wing through the Global Unions Council, in addition to the collapsing, former state socialist unions. Now it took over the once Christian-oriented WCL and brought eight previously unaffiliated national trade union confederations into its ranks. This was clearly a response to globalisation: 'The international trade union movement is adapting in order to remain a key player in an economic climate that is creating more losers than winners' (ICFTU 2006). But is this new-found spirit of political collaboration and practical action on the ground too late? Neoliberal globalisation implied the simultaneous weakening of traditional unionism's century-old national industrial base, the shift of that base to countries of the South (particularly China), the undermining of traditional job security and union rights, and the decline or disappearance of support from social-democratic parties, socially-reformist governments, and the most powerful inter-state agencies. Moreover, the traditional Northern unions were being confronted with a fact that they had not had to face previously, in the era of national/industrial relations/corporatist-type labour relations, namely that in this globalising world of labour, maybe only one worker in 18 was unionised. Finally, with the disappearance of their competitors in communist or national-populist unions, the ICFTU/GUF found themselves not only in an alien and hostile world, but also ideologically disoriented. Previously, they had been able to see themselves not only as representing the most advanced union model, but also as part of the 'free West', opposed to both communist and national-populist unionism. In the present era, they find themselves left behind by the globalisation of capital and by the decreasing political interest of the international hegemons.

First internationalisms

While the nineteenth century is generally read as the century of nationalism, internationalism emerged as early as 1875. From that point until the close of the century, 130 international nongovernmental organisations (NGOs) were formed, with the numbers formed between 1900 and the outbreak of the First World War in 1914 rising to a staggering 304 (Lyons 1963: 14). So while this period may end with the outbreak of national chauvinism and an inter-imperialist war, there was also a developing sense of international cooperation, not least in labour and socialist circles. As Eric Hobsbawm puts it, 'Internationalism is an integral part of bourgeois liberalism and progress in the nineteenth century' (1988: 3). The question arises as to whether internationalism is a discourse linked to a general theory of social evolution as part of inter-national development, or whether there is a specific labour or working-class variant of it.

The creation of the working class and of the early labour movement was, in essence, internationalist, for the simple reason that the era of the nation-state had not yet dawned. The mid-nineteenth century was a period of extensive and intensive labour movements (some 40 million workers migrated from Europe alone), both overseas and between neighbouring European countries. The trade union form of organisation was quite explicitly internationalist, not only because many of its leaders were formed through internationalism, but also because any form of nationalism would be as problematic as gender, religious, or racial divides. Michael Forman puts it most simply: 'As a class, the proletariat had to be internationalist to achieve its political and social goals, because the basis of its very existence *as a class* was an international system' (1998: 47). Even labour support for the democratic republic was on an internationalist, rather than a narrow nationalist, logic.

The first wave of labour internationalism in the mid-nineteenth century had various facets. At one level this early trade union internationalism was a simple response to the use by employers of overseas workers to undermine strikes and thwart trade union organisation. To this defensive motivation we can add the socialist ideal of the emancipation of global labour and the democratic ideal of national self-determination. Pragmatism and idealism could often go hand in hand in the development of labour organisation and ideologies. But another contradiction lay in the fact that this early internationalism required, if it was to be successful, the formation of strong *national* trade union movements. To some extent then, the very success of the early internationalism would lead to alternative national poles of attraction for the incipient working-class movements and its members.

An underlying trend in the 1875–1914 period is precisely the 'nationalisation' or national integration of the working class across Western Europe. Capitalist development of a national infrastructure and nation-state formation led to a progressive, if uneven, incorporation of the working class. As van der Linden puts it: 'In the transitional phase between 1870 and 1900 we thus see a decline of the possibilities for an effective old style working class internationalism' (2003b: 19). Thus, the very success of strong and viable national labour movements removed some of the urgency from the internationalism of the previous era. Working-class integration in key European nation-states such as France, Germany, and Britain may have strengthened the respective labour and socialist movements, but at the same time it undermined the internationalism that had played such a crucial role in the making of the European labour movements.

To refer to this first wave of internationalism as European is, at one level, a truism given that Europe is a geographic reality; on another level, however, it leads to the question of Eurocentrism, which has a very direct and contemporary relevance. Following Samir Amin, we should recognise that Eurocentrism is not 'simply the sum of the prejudices, errors and blunders of Westerners with respect to other peoples. If that were the case, it would only be one of the banal forms of ethnocentrism shared by all peoples of all times' (1989: 104). We need to conceive of Eurocentrism as the totalising and enduring dominant paradigm of Western social science. It is a worldview that dominates through the creation of subordinate Others. Ironically, this worldview is often reinforced by the very people who seek to challenge it. We need only think, for example, of anti-colonial positions that take a 'Western' model for granted. Eurocentrism is inextricably bound up with imperialism, colonialism, and racism, all of which it has helped to support with pseudo-scientific notions of modernisation and progress.

In organisational terms, Europe's internationalists came together in the First International in 1864, followed by the Second International in 1889. The International Working Men's Association, or First International, was conceptualised in a London pub among English trade unionists and visiting French delegates to the Great Exhibition, with the rationale being more 'economic' than political. It was essentially an instrument to build strike solidarity across national frontiers, and in this task it soon established its effectiveness. It was also successful in overcoming national or cultural differences, such as those between the Walloons and Flemish in the Belgian section. In 1866, the International launched a coordinated campaign in Europe and North America in pursuit of the eight-hour day, demonstrating the effectiveness of transnationalism in practice. Dimitris Stevis argues that the First International was quite like today's ecological organisations: 'with limited means it engaged in cross-border activism, promoted the formation of labour organizations, had significant ideological prestige and impact, and put the idea of labour internationalism on labour's agenda' (1998: 56).

A new chapter in labour transnationalism opened up with the formation of mass-based socialist parties in Western Europe in the 1880s. The Second International was formed in 1889 with internationalism as a key theme, symbolised in International May Day and International Women's Day demonstrations. Trade unionism began to grow rapidly in the 1900s, and by 1910 there were 28 different international trade union secretariats organising specific trades (e.g. builders, engineers, miners, transport workers, etc.) across national boundaries (Lyons 1963: 157). While the Second International had a much more solid social base than the First, its objectives were in some ways more limited, at least in terms of its commitment to internationalism. It organised national socialist political parties, distinct from the more ecumenical support sought by the First International. Its internationalism was geared specifically to achieving political harmonisation across national frontiers around socialist principles. It sought the reform of capitalism within national boundaries and not the world revolution that the First International preached and practised.

In his broad history of the West European Left in the twentieth century, Donald Sassoon concludes that for the leaders of the Second International in 1914:

> Internationalism was just a word, not a key component of a coherent strategic line ... Their understanding of international affairs was minimal. Their internationalism was a facade, not in the sense that they were opportunists as the Leninists believed, but in the sense that they did not imbue it with any strategic content.
>
> (1996: 29)

Nevertheless, the first wave of internationalism in Western Europe did have a lasting effect, creating an historic memory of considerable importance. The machinery of international cooperation would be rebuilt, and the European labour movement would eventually come out of the world wars more unified and coherent in its outlook than ever before.

Internationalism arose in the mid-nineteenth century at least partly in response to the broad socio-economic and political transformations of the era. Capitalism was spreading across the globe and the nation-states of the centre were consolidating. The 'universal interdependence of nations' generated by this process needed to be matched by what the *Communist Manifesto* of 1848 called the 'universal interdependence of peoples'. The theory and practice of internationalism had real roots, and universal political goals such as place, equality, and democracy were widely shared across national boundaries. As Alejandro Colás puts it, 'internationalism becomes both cause and consequence of the expansion of civil society' (Colás 2002: 57) during this era. International solidarity between peoples had material roots, but the principles of internationalism also had real material effects, such as undermining employers' efforts to divide the working class along national lines.

New internationalisms

In terms of the current strategy debates within the international trade union movement, Richard Hyman has found that, 'Thoughtful trade unionists have come to recognise that playing safe is the most risky strategy. The present is either the end of the beginning, or the beginning of the end' (2004: 23). Organised labour will become politically irrelevant if it does not drastically and thoroughly adapt to the new global order. There are those who are optimistic about the ability of the trade union movement to adapt.

Thus, Dan Gallin, former General Secretary of the International Union of Food and Allied Workers, declares:

> Those who are developing the concept of global social movement unionism, or of the global justice movement, are seeking to rebuild a labour movement with a shared identity and shared values – not the lowest common denominator, that is what we have today[,] and this movement as it is can only lose. Beyond the lowest common denominator, we need an alternative explanation of the world, alternative goals for society and a programme on how to get there that all can subscribe to. A new international labour movement, armed with a sense of a broader social mission, can become the core of a global alliance including all other social movements that share the same agenda. Such a movement can change the world. It can again be the liberation movement of humanity it set out to be, one hundred and fifty years ago.
>
> (2006: 10)

What the historical parallels with the late-nineteenth century and the emergence of the modern trade union movement teach us is that this necessary shift will not be a smooth and organic process. It is more likely that alternative social forces (the 'informal sector', for example) and geographical locations (the South generally, and China in particular) will challenge and subvert the current structures and strategies. There are signs that trade unions are looking towards the new social movements in more positive ways than in the past. Even in the US, as Dan Clawson shows, 'Labour's links with other [social movement] groups are denser and stronger than they have been for half a century' (2003: 205). This interaction has led to new, more progressive policies, including, for example, policies concerning undocumented immigrants. Frances O'Grady, deputy General Secretary of the British Trade Union Congress, has recognised that 'Growing globalisation has demonstrated ever more vividly that going it alone [for the unions] is not an option' (cited in O'Grady 2004), and that not only do unions need to engage seriously with the global justice movement, but if they wish to change the world they will need to start by changing themselves. Has this begun to happen?

A decade ago, the ICFTU declared that globalisation posed 'the greatest challenge for unions in the 21st Century' (ICFTU 1997). Since then, there has been a growing belief that labour needs to 'go global' to confront the new, more internationalised capitalist order. If the global economy is producing a global workforce, then global unions seem a logical development. Global economic power might be seen to impel the emergence of a global social counter-power. In Polanyian terms, the expansion of the market that lies at the heart of what we call globalisation generates a social countermovement by which society (and the social forces therein) protect themselves from the ravages of the free or unregulated market. These social relations, however, cannot be conceived without understanding how they are grounded in particular places. Thus, the spatial dimensions of transnational labour relations and transnational labour solidarity are crucial to our understanding. Furthermore, contending political projects inevitably contain a particular spatial vision. The forces of capital have their range of spatial fixes to maintain accumulation and healthy profit rates. Labour has, or needs to have, its own spatial vision and politics of place. Globalisation has imposed on us a particular vision of space: the 'shrinking globe', hypermobile investment, the communications revolution. Its contestation will also generate a new understanding of space: more networked, more interdependent, and perhaps more sustainable.

If we were to construct a basic social-spatial matrix to set the context for labour's varied and multidimensional responses to globalisation, it would look something like Figure 11.1. The various points of the diamond might be seen as poles of attraction, setting up force fields affecting the activity of labour in complex and intermingled ways. Thus, workers and unions operate within the parameters of the market (on the left), but they are also always-already embedded within social relations (on the right). Trade union strategies might thus be categorised in terms of whether they lean towards market discipline, or the social order. However, they are also pulled in different spatial ways, from the global (at the top) to the local (at the bottom), reflecting the different scales of human activity. Neither the Polanyian horizontal tension nor the vertical element of a politics of scale is wholly adequate, rather, these forces act in a combined, if uneven, manner.

The spatial turn in international labour studies should not be seen as a panacea, or as a reason to neglect more traditional social, political and, above all, historical forms of analysis and prognosis. There seems to be a tendency (perhaps inevitable) to prioritise, or place in a hierarchy, the 'scales' of human activity, as orthodox Marxists once did with the various 'levels' of capitalist society. Often this leads to binary oppositions and/or hierarchies being established, such as 'local is best' or labour 'must go global'. Furthermore, to just add 'space' to the old left trinity of race, gender, and class as determinants of human activity (see, for example, Herod 2001: 269) does not really subvert that well-established, but limited, paradigm. Overall, however, an intense focus on the interpenetration of the scales of human activity does contribute considerably to our understanding of the complexity of labour's position and strategies in the face of globalisation. As we displace the place–space ontological distinction, so we open up labour analysis and strategising in ways that acknowledge the complexity and fluidity of the world we live in.

In practice, the new trade union internationalism – as exemplified by the US/UK/German super-union referred to above – is set within the parameters of traditional industrial relations. Already the Global Unions Federations (GUF) (the former International Trade Secretariats) has moved towards setting up 'Global Framework Agreements' with some transnationals, the main purpose of which is defined as 'establish[ing] a formal ongoing relationship . . . which can solve problems and work in the interests of both parties' (ICFTU 2004). These international unions rightly see the transnationals as the major powers in the new global economy. Thus, they have moved back to 'free collective bargaining'-type strategies rather than relying on tripartite relations, including the state, to defend their interests. This is understandable as a syndicalist reaction, and it does seem to lead to a greater emphasis on traditional trade union activities, such as recruitment, union building, and the defence of basic labour rights. As a transformative strategy, however, it will most likely fail, insofar as it moves away from the broader counter-globalisation movements currently organising outside the workplace.

Labour internationalism has always taken different forms and these have rarely followed the mythical injunction to 'workers of all countries unite, you have nothing to lose but your chains'. In fact, from the period of the First International until 1968, it was, according to van der Linden (2003a), a 'national internationalism' that prevailed. That is to say it was based on a

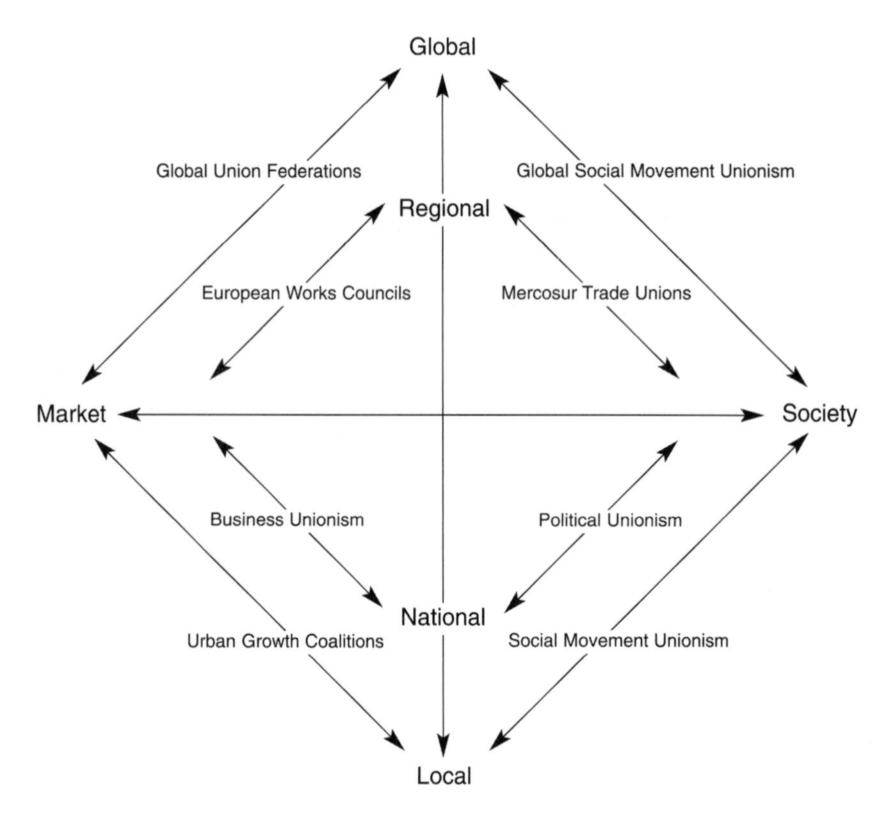

Figure 11.1 Labour's responses to globalisation.

narrow and Eurocentric conception of the 'international working class', and it was a form of solidarity between national trade union movements rather than a genuine transnationalism. In the period since 1968, we have seen the rise of new social movements, the collapse of communism, and the emergence of globalisation as a dominant societal paradigm. What this means in terms of internationalism is that we have probably entered a transitional phase akin to that associated with the formation of the First International, with new political and organisational forms emerging.

Traditional models of internationalism ignore the complex contingencies at play and the very real contradictions underlying its practice. For example, we might have to recognise that there are often narrow sectional interests lying behind 'internationalism', such as, for example, when US trade unions promote unionism in the South to dampen competition over wage levels with their own members. Also, we might find that the best way to combat globalisation is through a form of national alternativist trade union strategy. Thus, one of the new global unions, the International Federation of Chemical, Energy, Mine and General Workers Union (ICEM), concludes in a document arguing for 'global unionism' that 'priority must be given to supporting organising at local union level' (ICEM 1999: 25), thereby building union strength on the ground. There is, in reality, no 'one right way' to practise internationalism, and we need to recognise that it is a complex, shifting, and transitional phase we are currently experiencing.

It is perhaps tempting to see the Hardt and Negri (2004) concept of the 'multitude' as a radical alternative to industrial relations-oriented labour politics. The 'multitude' is not the same as the 'people' (seen as a more unitary category), the 'masses' (where differences are submerged), or the 'working class' (seen as less open and inclusive than the 'multitude'). Initially, Hardt and Negri simply define the multitude as 'all those who work under the rule of capital and thus potentially as the class who define the rule of capital' (ibid.: 106). While a broader conception of the working class has for some time been advocated by post-structuralist Marxists, the multitude goes further in presenting an image of radical immanentism as a spontaneous response to Empire, insofar as to revolt is natural to the human condition. The danger is that 'multitude' is so all-encompassing that it becomes self-explanatory and fails to show how specific social groups come together to contest capitalist globalisation in practice.

This task is tackled more productively, I would argue, by those engaged in bridging the gap between the organised labour movement and the 'new' social movements around environmental, place, and gender issues (see Clawson 2004; Waterman 2005). This is not a politics of nostalgia for an era when the 'class struggle' pitted clearly pre-defined antagonists into battle. It is a call for a politics of articulation between different sectors of the counter-globalisation movement on the basis of identifying democratic equivalents. Whether it is race/class, blue/green divides, or ever-present gender divisions, unity will not occur through some mystical submergence in a 'multitude'. Taking a broader view, we could say that the move from the hitherto dominant, neoliberal Washington Consensus to a putative post-Washington Consensus 'governance' problematic (see Broad 2004) depends on politics being removed from the equation so that we can all unite around 'globalisation with a human face'. Workers are resisting this on a daily basis, and their organisations are beginning to articulate a new labour politics for the current era of globalisation.

Transforming globalisation

It is now increasingly common to hear references to the 'collapse of globalism' (Saul 2006), a view informed by the fact that global peace has clearly not broken out and that the nation-state (and nationalism) remain very much alive and well. Indeed, for many authors globalisation has always been a necessary myth created by the architects of the post-Cold War neoliberal revolution (Hirst and Thompson 2000). In terms of economic internationalisation and financial openness, the classic Gold Standard period (1875–1914) more correctly merits the label globalisation. Today this essentially sceptical case about the novelty of globalisation seems more plausible than articulated by the few remaining true-believer globalists. However, it might be more prudent for us to follow the David Held *et al.* 'transformationalist' perspective: globalisation is driving rapid economic, political, social and cultural transformations across the globe, but the result of those changes is a contingent historical process replete with contradictions (1999: 7).

More recently Saskia Sassen (2006) has sought to develop a more mid-range social theory of globalisation, taking us beyond macro-level accounts that tend to simplify the complex social processes underway. In particular, this meso-level narrative helps to add 'social thickness' to our analysis of globalisation. By reducing globalisation to the hypermobility of finance capital and time-space compression, dominant accounts strip the global of its social determinants and conditioning factors. Sassen's approach also allows us to move beyond impoverished notions of the local and the global in both pro- and anti-globalisation literatures, which manage to equate the global with placelessness. Sassen's approach also leads us to focus on what she calls the 'countergeographies of globalisation' (ibid.: 370), whereby alternative networks develop a multiscalar politics that need not become cosmopolitan, in the classical sense, to act as powerful counter-forces to globalisation.

We can argue that there is, today, a tendency towards the formation of a global working class. For some 20 years now, there has been a tendential process towards the formation of a global labour market. Management consultant William Johnston declared at the start of the 1990s that, 'The globalisation of labour is inevitable' (1991: 126). Of course, in practice no more than one-fifth of the world's workers are directly linked to the global political economy in terms of labour relations. Yet the possibility of global unions is not diminished by this fact, especially when we take into account the much greater impact of what we call globalisation on labour relations worldwide. This leads even cautious labour scholars like Jeffrey Harrod and Robert O'Brien to conclude that 'a global labour force can be discerned, if it is defined as those workers connected to the global economy' (2002: 14).

There is, however, a powerful counter-tendency that in Ulrich Beck's Eurocentric language has been called 'Brazilianisation' (2000: 1). That is to say, while globalisation brings an ever greater number of workers within its remit, it is also creating greater diversity, disruption, and insecurity in the world of work. The pattern of employment once typical in countries such as Brazil – namely, the preponderance of 'informal' labour relations and great levels of income disparity – have now become generalised across the affluent North, albeit with particular nuances. So, while capitalist globalisation does tend towards the creation of an integrated global market, it also generates a dispersal tendency based on informalisation and flexibilisation. Clearly, labour's organisations cannot respond to this situation as they did in the North Atlantic during the so-called golden era of class compromise and the welfare state.

We need to be sensitive to the contradictory nature of responses to globalisation. Thus, for example, the same US trade unionists who demonstrated shoulder to shoulder with environmentalists at Seattle in 1999 under the 'Teamsters and Turtles Unite' banners against the WTO, would some months later demonstrate against the entry of China into the WTO under openly protectionist banners. Globalisation can call forth reactionary labour politics as much as progressive positions. It can be seen as the agent undoing a hitherto privileged labour situation, not least through the 'export of jobs' to low wage locations, creating a sense – and a reality – of downward mobility across wide swathes of the US working class, which once considered itself to be firmly 'middle class' in terms of lifestyle, differentials vis-à-vis African Americans, and social prospects. Workers in the USA – once secure in a class compromise state that provided reasonable social benefits in return for political stability – now need to make sense of their rapidly changing world. This rightist anti-globalisation discourse draws on long-standing populist traditions and the 'radical' critique of corporations in the USA. Articles by Ralph Nader on the evils of corporations, for example, appear in the same journals that carry far-right attacks on globalisation as the work of Lucifer.

The power of the local to impact the new global capitalism is clear. The local still matters, even while globalisation tends to obliterate space. But we need to go beyond the 'local-global paradox' if we are to construct a new internationalism for the current era of globalisation. The paradox refers to the fact that 'while economic relationships have become ever more *global* in scope and nature, political responses to economic globalization are becoming more *localized*' (Jonas 1998: 325). While this might be the case, it is not, I would argue, incompatible with the emergence of a new labour internationalism. Workers are clearly divided by national, regional, gender, ethnic, and other fault-lines. The growing internationalisation of capitalist rule may increase competition along national, regional, and even city lines. But globalisation is also creating a more numerous global working class and, arguably, a common focus for workers worldwide. Some workers and their organisations have responded with a 'new realism' that simply accepts an irreversible change in the balance of forces against workers. In other cases, national and regional alternatives have developed along traditional political mobilisation lines. Maybe we can develop a 'local transnationalism' based on the notion that workers' internationalism need not mirror the international structures of capitalism of either multinational corporations or the WTO.

If global capitalism today is characterised by uneven and combined development as much as it was in Marx's day, we are unlikely to see global unions springing up fully formed to confront it. The globalisation of the working-class condition has clearly not worked out in the way that Marxists assumed or hoped for. Instead of generalising and homogenising the condition of the industrial proletariat (of mid-nineteenth-century Britain), we see proletarianisation occurring without the Marxists' internationalist and revolutionary proletariat. Differentiation rather than homogenisation seems to be the rule. Local, ethnic, gender, and other identities are as important (maybe even more important) than those of class. It is the labour internationalists who still have a working class to win in the sense of winning hearts and minds, as is the case with the internationalism of women, of indigenous peoples, or of Africans. Given that the differentiated and dispersed working classes also have these other identities, a new working-class internationalism would seem to be dependent on an intimate articulation of *labour* internationalism with that of these *others* who are also, of course, workers. The question remains whether *trade union* internationalism can further this new internationalism.

By focusing on the complexity of transnational labour relations and contestation, we move beyond the paradigm of globalisation as subject. We must heed John Urry's warning that 'many globalisation analyses treat the emergent global properties as too unified and powerful' (Urry 2000: 40), producing a static and reductionist picture. In brief, 'many globalisation analyses . . . deal insufficiently with the *complex* character of emerging social relations' (ibid.: 39). This is less true today, with second or third generation globalisation studies focusing on global networks, communities, and flows that are fully cognisant of global complexity. In the new labour geography, for example, there is recognition of the fact that 'Building solidarity across space – especially internationally – is not a straightforward matter, but rather is fraught with complexities' (Herod 2001: 218). As Andy Herod reminds us, transnational labour practice is 'as much about geography as it is about class' (ibid.: 218).

In his 'search for international union theory', Harvie Ramsay concludes that 'in the end, the success of international unionism remains a contradictory and contingent matter' (1999: 215). There are many contradictions within the global working class, but not least there are the divisions based on social position and geographical location. There is tension between transnational labour activity 'from above' and local contestations of globalisation, which may take particularist and protectionist forms. There is also a huge element of contingency in terms of labour responding to capitalist strategies and structures that are always changing and taking on a huge variety of forms across space. Finally, we must remember the Gramscian dictum that the old is dying but the new has not yet fully developed in terms of transnational labour relations. Our conclusion might thus mirror Ramsay's, namely that 'This is not a message of hopelessness, but one which emphasises the complexity and difficulty of the international union project' (ibid.: 215).

As always, the development of a progressive alternative to a hegemonic project in crisis is a matter of political will. The transformationalist approach to globalisation can also be applied to this political project. During the first wave of globalisation (1875–1914) a form of transformative politics was articulated by Karl Kautsky with his notion of 'radical reform' designed to break the impasse between 'revolution' and 'reform'. Today, this type of politics is articulated most clearly by Brazilian political philosopher Roberto Mangabeira Unger. In a period when revolutionary change is unavailable as an option 'we are left to humanise the inevitable' (Unger 1998: 20) unless we adopt transformative politics. Reform, according to this conception, is seen as radical 'when it addresses and changes the basic arrangements of a society', refuses to take for granted dominant assumptions about society, and takes politics in an ever more democratic direction (ibid.: 18).

Today, within the international labour movement and the wider family of global anti-systemic movements, there is an ongoing debate on the 'new politics' of transformation. An alternative counter-hegemonic globalisation is being constructed, and it is generating an oppositional governance matrix. As with the post-1968 'new' social movements, this process is also challenging the positivist knowledge paradigm and the sanctity of what are taken to be scientific laws (e.g. neoliberal economics). For another world to be possible, another form of knowledge is needed. Subaltern groups are generating new forms of knowledge that challenge Northern (Eurocentric) capitalist epistemologies (see Sousa Santos 2006). The coloniality of power is being confronted by rival knowledges, and false universalisms are being rightfully contested.

References

Amin, S. (1989) *Eurocentrism*, London: Zed Books.

Beck, U. (2000) *The Brave New World of Work*, Cambridge: Polity Press.

Broad, R. (2004) 'The Washington Consensus Meets the Global Backlash: Shifting Debates and Policies', *Globalizations* 1(2): 129–154.

Castells, M. (1997) *The Power of Identity*, vol. II of *The Information Age*, Oxford: Blackwell.

Castree, N. (2000) 'Geographic Scales and Grass-Roots Internationalism: The Liverpool Docks Dispute, 1995–1998', *Economic Geography* 76(3): 272–292.

Clawson, D. (2003) *The Next Upsurge: Labor and the New Social Movements*, Ithaca, NY: Cornell University Press.

Clawson, D. *et al.* (2004) 'Symposium: The Next Upsurge: Labor and the New Social Movements', *Labor History* 45(2): 333–382.

Colás, A. (2002) *International Civil Society – Social Movements in World Politics*, Cambridge: Polity Press.

Dunn, B. (2006) 'Globalisation, Labour and the State', in C. Phelan (ed.) *The Future of Organised Labour: Labour Perspectives*, Oxford: Peter Lang, pp. 37–62.

Forman, M. (1998) *Nationalism and the International Labour Movement: The Idea of the Nation in Socialist and Anarchist Theory*, Philadelphia, PA: Pennsylvania University Press.

Freeman, R. (2006) 'China, India and the Doubling of the Global Labor Force: Who Pays the Price of Globalization?' Available at: www.zmag.org/content/showarticle.cfm?ItemID=8617

Gallin, D. (2006) 'Foreword', in C. Phelan (ed.) *The Future of Organised Labour: Global Perspectives*, Oxford: Peter Lang, pp. 7–10.

Gumbrell-McCormick, R. (2004) 'Putting the Labor into Labor Standards', *Labor History* 45(4): 522–529

Hardt, M. and Negri, A. (2004) *Multitude, War and Democracy in the Age of Empire*, New York: Penguin.

Harrod, J. and O'Brien, R. (2002) 'Organised Labour and the Global Political Economy' in J. Harrod and R. O'Brien (eds) *Global Unions? Theory and Strategies of Organised Labour in the Global Political Economy*, London: Routledge, pp. 3–28.

Haworth, N. and Hughes, S. (2002) 'International Labour and Regional Integration in the Asia-Pacific', in J. Harrod and R. O'Brien (eds) *Global Unions? Theory and Strategies of Organised Labour in the Global Political Economy*, London: Routledge, pp. 151–164.

Held, D., Mc Grew, A., Goldblatt, D., and Perraton, J. (1999) *Global Transformations: Politics, Economics and Culture*, Oxford: Oxford University Press.

Herod, A. (2001) *Labor Geographies, Workers and the Landscapes of Capitalism*, London: The Guildford Press.

Hirst, P. and Thompson, G. (2000) *Globalization in Question: The International Economy and the Possibilities of Governance*, Cambridge: Polity Press .

Hobsbawm, E. (1988) 'Opening Address. Working Class Internationalism', in F. van Holhoon and M. van der Linden (eds) *Internationalism and the Labour Movement*, Leiden: Brill, pp. 1–18.

Hyman, R. (2004) 'Agitation, Organisation, Diplomacy, Bureaucracy: Trends and Dilemmas in International Trade Unionism', *Labor History* 45(3): 137–154.

ICEM (1999) *Facing Global Power: Strategies for Global Unionism*, Durban: Second World Congress.

ICFTU (1997) *The Global Market: Trade Unionism's Greatest Challenge*, Brussels: ICFTU.

ICFTU (2004) *Framework Agreements with Multinational Corporations*, www.icftu.org

—— (2007) *Strength in Unity: A New International Trade Union Confederation Is* Born. Available at: www.icftu.org

IMF (2007) *World Economic Outlook: Spillovers and Cycles in the Global Economy.* Available at: www.imf.org

Jakobsen, K. (2001) 'Rethinking the International Confederation of Free Trade Unions and its Inter-American Regional Organisation', in P. Waterman and J. Wills (eds) *Place, Space and the New Labour Internationalisms*, Oxford: Blackwell, pp. 59–79.

Johnston, W. (1991) 'Global Work Force 2000: The New World Labor Market', *Harvard Business Review* March–April, pp. 115–127.

Jonas, A. (1998) 'Investigating the Local-Global Paradox', in A. Herod (ed.) *Organizing the Landscape: Geographical Perspectives on Labor Unionism*, Minneapolis, MN: University of Minnesota Press, pp. 325–350.

Lyons, F.S.L. (1963) *Internationalism in Europe, 1815–1914*, Leiden: A.W. Sythoff.

Moody, K. (1997) *Workers in a Lean World: Unions in the International Economy*, London: Zed Books.

Morgan, O. (2006) 'Birth of the First Global Super-union', *Observer*, 31 December.

O'Grady, F. (2004) 'Globalisation Makes Unions and Social Movements Natural Allies', *The Guardian*, Saturday 16th October.

Ramsay, P. (1999) 'In Search of International Union Theory', in J. Waddington (ed.) *Globalisation and Patterns of Labour Resistance*, London: Mansell, pp. 192–220.

Sassen, S. (2006) *Territory Authority Rights: From Medieval to Global Assemblages*, Princeton, NJ: Princeton University Press.

Sassoon, D. (1996) *One Hundred Years of Socialism*, London: I.B. Tauris.

Saul, J.R. (2006) *The Collapse of Globalism and the Reinvention of the World*, London: Atlantic Books.

Sousa Santos, B. (ed.) (2006) *Another Production is Possible: Beyond the Capitalist Canon*, London: Verso.

Stevis, D. (1998) 'International Labor Organizations, 1864–1997', *Journal of World-Systems Research* 4(1): 52–75.

Unger, R.M. (1998) *Democracy Realised: The Progressive Alternative*, London: Verso.

Urry, J. (2000) *Global Complexity*, Cambridge: Polity Press.

van der Linden, M. (2003a) *Transnational Labour History*, Aldershot: Ashgate.

—— (2003b) 'The ICFTU at the Crossroads: An Historical Interpretation', paper delivered to a conference on Labour and New Social Movements in a Globalising World System: The Future of the Past, Linz, September.

Waterman, P. *et al.* (2005) 'Symposium: Labor and the New Social Movements', *Labor History* 46(2): 195 – 244.

Index